I0099986

[*From "The Visitation of London, 1633-'34." Publication of the Harleian Society.*]

Goodwin.

Tower Street Ward.

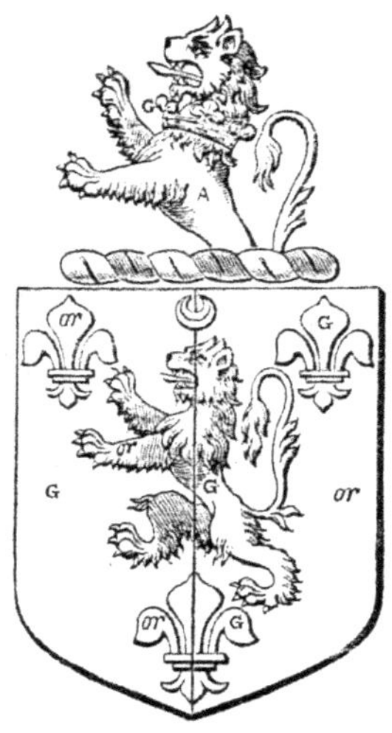

Respited for the difference in the Armes

Henry Goodwin of . . . . ╤ . . . . da. of . . . . = Mr Moore
com. Buckingham | his wife — second husband

Robert Goodwyn of Westminster ╤ Jane da. of Anthony Dollin of
and of Tower Streete | Henalt in Flanders

Peter Goodwyn of London ╤ Sara da. of John Hellard al's Highlord
salter a° 1633 | of London merchant

Gartrude wife to John Pigot of London grocer	2 Suzana — 3 Elizabeth — 4 Sara Goodwin	1 John Goodwin aged about 22 yeares 1633	2 Matthew — 3 Peter	4 James

PETER GOODWYN.

ARMS OF GOODWINS OF CO. BUCKS, ENGLAND, AND YORK CO., VA.

Per pale or and gu., a lion ramp., between three fleurs-de-lis counterchanged. Crest—A demi lion ramp. ar. gorged with an heraldic coronet gu. Motto—*De bon volore.*

—*Burke's "General Armory."*

SUPPLEMENT.

William and Mary College Quarterly

Historical Magazine.

The Goodwin Families in America.

Judge John S. Goodwin

HERITAGE BOOKS
2011

HERITAGE BOOKS
AN IMPRINT OF HERITAGE BOOKS, INC.

Books, CDs, and more—Worldwide

For our listing of thousands of titles see our website
at
www.HeritageBooks.com

A Facsimile Reprint
Published 2011 by
HERITAGE BOOKS, INC.
Publishing Division
100 Railroad Ave. #104
Westminster, Maryland 21157

Originally published
Richmond, Virginia
Whittet & Shepperson, General Printers
1897

— Publisher's Notice —
In reprints such as this, it is often not possible to remove blemishes from the original. We feel the contents of this book warrant its reissue despite these blemishes and hope you will agree and read it with pleasure.

International Standard Book Numbers
Paperbound: 978-0-7884-0205-0
Clothbound: 9978-0-7884-8892-4

TABLE OF CONTENTS.

SUPPLEMENT.

William and Mary College
Quarterly Historical Magazine.

Vol. VI. OCTOBER, 1897. No. 2.

THE GOODWIN FAMILIES IN AMERICA.

By Judge John S. Goodwin.

The Goodwins were among the very first of the English-speaking people to come to America. As the late Mr. Charles Francis Goodwin, of Brookville, Indiana, expressed it, "The Goodwins have *always* been here. It is still an open question whether the Indians or the Goodwins were the original inhabitants!"

Not only were they here at an early date, but the earliest ones were in Virginia. While some of those mentioned below did not leave families, their names are included, that the honor of priority may be given them. The years and names are as follows, and they thoroughly upset the "three-brothers" theory:

1607–'14.—Samuel Goodwin; was massacred at Jamestown.

1620.—Sir Francis Goodwin was a member of the Virginia Company. He died in England.

1620.—Reinold Goodwin, born in 1590, came to Elizabeth City county in *The Abigail* in 1620, and was living in 1624. Untraced.

1624.—Robert Goodwin, born in 1605, came to Elizabeth City county in *The Swan* in 1624. Untraced.

1632.—William and Ozias Goodwin, brothers, settled eventually in Hartford, Connecticut. A genealogy of this family has been published,* and it is the desire to trace its English origin—a matter which has, so far, eluded the most diligent search—which has led Mr. James J. Goodwin to preserve, with the intention of publishing, *all* Goodwin data found by Mr. Waters in his search for the English family of the Hartford Goodwins.

1633.—Christopher Goodwin settled in Charlestown, Massachusetts. Two manuscript records of this family are in existence.

**The Goodwins of Hartford, Connecticut;* compiled for James J. Goodwin, Hartford, Conn.

1635.—John Goodwin, November 20, 1635, was one of the "head rights" with William Wilkinson, and settled in Lynnhaven, Lower Norfolk, Virginia. Untraced.

1635.—Alexander Goodwin and Daniel Godwin, November 26, 1635, with eighteen others, were granted 1,250 acres in the county of Charles City, Virginia. Untraced.

1640.—Devereux Godwin or Goodwin settled in Old Kent, Maryland, and was a prominent man for many years, but no trace of his descendants has been found, except a son, Devorax Goodwin, Jr. Perhaps some of the Maryland families descend from him.

1648.—Major James Goodwin settled in York county, Virginia. His family and descendants are subjects of this sketch.

1652.—Daniel Goodwin settled in Kittery, York county, Maine, and his descendants are legion. Captain William F. Goodwin was engaged in compiling a genealogy of this family at the time of his death, in 1872. It is probable that it will be published at an early date.

1660.—Richard Goodwin married in 1666 in Essex Co., Massachusetts. This family is very numerous in the New England States. It is probably an offshoot of the Goodwins of Torrington, county Devon, England.

1660.—Edward Goodwin, of Essex county, Massachusetts, was the ancestor of a large family.

1700.—Rev. Benjamin Goodwin settled in Gloucester county, Virginia. His descendants, if any, are untraced.

1700–1800.—During this century a number of Goodwin families were established in the New England States, and in Pennsylvania, New Jersey, Delaware, Maryland, the Carolinas, and Georgia. In the search for the ancestry of Thomas Goodwin, data of all of these families have been gathered and preserved. None of them appear to be related to Major James Goodwin, and more detailed mention is not made of them at this time.

An Unsolved Problem.

In 1789, at Old Fort, now Brownsville, Fayette county, Pennsylvania, Samuel Goodwin, eldest son of Thomas Goodwin, Jr., was born. The yet unsuccessful attempt to trace the lineage of this family (Appendix A) has resulted in the gathering of all the data included in this publication, and, in fact, of almost complete records of all the Goodwin families in America.

MAJOR JAMES GOODWIN settled in York county, Virginia, but had land grants in Westmoreland county. Three of his sons are practically untraced. An hypothesis is suggested, that perhaps one or more of the sons and grandsons of Major James Goodwin went to Westmoreland county, crossed the river to St. Mary's and Calvert counties, Maryland, and that their descendants gradually worked northward with the tide of immigration into northern Maryland and southern Pennsylvania, and then westward along the trail which became the old National Road, and then, following the water courses, became, with their descendants, the pioneers of the great Ohio Valley.

Whether descendants of Major James or of Devereux Goodwin, or of other, and as yet unknown, immigrant ancestors, it appears that Old Fort, in western Pennsylvania, was the "storm centre." It was situated on the Redstone River, a tributary to one of the great branches of the Ohio River; and in those early days the river current was the most rapid conveyance. Concentred, then, within a circle of the radius of scarcely fifty miles, touching Maryland, Virginia (now West Virginia), and Pennsylvania, and having Old Fort for its centre, we find not less than nine families of Goodwins, none of them yet able to trace their original source. These families were:

1st. THOMAS GOODWIN, Jr., born in 1767, who, in 1788 or 1789, came along "the trail" with his bride; stayed for a few years at Old Fort, and then, with his young family and his household belongings, floated down the Ohio River to Cincinnati, and eventually settled at Brookville, Indiana, and became the ancestor of the GOODWINS OF BROOKVILLE. Appendix A.

2nd. AARON GOODWIN, born in 1753, but about whose place of birth his descendants differ, some claiming Hartford, Connecticut, but others, with perhaps better reason, laying the place in Virginia, removed from Virginia to the Cumberland Valley in Maryland, where he married; and in 1790, with his wife and family, he followed the exact footprints of Thomas, Jr., but without stopping long at Old Fort, and by flatboats went to Maysville, Kentucky, and eventually settled in Washington, Indiana, where he died in 1828, leaving descendants, mentioned in Appendix B.

3rd. JOHN GOODWIN, whose history prior to the time he was living near Wheeling, West Virginia, is wholly unknown as yet, removed, with part of his family, down the Ohio River, settling in Kentucky; but at least three of his sons afterward removed from near Wheeling and from Kentucky to Indiana; and his descendants are traced in Appendix D.

4th. SETH GOODWIN is said to have been born in Germany, and to have settled in York county, Pennsylvania, where he had sons John, in 1796, and William, and then removed to Washington county; and John and some of his children went to Greene county, across the river from Fayette. It is to be noted that John Goodwin, next above mentioned, had a son Seth of the same age as this Seth, and further investigation may combine this family with that of John Goodwin. It is, however, treated separately in Appendix E.

5th. JOSEPH GOODWIN, whose wife was born in Delaware, settled in Fayette county, Pennsylvania, about 1796, and his first son, Daniel, was born in 1800. His fourth son, William, "returned to Baltimore," and was killed by a fall while working on a public building.

6th. JOHN GOODWIN, brother of Joseph, and both sons of John Goodwin, Sr., settled "over the line," in West Virginia. This family is given in Appendix C.

7th. JOHN GOODWIN was born in Montgomery county, Maryland, in 1762. He served in Capt. William Lowther's company, of Virginia, from 1778 to 1780, and in Capt. Joseph Gregory's company, of Virginia, until 1782. He was pensioned in 1833, and then resided in Harrison county, (West) Virginia, having enlisted from Harrison county in 1778. See Appendix F.

8th. JAMES GOODWIN, private of the thirtieth Maryland, a soldier in the Revolutionary War, had land grant for fifty acres, number 1,784, which was located on a tract of land now called "Cherry Tree Valley," about seven miles north of Oakland, the county seat of Garrett county, Maryland; but James permitted the land to escheat to the State. Thomas Goodwin, Jr., is said to have had a brother James who went west.

9th. EDWARD GOODWIN resided near Simpson, in Taylor county, West Virginia. His son Gabriel was born about 1810. He was brother to John, mentioned in the 7th paragraph. See Appendix F.

The chief trouble found in tracing these families is that records were kept only of dates of birth, and not of places. They were pioneers, and their homes were "regions," "valleys," "districts," the name covering vast territories. Their old home ties were slight, and the life which they lived permitted them to dwell but little in the past. They were, as a rule, stern, silent men, always confronted with dangers, always with hardships; and their descendants know but little about them and their kin.

YORK COUNTY, VIRGINIA, GOODWINS.

The pedigree entered in the *Visitation of London* for 1633, and the abstracts of wills published in *The New England Historical and Genealogical Register*, Vols. XLVII. and XLVIII., of Robert Goodwin, Peter Goodwin, and John Pigot, show the following:

HENRY, of Buckinghamshire, had issue: ROBERT, who married Jane, the daughter of Anthony Dollin, of Henalt, in Flanders. Issue: PETER, a salter,* of Tower-Street Ward, London, who married Sarah, daughter of John Hillard, *alias* Highlord, of London, merchant. Issue: 1, Gertrude, who married, 1st, John Pigot, of London, merchant, who died in 1639; 2dly, Maurice Abbott, Esq.; 2, Susanna, who married ——— Stone; 3, Elizabeth, who married John Osborne; 4, Sarah, who married Wm. Elwood; 5, John, deceased before his father; 6, Mathew, eldest son in 1661, to whom his father gave his dwelling-house in "St. Margaret Patternes," in or near Tower street; 7, Peter; 8, *James*, "youngest son." The will of PETER GOODWIN was dated October 28, 1661, and was proved December 17, 1661, by the oath of James Goodwin, his son, one of the executors, power being reserved for Mathew and Peter, the other executors, etc. [So far the English authorities.]

In the early records of York county, Va., preserved at Yorktown (a copy of which, down to the year 1700, is in the State Library), the name of a James Goodwin appears as an early justice, with the title of major. He was justice from 1657 to 1662, and in 1658 he represented his county in the House of Burgesses. He lived on Back Creek. The identity of this James with the James of the English pedigrees is shown by two things: *First*, By the names of his children, which repeat the family names of the English people;

---

*The introduction to the *Visitation of Shropshire in* 1623, published by the "Harleian Society," contains an interesting account of the practice of the Heralds' College and the distinctions in society: "The simple state of society in the sixteenth and seventeenth centuries did not draw lines of demarcation at retail trades; great foreign merchants, such as we have now, had not yet been developed. War as a profession for younger sons had ceased; also the custom of attaching them to the *suites* of the greater nobility; and the consequence was, that they could only enter the learned professions, or be apprenticed to some ordinary retail trade, and so become members of one of these guilds; thus we find that the younger sons of extensive estates became tradesmen in the neighboring towns, and did not thereby cease to be members of the country gentry." So Peter Goodwin, in being a salter, did not cease to be a gentleman; and it was he who recorded his pedigree and arms with the Heralds' College in 1633.

and *Second*, By the fact that the York county books show that Major James Goodwin was present in York county on November 13, 1660, and that he reached England before April 30, 1661.* This would indicate that he returned to England after hearing of his father's death, and was present to swear to his father's will December 17, 1660. There was, between the date of the will and its proof in court, an interval of fifty days, which would have given time for the transmission of the news of Peter Goodwin's death to Virginia and for Major Goodwin's return and appearance in England. At the same time, the margin is not wide enough for us to suppose that his being in England about this time was the result of an accident.

Assuming this connection as proved, JAMES GOODWIN married, 1st, Rachel ——, whose tombstone on Back Creek, York county, Va., says that she was born in 1630, and died May 23, 1666, leaving, as it states, by Major Goodwin, five sons and two daughters. The tombstone bears an "impalement," by which is meant a division of the shield into two equal parts; the right, or dexter, representing the husband, and the left, or sinister, representing the wife. The right side in this case is too much worn to make out, but the left is divided *quarterly;* one and four, a bend; two and three, three bars. This quartering ought to give the names of the father and mother of Rachel Goodwin. Now, among those for whom Major Goodwin got "head rights," besides Mrs. Blanche Parry, Mrs. Ann Gooch, Robert Goodwin, John Goodwin, and "myself and wife," was one John Porter; and "three bars or" are the arms of Porter of County Warwick, England. With great confidence, then, it might be assumed that the mother of Rachel Goodwin was a Porter.† The other two quarters, containing each a bend, are too general for identification. Captain Gooch is called "brother" by Major James Goodwin; and Henry Gooch was, in 1660, the husband of Milicent Kinsey, widow of Robert Kinsey.

---

* In the York county records is the following:

"30th April, 1661. Capt. Henry Gooch and Mr. Robert Baldry are added to the Commission of Yorke County, and to be sworne at ye next Court, in the places of Coll. Xtopher Calthorpe & Majr. James Goodwin, who are removed, one to ye soward, ye other for England. Wm. BERKELEY."

† Off the mouth of the creek, near the tombstone, is an island still known as Goodwin's Island, which Samuel Chew deeded to James Goodwin. There is a lighthouse at the extreme point, called "Too's Point Lighthouse." Perhaps "Too's Point" is a corruption for "Chew's Point."

Henry Gooch,* who was also a magistrate of York county, Va., was manager of the estate of Major William Gooch, Esq., member of the Council, whose tomb is at "Temple Farm," where Cornwallis surrendered. This latter, who seems to have been an uncle of Governor William Gooch, and who died in 1655, left a daughter Ann, who married Captain Thomas Beale, of York and Richmond counties. Probably Ann Gooch, mentioned among Major Goodwin's head rights, was the wife of William Gooch and the mother of Anne Beale.

After the death of Rachel, Major James Goodwin married, 2dly, Blanche ——, probably Mrs. Blanche Parry, mentioned above. He died intestate, and his inventory was recorded January 6, 167$\frac{8}{9}$, showing £542 1*s.* 2*d.* On January 25, 169$\frac{1}{2}$, John and Peter Goodwin petitioned for their shares of their father's estate in the hands of their "mother-in-law" (step-mother), Mrs. Blanche Goodwin, and in the following month settlement was made with "seven children and y^e widow." In 1687 Mrs. Blanche Goodwin had given property to her "sons," John and Peter Goodwin, and daughter Susannah. Her will was proved September 22, 1701, and names sons Robert and Martin as executors; daughter, Elizabeth Blinkhorn; and grandchildren, James and Elizabeth Duke. Matthew Goodwin witnessed a deed from Peter to Martin in 1701.

Children—All, Presumably, by First Wife.

I. *Robert*, married Anne ———; II. *John*, married Elizabeth Moore; III. *Peter*, married Rebecca Tiplady; IV. *Matthew*; V. *Martin*, married Barbara ——; VI. *Susannah*, married —— Duke; VII. *Elizabeth*, married ——— Blinkhorn.

No children by second wife.

Robert Goodwin (James) was married before 1696 to Anne ——. By occupation he was a planter. They resided in Hampton parish, York county, Va., and in 1696 Robert was grantee in a deed from Peter Goodwin, the witnesses being John, Matthew, and Martin. A Robert was mentioned in 1711 as being one of the patrons of a private school. Anne Goodwin was permitted to keep an ordinary in 1715. A few years later she had married Joseph Frith, and was devisee of her son Martin, deceased, *one* of the orphan children of Robert Goodwin, deceased.

---

* Henry Gooch became lieutenant-colonel, and was a supporter of Bacon in 1676. (See "Gooch Family," QUARTERLY, IV.)

For probable descendants of Robert Goodwin, see Appendix H.
Children: i. Martin, d. s. p.

Capt. John Goodwin (James) was born in England; was married to Elizabeth Moore, a daughter of Augustine and ——— Moore, of Elizabeth City county, Va. By occupation he was a planter. They resided in York parish, York county, Va. John was security of Robert Reade as sheriff in 1689; churchwarden of the lower precincts of York parish in 1694; justice in 1699, with the title of captain, etc. He died in 1701, and his wife qualified on his estate. Elizabeth (Moore) Goodwin died in 1718–'19.

Children: i. Elizabeth, married, 1st, William Moss; 2dly, Robert Kerby; ii. James, married Mildred Reade; iii. Rachel, married Charles Wise; iv. Susannah; v. John (Colonel).

Elizabeth Goodwin (John, James) was born in York county, Va.; was married, first, to William Moss. Elizabeth (Goodwin) Moss married, secondly, Robert Kerby. *Moss* child: i. Edward.* *Kerby* children, if any, unknown.

James Goodwin (John, James) was born in York county, Va.; was married to Mildred Reade, a daughter of Robert Reade, gent., son of Col. George Reade, Secretary of State. By occupation he was a planter. They resided in York county, Va. James Goodwin's will, proved November 16, 1719, mentions "the child my wife now goes with." Mildred (Reade) Goodwin married, 2ndly, Col. Lawrence Smith. (See "Temple Farm," WILLIAM AND MARY COLLEGE QUARTERLY, Vol. II., No. I.) *No surviving child.*

Rachel Goodwin (John, James) was born in York county, Va.; was married to Charles Wise. They resided in York county. Rachel (Goodwin) Wise's will was proved February 15, 1719. *Wise* child: i. Frances.

Col. John Goodwin (John, James) was born in York county, Va.; was married to ———. By occupation he was a planter. They resided in York-Hampton parish. He was justice, captain, colonel, etc. Will proved February 16, 176$\frac{7}{8}$. Children: i. Elizabeth, born 1711, married Edward Moss, Jr.; ii. Rebecca, married James Goodwin; iii. Peter, died in 1763, unmarried; iv. John (Captain), married Rebecca ——— ?

Elizabeth Goodwin (John, John, James) was born in 1711, in York county, Va.; was married to Edward Moss, Jr., a son of Ed-

* Edward Moss, "eldest son," died in 1738, leaving a daughter, Diana, who was eighteen years old in 1754.

ward Moss. They resided in York county. Edward Moss, Jr., died in 1754, and administration was granted to his wife April 6. She died in 1760.

"Ordered, that Albritton Wagstaffe pay to Peter Goodwin 11£ 10*s*. for Elizabeth Goodwin, who had come of age December 15, 1729." (York County Records.)

Moss children: i. John; ii. Sheldon; iii. Anne; iv. Lucy; v. Diana, married Capt Thomas Chisman; vi. Elizabeth, married ——— Toomer.

Rebecca Goodwin (John, John, James) was born in York Co., Va.; was married to James Goodwin, a son of Captain John and Elizabeth (Doswell) Goodwin (Peter,[2] James[1]). By occupation he was a planter. They resided in Hanover county, Va. *Goodwin* children: i. John, born before 1759; ii. Martin, born after 1763.*

Captain John Goodwin (John, John, James) was married to Rebecca ———? They resided in York county. Children: i. Peter; ii. Margaret; iii. Mollie; iv. Elizabeth, born July 26, 1772; † v. Nancy.

Peter Goodwin (John, John, John, James) was married to Frances Chapman or Toomer. By occupation he was a farmer. They resided in York county. Children: i. John, died unmarried; ii. Peter, drowned young; iii. Harold, born 1800; died January 10, 1878, unmarried; iv. Jefferson, died unmarried; 12. v. Mary, married John Garrett; vi. Frances, died unmarried; vii. Louisa, died unmarried; viii. Rebecca, died unmarried; ix. Elsie, died unmarried; x. Elizabeth, died unmarried; xi. Caroline, died unmarried. (Dr. Tyler doubts the identity of this Peter with Peter, son of Captain John.)

Mary Goodwin (Peter, John, John, James) was born in York county; was married to John Garrett. Child: i. Frances Elizabeth, married Robert I. Williams.‡

Peter Goodwin (James) was married, before 169$\frac{6}{7}$, to Rebecca Tiplady, a daughter of Captain John Tiplady, justice of the peace for York county, and son of John and Ruth (Beale) Tiplady.

---

* See note to page 12 for John and Martin.

† Elizabeth, daughter of John and Rebecca Goodwin, born July 26, 1772. (Parish Register of Charles, or New Pocosin.) On March 22, 1787, a Martin Goodwin signed a bond to marry Elizabeth Goodwin in York county.

‡ Their daughter, Frances, is the wife of W. T. Moss, attorney, Newport News, Virginia.

By occupation he was a planter. They resided in York county; then, at Warranuncock Island; then, in New Kent county, removing to King and Queen; and afterwards, in King William county. His will was proved in York county March 20, 173½. Children: i. John (Captain), baptized December 25, 1698; married, 1st, Elizabeth Doswell; 2ndly, Anne ——; ii. Elizabeth, baptized 1700–'1; iii. Peter, married Mrs. Mary (Robinson) Calthorpe; iv. James, married, 1st, Diana Chisman; 2ndly, Mrs. Elizabeth (Chapman) Chisman; v. Rachel, married ——— Charles; vi. Anne.

Captain John Goodwin (Peter, James) was baptized December 25, 1698, in St. Peter's parish church; was married, 1st, to Elizabeth Doswell, who was born December 23, 1709, a daughter of John and Elizabeth (Nutting) Doswell; she a daughter of Captain Thomas Nutting. By occupation he was a planter. They resided in York county. He married, 2ndly, Anne ———. His will was proved May 21, 1759. He had stock in King William and a plantation in Hanover county.

Children by first wife: i. John; ii. James, married Rebecca Goodwin; iii. Peter; iv. Thomas, married Theodosia ———; v. Reuben; vi. Susannah, untraced; vii. Elizabeth, untraced; viii. Mary, untraced; ix. Anne, untraced. Children by second wife: x. Rebecca, untraced; xi. Alice, untraced.

John Goodwin (John, Peter, James) was born in York county, Virginia; was married to ———. By occupation he was a farmer. They resided in Hanover Co. It is not definitely known whether this John Goodwin is John, the son of Captain John and Elizabeth (Doswell) Goodwin. Captain John owned a plantation in Hanover county. In 1782, John, Reuben, and Rebecca Goodwin owned 415, 385, and 348 acres, respectively, in Hanover, and resided there. Captain John's will mentions Frances and Mary, children of *his* son John. This John had two daughters, but it has not been possible to ascertain their first names. Children: i. Daughter (Frances?), married ——— Moss; ii. daughter (Mary?), married Wilson Trevelian; iii. James, died an aged man, unmarried; iv. Reuben, married, 1st, Sally Day; 2ndly, Mrs. Sallie (Bradford) Grantland; v. Cyrus, married Nancy Timberlake; vi. John, resided in Yorktown, Va., untraced.

Reuben Goodwin (John, John, Peter, James) was born in York county, Va.; was married, 1st, to Sally Day. Children *by first wife:* i. Lewis, died unmarried; ii. John, married a French lady in New Orleans, and died *sine prole* about 1833; iii. Elizabeth, married

William Tompkins; iv. Sallie, married ——— Brown; v. Fanny, married Lewis Goodwin, of Yorktown, her cousin. Perhaps he was son of her father's brother John, who lived in Yorktown; vi. Nancy, died unmarried; vii. Mary (Polly), married Colonel John D. Andrews. *Reuben Goodwin* was married, 2ndly, to Mrs. Sallie (Bradford) Grantland, a daughter of —— and —— (Terry) Bradford.* They resided near Andrews post-office, Spotsylvania county. Reuben Goodwin served in the Revolutionary War, losing a leg through a wound. He died about 1810. Children *by second wife:* i. Eliza, married John Castlen; ii. Reuben Bradford, died unmarried.

Elizabeth Goodwin (Reuben, John, John, Peter, James) was married, at her father's home in Hanover county, to William Tompkins, who was born in 1787, in Caroline county, Virginia, a son of Robert and Anne (Dickinson) Tompkins. By occupation he was a farmer, and in religion an Episcopalian. They resided in Spottsylvania county. Elizabeth claimed cousinship with Littleton Goodwin and his wife (these two were cousins). Elizabeth (Goodwin) Tompkins died in 1832; William Tompkins died in 1858. *Tompkins* children: i. Sarah Day, born November 24, 1800; died unmarried; ii. Hardenia L., born March 22, 1802; married George Parker; iii. Emily, born 1804; iv. Susan Goodwin,† born November 9, 1805; married, 1st, Gottlob Rumbolz; 2ndly, ——— Hayton; v. Benjamin J., born May 17, 1807; married Achsah Hamilton; vi. Reuben R., born January 5, 1811; married Susan Hamilton; vii. Francis A.,‡ born December 5, 1814; married Claudius Tompkins.

Eliza Goodwin (Reuben, John, John, Peter, James), born 1801 in Hanover county, Va.; was married in 1819 at Richmond to John Castlen, born in 1788 in Hanover county, a son of John and Elizabeth (Timberlake) Castlen. (John Castlen, Sr., came from England.) By occupation he was a farmer; in politics a Democrat, and in religion an Episcopalian. They resided in Macon, Ga., where John Castlen died in 1860. Eliza (Goodwin) Castlen died in 1889 in Bollingbrook, Ga. *Castlen* children: i. John Bradford, born 1820, married Mary H. Holt; ii. Sarah Elizabeth, born 1825,

---

* Reuben Goodwin's second wife is also given as Mrs. Sally (Terry) Grantland, daughter of ——— and ——— (Timberlake) Terry, and as Mrs. Sally (Bradford) Grantland, daughter of ——— and ——— (Terry) Bradford, and as Mrs. Sally (Bradford) Grantland, daughter of John and Sallie (Crump) Bradford. She died in Milledgeville, Ga., in 1847, aged 92.

† Living, November, 1896, in Lincoln, Neb. ‡ Living in Andrews, Va.

married 1st, George Clarke; 2d, Thomas Cauthorn; iii. William H. P., born 1827, married Mary Woodward; iv. Ann Eliza, born 1830, married Peyton Cocke; v. (Dr.) Fleming Grantland, born 1833, married Eppie Maria Bowdre; vi. Edwin Samuel, born 1835, married Mattie Harrison; vii. Mary Catherine, born 1838, married A. P. Cherry; viii. Carrie Virginia, born 1840, married John S. Timberlake; ix. Bradford Goodwin, born 1845, married Fannie Burns; x. Marcellus, born 1847, married Juliette Harrison.

James Goodwin (John, Peter, James) was married to Rebecca Goodwin, a daughter of John Goodwin (John,[2] James[1]). They resided in Hanover county, Va. Children: i. John, born before 1759; ii. Martin,* born after 1763.

Thomas Goodwin (John, Peter, James) was married to Theodosia ———. "Thomas Goodin died at Isaac Pipper's 23[d] May, 1761." (Abingdon (Gloucester county) Parish Register.) Their children were baptized in Saint Peter's parish, New Kent. Children: i. William, born January 2, 1748; untraced; ii. Thomas, born September 10, 1758; untraced.

Reuben and *Peter Goodwin* (John, Peter, James) were born in York county, Va. By occupation they were farmers. Reuben resided in Hanover county, dying about 1816. One or the other of these was the father of the child mentioned below. Child: i. John Doswell.

John Doswell Goodwin (Peter or Reuben, John, Peter, James) was born in Virginia. They resided in Virginia until about 1825, when they removed to Eastern Tennessee (?) Children: i. William Banks, born June 27, 1804; married Catherine Buckallew; ii. Overton, resided in Arkansas; iii. Beal, resided in Alabama; iv. Peter, resided in Tennessee; no responses from his descendants; v. John Doswell, killed in Virginia while young.

William Banks Goodwin (John Doswell, Peter or Reuben, John, Peter, James) was born June 27, 1804, in Virginia; was married in 1825 to Catherine Buckallew, who was born September 1, 1801. They resided in Virginia, removing to eastern Tennessee in 1825. William Banks Goodwin died April 9, 1869; Catherine

---

* MARTIN GOODWIN and Elizabeth Goodwin were married in 1787, and resided in York county. Captain John and Rebecca (———) Goodwin baptized a daughter, Elizabeth, July 26, 1772, in York county.

JOHN GOODWIN is mentioned in his father's will, made in 1759, and in the will of his father's brother Peter, made in 1763. These dates indicate that John was born prior to 1759, and Martin subsequent to 1763. Martin is mentioned in his mother's father's will, proved February 16, 176$\frac{7}{8}$.

(Buckallew) Goodwin died August 15, 1878. Children: i. Jane, born 1827; married, in 1850, Lewis Waller; three sons and three daughters; ii. Mary (Polly), born in 1830; married George W. Monger; four sons; iii. Peter W., born December 10, 1832; married America Waller; iv. Andrew J., born 1834; married Evaline Pickel; three sons and three daughters; v. John Doswell, born in 1836; married Mary Billingsley; two sons and one daughter. No further information furnished, except as to Peter W.

Peter W. Goodwin (William Banks, John Doswell, Peter or Reuben, John, Peter, James) was born December 10, 1832; was married, December 11, 1856, to America Waller, who was born December 2, 1835. Peter W. Goodwin died January 25, 1892; America (Waller) Goodwin died May 5, 1893. Children: i. John B., born February 21, 1858; married Malinda E. Stowe; ii. William B., born October 8, 1859; died July 22, 1860; iii. Thomas E., born May 2, 1863; teacher; unmarried; iv. Joseph Lee, born November 14, 1876; resides at Kingston, Tenn.; unmarried.

John B. Goodwin (Peter W., William Banks, John Doswell, Peter or Reuben, John, Peter, James) was born February 21, 1858; was married September 30, 1884, to Malinda E. Stowe, who was born November 6, 1866. They reside in Kingston, Tenn. Children: i. Ada Frank, born September 9, 1885; ii. Dorcas Edna, born January 5, 1887; died September 5, 1887; iii. Luther Vilas, born March 11, 1888; iv. Bertha B., born October 23, 1889; died June 24, 1890; v. Lady Kate, born April 29, 1892.

Peter Goodwin (Peter, James) was married to Mrs. Mary (Robinson) Calthorpe, a daughter of John Robinson, and widow of Elimalech Calthorpe. They resided in York county. Peter Goodwin exhibited the orphan accounts of Mary and Frances Calthorpe September 19, 1743. Children: i. Peter, born July 4, 1738; died January 4, 1739; ii. John, born December 8, 1739; married Mary Allen Chapman; iii. Rebecca, born 1740; iv. Mary, born 1746; v. Anne, born 1747; married William Hardrick (?)

John Goodwin (Peter, Peter, James) was born December 8, 1739, in Charles parish, York county, Va.; was married to Mary Allen Chapman, a daughter of John and Anne (Hansford) Chapman. They resided in New Pocosin (or Charles) parish, York county. Anne Chapman's will, proved December 17, 1770, mentions her daughter, Mary Allen Goodwin, and granddaughter, Anne Goodwin. Perhaps Peter of 1768 did not survive, as he is not mentioned in his grandmother's will. Children: i. Anne; ii. Peter, born August 6, 1768.

James Goodwin (Peter, James), born in York-Hampton parish, York county, Va.; was married, 1st, to Diana Chisman, born October 12, 1715, a daughter of John and Eleanor (Howard) Chisman. Diana died November 30, 1735. He was a planter. They resided in York-Hampton parish. James Goodwin married, 2ndly, Mrs. Elizabeth (Chapman) Chisman, who was born December 28, 1709, in York county, a daughter of John and Elizabeth (——) Chapman and widow of Edmund Chisman. James Goodwin died November 8, 1757.

ABSTRACT OF DEED.—Benjamin Dumas and Frances, his wife, of the county of Louisa, of the one part, and James Goodwin, of the county of York, of the other part. Four hundred pounds of lawful money of Virginia; 600 acres. Dated February 3, 1750; admitted to record March 26, 1751.

JAMES LITTLEPAGE, Clerk.

The property adjoins that of Bickleys, on the east side of the river; also, that of Robert Garland. Probably this land is the same that was owned by Charles Q., conveyed to him by John Chapman Goodwin.

Child by first wife: i. John, born November 17, 1735; married Elizabeth Doswell. Children by second wife: ii. Peter, married, 1st, Sarah Coleman; 2ndly, Sarah Coghill; iii. Robert, born 1739; married Jane Tulloch; iv. James, married Margaret ——; v. Rebecca, married —— Mask; untraced; vi. Diana, married —— Bailey; had children, Wilson and Elizabeth, untraced; vii. Elizabeth, married Robert Blackwell ("Elizabeth Blackwell went from Crab Neck Nov. 15, 1765."—*James Goodwin's Bible Record*); viii. Rachel, married Edward Mallory; untraced.

John Goodwin (James, Peter, James), born November 17, 1735, in York county, Va.; was married to Elizabeth Doswell, born 1743, a daughter of Thomas and Rebecca (Drummond) Doswell; she a daughter of a son of William Drummond, Governor of the Carolinas. He was a farmer. They resided in Hanover county, Va. John Goodwin took the oath as lieutenant, and Thomas Chisman as captain, March 21, 1768. John Goodwin died May 15, 1783. Elizabeth (Doswell) Goodwin died February 16, 1814, in her seventy-first year. Children: i. Diana Chisman, born February 1, 1760; married William Overton Harris; ii. Mary, born July 3, 1763; married John Harris; iii. Thomas, born May 25, 1765; married Temperance Harris; iv. James, born November 28, 1768; married Fanny Harris; v. Frances, born May 31, 1772; married Robert Clough, and died without issue; vi. William Doswell, born July 28, 1774; married Mary Cosby; vii. Edmund Chisman, born

October 30, 1776; married 1st, Miss Anderson; 2d, Elizabeth Waddy; 3d, ———; viii. Elizabeth Doswell, born July 28, 1779; died January 12, 1781; ix. Elizabeth Doswell, born September 3, 1781; married Littleton Goodwin.

Diana Chisman Goodwin (John, James, Peter, James), born February 1, 1760, in Hanover county, Va.; was married to Col. William Overton Harris, born January 13, 1753, a son of Overton and Ann (Nelson) Harris; he was a farmer. They resided about two miles from Taylorsville, in Hanover county, at "Cedar Hill." Col. William Overton Harris died January 26, 1802. Diana Chisman (Goodwin) Harris died in 1850. "Mary Garland Harris and Thomas Baker Cosby were married on Wednesday, January 18, 1812." (Family Bible.) *Harris* children: i. William Overton,* born November 22, 1785; married 1st, Eliza B. Gwathmay, 2nd, Lucy Robinson Butler; ii. Elizabeth Doswell, born September 28, 1788; married ——— White; iii. Mary Garland, born November 20, 1791; married Thomas Baker Cosby; iv. Frances Goodwin, born August 31, 1796; married Rev. Walker Taliaferro; v. Ann Nelson, died October 9, 1799; vi. John Goodwin, died February, 1793.

Mary Goodwin (John, James, Peter, James), born July 3, 1763; was married to John Harris, a son of Overton and Ann (Nelson) Harris. Elizabeth Doswell (Harris) Blunt was mother of Mrs. Martha A. Parr, and John Overton Harris was father of Miss Edmonia V. Harris, to both of which ladies credit is due for information furnished. *Harris* children: i. Ann Nelson, born 1785–'86; died unmarried; ii. Elizabeth Doswell, married Capt. Francis Blunt; iii. Diana Chisman, married Garland Bumpass; iv. Mary Goodwin, married Roger Thompson; v. Jemima B., married William Dabney; vi. Sarah Overton, married James Winston; vii. John Overton, born 1799; married Nancy Hill; viii. Thomas Doswell, born 1801; ix. Maria Drummond, born 1803; married Genet Anderson; x. Martha W., born 1805; married Zachery Terrell.

Thomas Goodwin (John, James, Peter, James) was born May 25, 1765, in Hanover county; was married in 1789 to Temperance Harris, who was born in Hanover county, a daughter of Overton and Ann (Nelson) Harris. He was a farmer; and in religion a Baptist. They resided in Nelson county. Thomas Goodwin

---

* B. B. Harris, eldest son, resides (1897) in San Bernardino, Cal., having resided in California since 1849.

served an unfinished term of enlistment for his father in the Continental army. He was a Revolutionary pensioner. He died April, 1838, in Nelson county, Va. Children: i. John, born 1790; died 1823 unmarried; ii. Overton, born 1792; died August, 1818, unmarried; iii. Thomas Cary (Chisman), born September 1, 1794; married Lucinda Montgomery; iv. Ann Nelson, born 1796; married Charles P. Rodes; v. James Doswell, born September 10, 1798; married Catharine Watts; vi. Nelson, born 1800; died young; vii. William, born 1803; viii. William Harris, born September 18, 1805; married Bertha W. Harris; ix. Edmund Chisman, born April 4, 1807; married 1st, Maria F. Ware, 2nd, Mary Small.

Thomas Cary (*Chisman*) *Goodwin* (Thomas, John, James, Peter, James) was born September 1, 1794, in Amherst county, Va.; was married October 11, 1820, at Glenthorn, Nelson county, Va., to Lucinda Montgomery, who was born September 30, 1795, in Nelson county, Va., a daughter of Capt. Joseph and Jane (Woods) Montgomery. He was a farmer; in politics an old line Whig, and in religion an Episcopalian. They resided in Nelson county, Va., removing in 1825 to Amherst county. Capt. Joseph Montgomery served in the Continental army. Thomas C. Goodwin was baptized Thomas Chisman, but owing to the same middle name being given to his youngest brother, Edmund C., he changed the name to Cary. He served in the war of 1812, and died January 6, 1864. Children: i. Jane Ann, born July 9, 1822; married Isaac Newton Drummond; ii. Temperance Pauline, born July 25, 1825; died February 21, 1850, unmarried; iii. Elizabeth Doswell, born October 17, 1827; married G. W. A. Raine; iv. Thomas Joseph Montgomery, born July 19, 1830; married Louisa H. Bailey; v. John Overton, born September 12, 1834; died 1843.

Jane Ann Goodwin (Thomas Cary, Thomas, John, James, Peter, James) was born July 9, 1822, at Glenthorn, Nelson county, Va.; was married October 15, 1845, at Cedar Hill, Amherst county, Va., by Rev. Pitt Woodruff, to Isaac Newton Drummond, who was born May 10, 1820, in Amherst county, Va., a son of Zacharias and Isabella (Taliaferro) Drummond. By occupation he was a farmer; in politics a Democrat and in religion a Baptist. They resided in Amherst county, Va. Isaac Newton Drummond was captain of the militia, and died in Orange county, Va., during the Civil War from exposure and cold. *Drummond* children: i. Charles Overton, born September 9, 1846; married in Buchanan, Texas; ii. Newton, born September 11, 1848; married ——

Waterhouse; iii. Frances Jane, born March 2, 1852; iv. Elizabeth Doswell, born June 17, 1853; married ——— Smith; v. Julia, died in infancy; vi. Edward, born August, 1862.

Elizabeth Doswell Goodwin (Thomas Cary, Thomas, John, James, Peter, James) was born October 17, 1827, at Cedar Hill, Amherst county, Va.; was married Aug. 7, 1847, at Cedar Hill, Va., by Rev. Pitt Woodruff, to George William Augustus Raine, who was born May, 1820, in Appomattox county, Va., a son of John and Eliza (Woodson) Raine. By occupation he was a farmer and hotel proprietor. They resided at Appomattox Court House, Va. Elizabeth Doswell (Goodwin) Raine died April 3, 1874, in Bristol. *Raine* children: i. Ida T. M., born April 6, 1852; married Robert W. Dawson; ii. Ann Eliza, died in infancy.

Thomas Joseph Montgomery Goodwin (Thomas Cary, Thomas, John, James, Peter, James) was born July 19, 1830, in Nelson county, Va.; was married December 22, 1870, at Bristol, Tenn., by Rev. George A. Caldwell, to Louisa Haskins Bailey, who was born April 16, 1843, in Albion Castle, Prince Edward county, Va., a daughter of Joseph Richard and Julia Ann (Womak) Bailey. By occupation he was a farmer, in politics a Republican, and in religion a Methodist. They reside in Allwoods, Amherst county, Va. Mr. Goodwin has rendered very considerable assistance in compiling the records of his branch of the family. Children: i. Thomas Cary, born October 3, 1871; ii. Joseph Richard, born July 27, 1873; iii. Lucinda Montgomery, born May 22, 1878; iv. Julia Ann, born August 5, 1880; v. John Overton, born August 20, 1882.

Ann Nelson Goodwin (Thomas, John, James, Peter, James) was born 1796 in Amherst county, Va.; was married 1818 in Nelson county, Va., to Charles Preston Rodes, born 1794, a son of John Rodes. By occupation he was a farmer, in politics a Democrat, and in religion a Methodist. They resided in Nelson county, Va. Charles Preston Rodes died February 12, 1864. Ann Nelson (Goodwin) Rodes died October 28, 1882. (The name is given by others as "Rhodes.") No children.

James Doswell Goodwin (Thomas, John, James, Peter, James) was born September 10, 1798, in Amherst county, Va.; was married October 15, 1825, in Nelson county, Va., by Rev. James Boyd, to Catherine Watts, who was born February 6, 1806, in Amherst county, Va., a daughter of Charles and Elizabeth (Dillard) Watts. By occupation he was a farmer and merchant, in politics a Democrat, and in religion a Protestant Episcopalian. They resided in Nelson county, Va., until 1845; removed then to Ralls county, Mo., and afterwards, in 1851, to Fayette county, Tenn. James Doswell Goodwin died June, 1869, in Memphis, Tenn., and is buried in Elmwood Cemetery. Catherine (Watts) Goodwin died January 27, 1851, in Ralls county, Mo., and is buried near Hydesburg, Mo. Children: i. Maria Louise, born October 6, 1826; married Leroy P. Stewart; ii. John Watts, born August 6, 1831; married Elizabeth Rose Bailey; iii. Virginia Ella, born January 31, 1843; married Charles T. Hodges; iv. James Overton, born June 14, 1846; died July, 1876, unmarried; v. Mary Catherine, born May 27, 1849; died July, 1860, unmarried; and three others who died in infancy.

Maria Louise Goodwin (James Doswell, Thomas, John, James, Peter, James) was born October 2, 1826, in Lovington, Nelson county, Va.; was married in 1856, in Fayette county, Tenn., to Leroy P. Stewart. *Stewart* children: i. Annie, married J. Z. Tankersley; ii. Lula, married D. H. Rosseau; iii. Leroy; iv. Jennie Catherine.

John Watts Goodwin (James Doswell, Thomas, John, James, Peter, James) was born August 6, 1831, in Nelson county, Va.; was married October 25, 1870, at Early Grove, Miss., by Rev. W. K. Douglas, to Elizabeth Rose Bailey, who was born August 5, 1839, in Fayette county, Tenn., a daughter of Dr. Isham G. and Susan Bird (Smith) Bailey. By occupation he was a merchant, and treasurer of Little Rock & Memphis Railroad, in politics a Democrat, and in religion an Episcopalian. He resided in 1897 in Little Rock, Ark. Children: i. John Bailey, born August 16, 1875; ii. William, born July 26, 1877; iii. Bessie, born September 24, 1879.

Virginia Ella Goodwin (James Doswell, John, James, Peter, James) was born January 31, 1843, in Nelson county, Va.; was married June 13, 1858, in Fayette county, Tenn., to Charles T. Hodges. *Hodges* children: i. Kate, born November 16, 1859, married Henry McDonald; ii. Virginia Olivia, born August 18, 1861; iii. Anna Rives, born September 5, 1865, married T. B. Crow; John Goodwin, born November 4, 1867, married Minnie King; v. William Franklin, born July 14, 1870, married Arnold Lange; vi. Charles McMultin, born March 12, 1873.

William Henry Goodwin (Thomas, John, James, Peter, James) was born September 19, 1805, in Nelson county; was married November 20, 1827, in Louisa county, to Bertha Wood Harris, born October 22, 1802, in Louisa county, a daughter of Nelson and —— (Pryor) Harris. She died October 23, 1848. He was married, second, to Mrs. Carrington. His name is also given as William *Harris* Goodwin. By occupation he was a farmer and stock-raiser, in politics a Democrat, and in religion a Methodist. They resided at Arrington Depot, Nelson county, Va. Children by first wife: i. Nelson Harris, born October 5, 1828, married Sarah Nicholas; ii. Edwin Williams, born October 7, 1830, resided in Arrington, Va., unmarried; iii. Mary Ann, born November 26, 1832, married James C. Pettit; iv. India Bertha, born July 26, 1835, married John W. Wheeler; v. Martha (Pattie) Pryor, born April 11, 1838, married Rev. James E. Gates. No children by second wife.

Nelson Harris Goodwin (William Henry, Thomas, John, James, Peter, James) was born October 5, 1828, in Nelson county, Va.; was married 1864, in Albemarle county, Va., to Sarah Nicholas, born in 1840, in Albemarle county, Va., a daughter of John and —— (Moore) Nicholas. By occupation he was a farmer, in politics a Readjuster, and in religion a Methodist. They resided in Nelson county, Va. Nelson Harris Goodwin was deputy-sheriff of Nelson county many years. He died in 1883 of paralysis, honored and respected by all who knew him. Children: i. John W., born April 23, 1867; ii. Charles W., born January 27, 1869, married —— Woodson; iii. Sarah E., born September 11, 1871; iv. Martha (Pattie) T., born February 25, 1877; v. Josephine N., born February 22, 1879; vi. Charlotte E., born February 5, 1881; vii. Nelson Harris, born May 13, 1883.

Mary Ann Goodwin (William Henry, Thomas, John, James, Peter, James) was born November 26, 1832, in Nelson county, Va.; was married in 1868, in Nelson county, Va., to James C. Pettit, who was born in 1830, in Amherst county, Va. By occupation he was a farmer, in politics a Democrat, and in religion a Methodist. They resided near Roseland, Nelson county, Va. *Pettit* child: i. James, born 1870.

India Bertha Goodwin (William Henry, Thomas, John, James, Peter, James) was born July 26, 1835, in Nelson county, Va.; was married in 1878 in Nelson county, Va., to John W. Wheeler, born in Henrico county, Va. In politics a Democrat. She resided near Arrington, Nelson county, Va. Wheeler children names not furnished.

Martha (*Pattie*) *Pryor Goodwin* (William Henry, Thomas,

John, James, Peter, James) was born April 11, 1838, in Nelson county, Va.; was married in 1875 in Nelson county, Va., to Rev. James E. Gates, born 1823 in Virginia. By occupation he was a minister, in politics a Democrat, and in religion a Methodist. They resided in 1893 in Culpeper county, Va. *Gates* child: i., James, born 1876.

Edmund Chisman Goodwin (Thomas, John, James, Peter, James) was born April 4, 1808, in Nelson county, Va.; was married first, in 1838, in Nelson county, Va., to Maria F. Ware, born in Nelson county, Va. Maria (Ware) Goodwin died September 5, 1845. He was married, second, August 13, 1846, to Mary Ann Small, born April 18, 1824, a daughter of John and Sallie (Fitzpatrick) Small; she died May 15, 1863. Edward C. was a farmer, a Democrat, and a Baptist. He resided in Nelson county, where he died in 1875. Children by first wife: i. John Wesley, born 1840, died in West Virginia in Civil War, unmarried; ii. William Henry, born August 24, 1845, married Margaret W. Plunkett. Children by second wife: iii. Sarah Temperance, born June 5, 1847, married John Perry Hughes; iv. James Napoleon, born July 27, 1848, resides Kansas City, Mo., unmarried; v. Mary Hester, born February 11, 1852, married Samuel S. Johns.

William Henry Goodwin (Edmund Chisman, Thomas, John, James, Peter, James) was born August 24, 1845, in Nelson county, Va.; was married November, 1866, in Nelson county, Va., by Rev. Thomas W. Roberts to Margaret Watts Plunkett, born 1842 in Nelson county, Va., a daughter of Willis R. and Mahala R. (Dillon) Plunkett. By occupation he was a farmer, in politics a Republican, and in religion a Baptist. They reside near Afton, Nelson county, Va. Children: i. Thomas Joseph, born December 2, 1867, married ——— Harris; ii. Clancy Mornington, born September 18, 1869; iii. Alma, born June 25, 1871; iv. Kemnie Elsie, born August 8, 1873, married Thomas E. Mays; v. William David, born May 28, 1876; vi. John Overton, born March 27, 1878; vii. James Jeter, born June 17, 1880; viii. Charles Preston, born June 17, 1880; ix. Henry Clay, born August 17, 1883.

Sarah Temperance Goodwin (Edmund Chisman, Thomas, John, James, Peter, James) was born June 5, 1847, in Nelson county; was married March 4, 1863, in Nelson county by Rev. Thomas W. Roberts to John Perry Hughes, who was born February 12, 1841, in Nelson county, a son of Breckenridge and Elizabeth (Perry) Hughes. They resided in Slaughter, Va., where she died

January 19, 1894. *Hughes* children: i. Charles Goodwin, born July 14, 1865, married Eliza C. Damron; ii. Herbert Breckenridge, born December 31, 1866, killed on railroad December 12, 1889; iii. John Lester, born November 1, 1868; iv. Claude Metford, born February 23, 1870; v. Napoleon Quinton, born November 17, 1871; vi. Carlton Temperance, born January 25, 1874, died July 15, 1874; vii. Maude Pauline, born April 10, 1875, resides Aylmer, Virginia; viii. Annie Blanche, born September 29, 1877; ix. Bessie Hazleton, born February 23, 1879; x. Edwin Parker, born June 22, 1881; xi. Mary Elizabeth, born December 17, 1883; xii. Hope Vernal, born June 13, 1885.

Mary Hester Goodwin (Edmund Chisman, Thomas, John, James, Peter, James) was born February 11, 1852, in Nelson county, Va.; was married 1867, in Nelson county, Va., by B. M. Wailes to Samuel S. Johns. By occupation he was a mechanic, in religion a Baptist. They resided in 1897 in Charleston, Ill. *Johns* children: i. Bessie Goodwin, born December 12, 1869; ii. Percy Manton, born March 28, 1872, resides Charleston, Ill.; iii. Augustus Bradford, born August 24, 1873.

James Goodwin (John, James, Peter, James) was born November 28, 1768, in Hanover county, Va., was married to Fanny Harris, a daughter of Overton and Ann (Nelson) Harris. Children: i. Elizabeth Ann (Nancy), married —— Dandridge; ii. William Harris, married —— Harris, and died *sine prole;* iii. Fanny Thompson, died unmarried; iv. James, died unmarried; v. Diana, died unmarried.

William Doswell Goodwin (John, James, Peter, James) was born July 28, 1774, was married November 12, 1814, by Rev. Rowzie to Mary Wingfield Cosby, who was born March 7, 1793, in Louisa county, Va., a daughter of Wingfield and Anna (Baker) Cosby. By occupation he was a farmer. They resided in Hanover county. William Doswell Goodwin was a soldier in the war of 1812, and died December 12, 1827, in Hanover county, Va. Mary Wingfield (Cosby) Goodwin died September 28, 1872. Miss Maria Wingfield Goodwin has furnished copies of Bible and family records of this branch. Children: i. Ann Elizabeth, born October 13, 1816, married Alfred Dukes; ii. John Wingfield, born February 6, 1818, married Diana Dorothea Goodwin; iii. Mary Overton, born December 18, 1819, died February 17, 1820; iv., Sarah Frances, born May 3, 1822, married William Harris Cosby; v. Maria Wingfield, born May 10, 1823, resides Tyler P. O., Va., unmarried; vi. Martha Overton, born March 7, 1825, died February 24, 1826; vii. Julia Ann, born May 2, 1827, married William Hugh Goodwin.

Ann Elizabeth Goodwin (William Doswell, John, James, Peter, James) was born October 13, 1816, in Hanover county, Va.; was married to Alfred Dukes. *Dukes* children: i. William Burnley; ii. Mary Goodwin, married John A. Garrett; iii. Elizabeth Ann, unmarried; iv. Sarah Wingfield, married D. Rhion; v. Philip St. John.

John Wingfield Goodwin (William Doswell, John, James, Peter, James) was born February 6, 1818, in Hanover county, Va.; was married January 19, 1842, by Rev. —— Faulkner, to Diana Dorothea Goodwin, who was born July 11, 1820, a daughter of Littleton and Elizabeth Doswell (Goodwin) Goodwin; he, son of Peter,[4] James,[3] Peter,[2] James[1]; she, daughter of John,[4] James,[3] Peter,[2] James.[1] By occupation he was a farmer. They resided in Hanover county. Diana Dorothea Goodwin died January 7, 1864; John Wingfield Goodwin died April 25, 1878; William Littleton Goodwin died at his grandmother's, Mrs. Mary Wingfield (Cosby) Goodwin. He was a soldier in the Confederate army; was captured after the fall of Richmond, and was kept a prisoner at Newport News for some time, where his health was utterly wrecked. Children: i. William Littleton, born November 7, 1843, died June 8, 1868, unmarried; ii. Thomas Cosby, born March 21, 1846, resides in Reidsville, N. C.; iii. Elizabeth Doswell, born November 9, 1848, died February 20, 1849; iv. Nannie Washington, born March 19, 1850; v. Virginia Hawes, born March 6, 1853; vi. Mary, born December 1, 1854; vii. Edward, born September 16, 1856, died April 28, 1862; viii. John Walter, born November 22, 1859, resides in Hinton, W. Va.; ix. Charles Doratheus, born May 1, 1861.

Charles Doratheus Goodwin (John Wingfield, William Doswell, James, John, Peter, James) was born May 1, 1861; was connected with the Chesapeake and Ohio Railroad. He resided in Richmond, Va., and contributed both time and money to the compiling of these records. He died in 1895, and had delayed sending his own family data, giving his time to collecting that of the earlier generations. No reply has been made to numerous letters asking for information concerning him and his family.

Sarah Frances Goodwin (William Doswell, John, James, Peter, James) was born May 3, 1822, in Hanover county, Va.; was married December 7, 1848, in Hanover county, Va., by Rev. ——

Cook, to William Harris Cosby, who was born October 19, 1812, in Hanover county, Va., a son of Thomas Baker and Mary Garland (Harris) Cosby; she a daughter of Col. William Overton Harris and Diana Chisman Goodwin, John,[4] Peter,[3] James,[2] James.[1] By occupation he was a merchant and farmer, in politics a Democrat, and in religion a Baptist. They resided in Hanover and Albemarle counties, Va. William Harris Cosby was married first to a Miss Marshall, of Orange county, Va. *Cosby* children: i. William Goodwin, born November 12, 1851, married —— Briggs; ii. Sue Lee, born September 18, 1853, married Dr. J. S. Daniel, of North Carolina; iii. Charles Walker, born December 3, 1856, married —— Martin; iv. Linnie Boyd, born May 2, 1861, unmarried; v. Morris Wellford, born October 12, 1866, married Mrs. —— Alexander.

Julia Ann Goodwin (William Doswell, John, James, Peter, James) was born May 2, 1827, in Hanover county, Va.; was married ———— 27, 1853, in Hanover county, Va., to William Hugh Goodwin, who was born September 22, 1829, in Louisa county, Va., a son of Dr. William and Frances Jane (Goodwin) Goodwin; he a son of Hugh,[5] Robert,[4] James,[3] Peter,[2] James[1]; she a daughter of John Chapman,[5] Robert,[4] etc. They resided in Louisa Courthouse, where she died April 13, 1893. *Goodwin* children: i. Mary A., married Malcolm Hiter; ii. Frances Jane, married Thomas Winston; iii. William D.; iv. H. B.; v. John C.; vi. Julia M.; v. Maria; viii. Amelia.

Edmund Chisman Goodwin (John, James, Peter, James) was born October 30, 1776, in Hanover county, Va.; was married, first, to Miss —— Anderson; he was married, second, to Elizabeth Waddy, and, third, to —— ——. He was a farmer, and resided in Haywood county, Tenn. Mr. Otha King, Searcy, White county, Ark., is said to be able to furnish information concerning Edmund, but all letters to him remain unanswered. Children by first wife: i. Eliza; ii. Sarah. Child by second wife: iii. John. Child by third wife: iv. Karrenhappock Rebecca.

Elizabeth Doswell Goodwin (John, James, Peter, James) was born September 3, 1781, in Hanover county, Va.; was married January 19, 1797, to Littleton Goodwin, a son of Peter and Sarah (Coghill) Goodwin, James,[3] Peter,[2] James.[1] They resided on the Oakley Home farm, Caroline county. Elizabeth Doswell (Goodwin) Goodwin died June 27, 1849, in Caroline county, Va. *Goodwin* children: i. Peter Doswell, married Mrs. Fannie Bullard; ii. Sarah

Coghill, married John Woodford; iii. Elizabeth Doswell, married Charles Augustine Lewis; iv. Ann Maria, born February 20, 1805, married Rev. Thomas Smith; v. Littleton, born October 5, 1807, married Caroline A. H. Chiles; vi. Mary Frances, died in infancy; vii. Clara Hawes, died unmarried; viii. Eleanor Harwood, died in infancy; ix. John Thomas, born June 8, 1818, married Ann Elizabeth Goodwin; x. Diana Dorothea, married John Wingfield Goodwin.

Elizabeth Doswell Goodwin was a small woman with light hair and blue eyes. Great strength of character, blended with sweetness of disposition, made her firm in discharge of duty and easy of approach. Besides attending to her own large family, she and "Uncle Littleton" always had room for the orphan children of both families. She was the "lady of the manor" in the age in which she lived in her vicinity, and was especially kind to the poor. In cases of sickness she would send dainties to them by her black servants, prettily arranged on a silver waiter, much to the disgust of the "blacks," who thought it all nonsense for "Miss Betsy to be sending dem t'ings to dem low down po' white trash." But her idea was to "elevate those in a lower social scale." During the late war, one family thus served for generations, came to the rescue of her son and grandchildren when left impoverished entirely without luxury and almost without necessities. Thus "bread on the water returneth after many days."

Her mother, Sarah Coghill, used to say, "We're next in coat of arms to the king," and tell of an old satin cloak, yellow lined with pale green.

One of the grandmothers fought a British officer away from Oakley, Caroline county (P. O. Paige), with a linen table cloth, just as it was saturated by the laundress.

Oakley contains an old saddle on which one of the Goodwins used to ride to Yorktown. Notwithstanding its extreme age, it is in a good state of preservation.

The tankard, which was marked with the Goodwin coat of arms, was buried in three wars—Revolution, 1812, and the late war—each time with money in it. Miss Mary Goodwin, of Fredericksburg, Va., sold it just after the war for bread, she said. She was condemned by many for not offering it to members of the family instead of selling to a stranger; but she was too proud to let them know her necessity. I know of no one who can give a description of it.

Peter Goodwin (James, Peter, James) was born, probably, in Caroline county, on "Oakley" farm; was married, 1st, to Sarah Coleman, a daughter of —— and —— (Hawes) Coleman. Peter married, 2ndly, Sarah Coghill, a daughter of Frederick and —— (Hawes) Coghill,[3] (Frederick,[2] James Coghill[1]). The mothers of Peter's wives were sisters. He resided on the "Oakley" farm, in Caroline county, Va., where he and his wives and his parents are buried. Children by first wife: i. James Coleman, born March 29,

1761; married Nancy Graves; ii. a daughter, married a Coleman; iii. a daughter, married Hawes Coleman, Jr., and died *sine prole.* Children by second wife: iv. Thomas, born October 9, 1770; married Ann Maria Smith; v. Littleton, married Elizabeth Doswell Goodwin; vi. Harwood, born September 3, 1775; married Sarah Minor; viii. Elizabeth Garland, married Henry Coleman.

James Coleman Goodwin (Peter, James, Peter, James) was born March 29, 1761, in Virginia; was married, September 6, 1782, in Virginia, to Nancy Graves, born May 27, 1765, a daughter of Thomas and Frances (Coleman) Graves. By occupation he was a farmer. They resided in Caroline county, Virginia, removing to Fayette county, Ky., where James Coleman Goodwin died February 9, 1814, and Nancy (Graves) Goodwin died August 12, 1844. Children: i. Sarah Coleman, born February 25, 1785; married Frank Flournoy; ii. Joseph Graves, born February 26, 1789; married, 1st, Frances C. Graves; 2ndly, Rachel Downey; iii. Lloyd King, born November 12, 1791; married Mary Jane Graves; iv. Mary (Polly) Coleman, born June 1, 1802; married Lewis Barber.

Sarah Coleman Goodwin (James Coleman, Peter, James, Peter, James), was born February 25, 1785, in Pendleton county, Ky.; was married, September 25, 1800, to Frank Flournoy, born January 18, 1773, in Culpeper (?) county, Va., a son of Mathews Flournoy. They resided in Scott county, Ky., where she died June 20, 1858. *Flournoy* children: i. James, unmarried; ii. Gideon; iii. Frank; iv. Robert; v. Walker; vi. Llewellen; vii. Sarah; viii. Ann.

Joseph Graves Goodwin (James Coleman, Peter, James, Peter, James), born February 26, 1789, in Pendleton county, Ky., was married, first, December 25, 1810, to Frances Coleman Graves, born October 26, 1793, in Spotsylvania county, Va., a daughter of Joseph and Mary (Goodwin) Graves; she a daughter of Robert,[4] James,[3] Peter,[2] James.[1] He married, 2ndly, Rachel Downey, a daughter of William Downey. Joseph Graves Goodwin resided near Lexington, Ky., where he died June 23, 1872. Children by the first wife: i. Joseph J., born March 25, 1816; married Lucy Graves; ii. Dr. Benjamin G., born October 25, 1818; died unmarried; iii. John T., born November 24, 1820; married Serena Cartwright, and died *sine prole;* iv. Mary (Polly) Frances, born December 28, 1822; married William Bowman, and died *sine prole.* Children by second wife: v. William Montgomery, born August, 1833; died aged sixteen years; vi. Breckenridge Payne, born 1836; died aged five years; vii. Martha Montgomery, born March 9,

1838; married Joseph Marshall, M. D.; viii. Rachel Josephine, born May 5, 1840; married John W. Muir; ix. Ella Jane, born December, 1842; died young.

Joseph J. Goodwin (Joseph Graves, James Coleman, Peter, James, Peter, James), born March 25, 1816, married Lucy Graves. Joseph J. Goodwin died February 14, 1863. Children: i. J. G.; ii. T C.; iii. Elizabeth, married ——— Brown; iv. Mary (Polly), married ——— Saffrans.

Martha Montgomery Goodwin (Joseph Graves, James Coleman, Peter, James, Peter) was born May 9, 1838, near Lexington, Ky.; was married September 25, 1855, at Lexington, by Rev. Joseph Bullock, to Joseph Marshall, M. D., who was born June 24, 1832, in Lexington, a son of Robert and Elizabeth (Evans) Marshall. By occupation he was a physician, in politics a Democrat, and in religion a Presbyterian. They resided in Lexington, Ky., Davenport, Iowa, and (1897) Normal, Ill. *Marshall* children: i. Ella J., born August 19, 1856, married I. D. Horner; ii. Ida Elizabeth, born November 21, 1858, married J. K. Waddington; iii. Rachel Josephine, born October 13, 1865, married T. H. Lindley; iv. Robert, born September 27, 1867, married Maude Owsley; v. Sara Rodes, born May 11, 1872; vi. Edwin Shelby, born May 14, 1874.

Lloyd King Goodwin (James Coleman, Peter, James, Peter, James) was born November 17, 1791, in Pendleton county, Ky.; was married August, ——, to Mary Jane Graves, who was born January 14, 1796, in ———, Va., a daughter of Joseph and Mary (Goodwin) Graves; she a daughter of Robert Goodwin,[4] James,[3] Peter,[2] James.[1] By occupation he was a farmer, in politics a Democrat, and in religion a Presbyterian. Lloyd King Goodwin was a very successful farmer, and by industry and frugality became quite wealthy. He never sought political distinction of any kind. He was an honorable gentleman, and a grand old man; both himself and his wife living to a green old age. Children: i. Mary Ann, born October 17, 1814, married William Hayes; ii. Frances Jane, born March 1, 1817, married Frank Brown; iii. Hardenia Bunly, born September 2, 1819, married William Harris Coleman; iv. Elizabeth, born March 17, 1822, married Pike M. Thompson; v. Barbara, born April 27, 1825, married Spencer Coleman Tyler; vi. George Joseph, born November 8, 1826, married Eliza M. Jamison; vii. Nancy, born May 29, 1830, married Joseph L. Cartwright; viii. James Lucien, born April 5, 1832, unmarried; ix. Benjamin Lloyd, born September 29, 1836, unmarried; x. Lucina Victoria, born September 20, 1838, married Thompson Hildreth.

Mary Ann Goodwin (Lloyd King, James Coleman, Peter, James, Peter, James) was born October 17, 1814, in Fayette county, Ky.; was married February 11, 1830, in Fayette county, Ky., to William Hayes, a son of William Hayes. By occupation he was a farmer, in politics a Democrat, and in religion a Christian. They resided in Fayette county, Ky. *Hayes* children: i. Mary Jane; ii. Robert; iii Lucy Ann; iv. Margaret; v. William; vi. Alexander C.; vii. Ann; viii. Joseph; ix. James; x. Samuel.

Frances Jane Goodwin (Lloyd King, James Coleman, Peter, James, Peter, James) was born March 1, 1817, in Fayette county, Ky.; was married November 5, 1835, by Thomas P. Dudley, to Frank Brown. By occupation he was a farmer, and in religion a Baptist. They resided in Clark county, Ky. *Brown* children: i. Amanda; ii. Joseph L.; iii. Mary H.; iv. Thomas; v. Benjamin; vi. Henry R.

Hardenia Bunly Goodwin (Lloyd King, James Coleman, Peter, James, Peter, James) was born September 2, 1819, in Fayette county, Ky.; was married April 24, 1838, by Thomas P. Dudley, to William Harris Coleman, a son of Robert Coleman. By occupation he was a farmer, in politics a Democrat, and in religion a Baptist. They resided in St. Louis county, Mo. *Coleman* children: i. Carolina, married Thomas Locker; ii. Elizabeth, unmarried; iii Dinah; iv. Jane, married —— Fields; v. Belle, married Henry Lay; vi. Lily, married Robert G. Coleman.

Elizabeth Goodwin (Lloyd King, James Coleman, Peter, James, Peter, James) was born March 17, 1822, in Fayette county, Ky.; was married October 15, 1843, by William Rash, to Pike M. Thompson. By occupation he was a farmer, in politics a Democrat, and in religion a Baptist. They resided in Saline county, Mo. *Thompson* children: i. John W., married —— Graves; ii. Lloyd G., married Nannie Brown; iii. Lucien, married —— Johnson; iv. Ruth, married —— Bush; v. Pike M.; vi. Elizabeth, married —— Richardson; vii. Laura, married —— Saltonstall.

Barbara Goodwin (Lloyd King, James Coleman, Peter, James, Peter, James) was born April 27, 1825, in Fayette county, Ky.; was married May 1, 1847, in Fayette county, Ky., by Thomas P. Dudley, to Spencer Coleman Tyler, a son of Henry Tyler. By occupation he was a farmer, in politics a Democrat. They resided in St. Charles county, Mo. *Tyler* children: i. George L., married Mary Cartwright; ii. Lucien; iii. Dinah, married —— Martin; iv. Lucinda, married George Cartwright; v. Huldah, married —— Cottle; vi. Joseph; vii. Spencer.

George Joseph Goodwin (Lloyd King, James Coleman, Peter, James, Peter, James) was born November 8, 1826; was married December 13, 1849, in Montgomery county, Ky., by Elder B. E. Allen, to Eliza M. Jamison, who was born November 4, 1829, in Montgomery county, Ky., a daughter of Milton and Sarah (Badger) Jamison. By occupation he was a farmer, and in politics a Democrat. They resided in Fayette county, Ky., removing to Lexington, Ky. Children. i. George Miller; ii. William Moore; iii. Benjamin Lloyd; iv. Milton Jamison; v. David Badger; vi. Edward Lane; vii. Hugh Smith; viii. Mary Caroline.

Nancy Goodwin (Lloyd King, James Coleman, Peter, James, Peter, James) was born May 29, 1830; was married December 2, 1847, by Thomas P. Dudley, to Dr. Joseph L. Cartwright, a son of James and Adeline (Graves) Cartwright; she a daughter of Joseph and Mary (Goodwin) Graves. By occupation he was a physician, in politics a Democrat, and in religion a Christian. *Cartwright* children: i. James L.; ii. George L., married Lucinda Tyler; iii. Mary V., married George Tyler.

Lucina Victoria Goodwin (Lloyd King, James Coleman, Peter, James, Peter, James) was born September 20, 1838; was married April 5, 1860, to Thompson Hildreth. *Hildreth* children: i. Joseph; ii. Victor; iii. Walter; iv. Helen; v. Lawrence.

Mary Coleman Goodwin (James Coleman, Peter, James, Peter, James) was born June 1, 1802; was married in Fayette county, Ky., by Thomas Dudley, to Lewis Barbee. *Barbee* children: i. James; ii. Porter, married Mary Harris; iii. Benjamin, unmarried.

Miss ——— *Goodwin* (Peter, James, Peter, James) was born in "Oakley," Caroline county; was married to Hawes Coleman, Jr., a son of John and Nicie (Hawes) Coleman. They resided in Caroline county, Va. Mrs. (Goodwin) Coleman died ———. Hawes Coleman, Jr., so-called on account of having an uncle, Hawes Coleman, married second, Miss ——— Harris, and had William H., Hawes N., Mary and John Joy. He married third, Nancy Overton; no children.

Thomas Goodwin (Peter, James, Peter, James) was born October 9, 1770, in "Oakley," Caroline county, Va.; was married October 2, 1792, at Fredericksburg, Va., to Ann Maria Smith, who was born 1774, in Fredericksburg, Va., a daughter of William and Mary Smith, she of Dublin, Ireland. By occupation he was a merchant, in politics a Whig, and in religion an Episcopalian. They resided in Fredericksburg, Va. Ann Maria (Smith) Goodwin was a Roman Catholic. The family Bible gives Thomas as born in "the parish of St. Maguerites." Children: i. William Peter, born 1793; married first, Caroline Heiskell, second, ———; ii. Sarah, born 1795; unmarried; iii. Charles, born June 30, 1797; married Janet Gordon Carmichael; iv. Thomas (Doctor), born 1799; died unmarried; v. Arthur, born 1801; married Anne Thom; vi. Littleton, born 1803; married Ann Maria Smock; vii. John Harwood, born 1805; married Mary Hart; viii. Mary, born 1809; ix. Elizabeth, born 1811; x. Ann Maria Smith, born 1813; married John Hart.

Col. William Peter Goodwin (Thomas, Peter, James, Peter, James) was born 1793 in Fredericksburg, Va.; was married first at Fredericksburg, Va., to Caroline Heiskell, who was born in Fredericksburg, Va., a daughter of Ferdinand Heiskell. Caroline (Heiskell) Goodwin died ———. He married second ———. He was a merchant and farmer, in politics a Democrat, and in religion an Episcopalian. He resided in Fredericksburg, Va. Children by first wife: i. Ann Elizabeth, married John Thomas Goodwin; ii. Maria Margaret, died unmarried; iii. Evalina Caroline Sarah, married Arthur Rose Hart. Children by second wife; iv. Ann Maria Smith, married Edgar Wilton Harrison; v. William Macy Byrd, married Nancy Holliday.

Ann Elizabeth Goodwin (William Peter, Thomas, Peter, James, Peter, James) was born April 27, 1818, in Fredericksburg, Va.; was married December 19, 1838, at Fredericksburg, by Rev. Edward McGuire, to John Thomas Goodwin, who was born June 8, 1818, in Oakley, a son of Littleton and Elizabeth Doswell (Goodwin) Goodwin. He a son of Peter,[4] James,[3] Peter,[2] James.[1] She a daughter of John,[4] James,[3] Peter,[2] James.[1] By occupation he was a farmer, in politics a Democrat, and in religion an Episcopalian. They resided in Oakley, Caroline county, where she died June 16, 1872. *Goodwin* children: i. Caroline Heiskell, born April, 1841; resides in Berryville, Va.; unmarried; ii. Littleton Clarence, born September 1, 1843; died unmarried; iii. William Peter, born November 19, 1845; married Mary Byrd Goodwin; iv. Elizabeth Glassell, died in infancy; v. Sarah Byrd, born February 8, 1850;

married William J. Lacy; vi. Evelina Lewis, born September 11, 1852; married Bartelott Davies; vii. John Thomas, died in infancy.

Charles Goodwin (Thomas, Peter, James, Peter, James), born June 30, 1797, in Fredericksburg, Va., was married December 21, 1819, at Fredericksburg, Va., by Rev. E. C. MacGuire, to Janet Gordon Carmichael, born February 6, 1802, in Fredericksburg, Va., a daughter of James Carmichael. By occupation he was a bank officer, in politics a Democrat, and in religion an Episcopalian. They resided in Fredericksburg, Va., until about 1838, and thereafter in Baltimore, Md. Children: i. Thomas, born September 8, 1820, married Ellen Ayers; ii. James Carmichael, born September 17, 1823, died July 25, 1830; iii. Eleanor Carmichael, born August 28, 1825, married George R. W. Allnutt; iv. Edward Hackley Carmichael, born November 22, 1826, married Mary Van Bibber; v. Sarah Ann, born August 23, 1829, unmarried.

Thomas Goodwin (Charles, Thomas, Peter, James, Peter, James) was born September 8, 1820, in Fredericksburg, Va., was married January 13, 1846, at Baltimore, by Rev. Thomas Atkinson, to Ellen Ayers, born February 21, 1825, in Baltimore, a daughter of Jacob and Sidonia (Sellman) Ayers. By occupation he was a merchant, in politics a Democrat, and in religion an Episcopalian. He resided in Fredericksburg until his 16th year, and thereafter in Baltimore. Children: i. Charles, born October 30, 1846, married first, Louisa Lawrence, second, Sarah Lawrence; ii. Jacob Ayres, born May 19, 1849, married first, Lillie Alexander, second, Mary Alexander; iii. Janet Gordon, born September 13, 1850, married J. Kelty Smith; iv. Charlotte Elizabeth, born July 14, 1853, married first, William H. Smith, second, J. Vansant Smith; v. Sarah Anne, born July 15, 1855, unmarried; vi. Ellen Thomas, born February 21, 1858, unmarried; vii. Thomas, born May 12, 1864, resides in Memphis, Tenn.

Charles Goodwin (Thomas, Charles, Thomas, Peter, James, Peter, James) was born October 30, 1846, in Baltimore, was married first, October 27, 1869, at Baltimore, by Rev. E. H. C. Goodwin, to Louisa A. Lawrence, born May 28, 1850, in Baltimore, a daughter of France L., and Hannah R. (Thomas) Lawrence. He was married second, April 22, 1884, by Rev. William Kirkers, at Baltimore, to Sarah E. Lawrence, born February 10, 1854, a sister to his first wife. By occupation he was a merchant, in politics a Republican, and in religion an Episcopalian. He resided in Baltimore. Children by first wife: i. Charles, born July 17, 1870; ii. Ethel, born August 17, 1872, died July 21, 1874; iii. Madge, born December 28, 1874, died July 20, 1875. Children by second wife: iv. France Lawrence, born August 20, 1885; v. W. H. Baldwin, born October 18, 1889.

Rev. Edward Hackley Carmichael Goodwin (Charles, Thomas, Peter, James, Peter, James) was born November 22, 1826, in Fredericksburg, Va., was married October 26, 1858, at Westminster, Md., by Dr. Thomas Richey, to Mary Peterson Van Bibber, born March 9, 1839, in North River, Gloucester county, Va., a daughter of Andrew and Betty Carter (Garretson) Van Bibber. By occupation he was an Episcopal minister. They have resided for about twenty-five years on Governor's Island, New York. Children: i. Frederic Van Bibber, born August 4, 1859, married Elisabeth Hungerford; ii. William Dallas, born March 21, 1861, married Mary Van Nest Thompson; iii. Betty Carter, born December 2, 1863, resides at Governor's Island; iv. Edward, born March 18, 1866, married Mary Myrtle Zollner; v. Mary Verena, born January 9, 1869, resides at Governor's Island; vi. Paul, born February 25, 1876, resides at Governor's Island.

Arthur Goodwin (Thomas, Peter, James, Peter, James) was born in 1801 in Fredericksburg, Va., was married in 1834 at Fredericksburg, Va., by Rev. C. C. McGuire, to Ann Thom, born 1808 in Fredericksburg, Va., a daughter of Reuben J., and Eleanor (Reat) Thom. He was an Episcopalian. They resided in Fredericksburg. Their daughter, Miss Nannie S. Goodwin, of Fredericksburg, has collected and furnished much of the family data. Arthur Goodwin was a banker, and owned, among other pieces of real estate, the Washington farm, where the cherry tree incident is said to have taken place. This farm now constitutes the most thickly settled part of Fredericksburg. The Washington house was sold, but Miss Nannie and her two sisters dwell in the adjoining house, which they have furnished almost wholly with antique furniture inherited from the earlier generations, the effect being very quaint and beautiful. Children: i. Eleanor Reat, born 1835, married James Hamilton Wilson; ii. Mary Allen; iii. Ann Smith, resides in Fredericksburg, Va.; iv. Elizabeth Carmichael; v. Arthur; vi. Janet Gordon; vii. Arthur Thomas; viii. Reuben Thom; ix. Catherine Ware.

Eleanor Reat Goodwin (Arthur, Thomas, Peter, James, Peter, James) was born in 1835 in Fredericksburg, Va., was married in

1863 at Richmond, Va., by Rev. Joshua Peterkin, to James Hamilton Wilson, who was born in Charleston, S. C., a son of Hugh. By occupation he was a banker, in politics a Democrat, and in religion an Episcopalian. *Wilson* children: i. Son; ii. Anne Elizabeth; iii. Sarah McLeod.

Littleton Goodwin (Thomas, Peter, James, Peter, James) was born 1803 in Fredericksburg, Va., was married at Fredericksburg, Va., to Ann Maria Smock, a daughter of William and Sarah (Richards) Smock. He was an Episcopalian. Children: i. Thomas E.; ii. Caspar Wistar; iii. Littleton.

John Harwood Goodwin (Thomas, Peter, James, Peter, James) was born 1805 in Fredericksburg, Va., was married to Mary Hart, a daughter of Charles and Nancy (Rose) Hart. Children (names not furnished).

Ann Maria Smith Goodwin (Thomas, Peter, James, Peter, James) was born 1813 in Fredericksburg, Va., was married at Fredericksburg, Va., by Rev. E. C. Maguire, to John Hart, who was born in Hartwood, Fauquier county, Va., a son of Charles and Nancy (Rose) Hart. By occupation he was a farmer. They resided in Fauquier county, Va. *Hart* children: i. Thomas Goodwin; ii. Robert Allison; iii. John Goodwin; iv. Laura Chapman; v. Nannie Smith; vi. Charles Henry; vii. Alexander; viii. Arthur Rose; ix. Benjamin; x. Nannie; xi. Susan.

Littleton Goodwin (Peter, James, Peter James) was born about 1778 in "Oakley," Caroline county, Va., was married January 19, 1797 to Elizabeth Doswell Goodwin, who was born September 3, 1781, in Hanover county, Va., a daughter of John and Elizabeth (Doswell) Goodwin,[4] James,[3] Peter,[2] James.[1] By occupation he was a farmer. They resided on "Oakley" farm in Caroline county, Va., where Littleton Goodwin died about 1824, aged 46. His wife died in 1849. Children: i. Peter Doswell, married Mrs. Fannie (Woolfolk) Bullard; ii. Sarah Coghill, married John Woodford; iii. Elizabeth Doswell, married first, William Woodford, second, Charles Augustine Lewis; iv. Ann Maria, born February 20, 1805, married Rev. Thomas Smith; v. Littleton, born October 5, 1807, married Caroline A. H. Chiles; vi. Mary Frances, died in infancy; vii. Clara Hawes, died unmarried; viii. Eleanor Harwood, died in infancy; ix. John Thomas, born June 8, 1818, married Ann Elizabeth Goodwin; x. Diana Dorothea, married John Wingfield Goodwin.

Sarah Coghill Goodwin (Littleton, Peter, James, Peter, James), born on "Oakley" farm, was married to John Woodford. *Woodford* children: i. Katesby,* married John C. Willis; ii. John Battle; iii. Elizabeth Meriwether.

Elizabeth Doswell Goodwin (Littleton, Peter, James, Peter, James), born at "Oakley," was married to Charles Augustine Lewis. Elizabeth Doswell Goodwin married, 1st, William Woodford, who died *sine prole*. *Lewis* child: i. Elizabeth Meriwether, married Rodes Massie.

Ann Maria Goodwin (Littleton, Peter, James, Peter, James), born February 20, 1805, at "Oakley," Caroline county, Va.; was married, January 16, 1823, at "Oakley," Virginia, by Rev. William McGuire, to the Rev. Thomas Smith, born November 19, 1799, in "Office Hall," King George Courthouse, Va., a son of Caleb and Mary (Waugh) Smith (cousins). By occupation he was a lawyer and a minister, in politics a Democrat, and in religion an Episcopalian. They resided in King George county, in Alexandria, and in Smithfield, Va., and in Parkersburg, W. Va. He died April 4, 1847. His wife died April 16, 1885.

Lieutenant Caleb Smith, U. S. A., was wounded at the battle of Molina del Rey (Mexican War), then a mere youth; was promoted on the field for bravery, and was complimented by General Scott. At the opening of the Civil War he resigned his commission, and entered the Confederate States army. He was wounded at Bull Run, and again was promoted on the field. He died a Christian. A contemporary thus described him: "High-minded and noble to an unusual degree, he was, intellectually, second to no man in Virginia. His Christian life was sincere, and his influence unbounded. His death was a severe loss to all who knew him."

Smith children: i. a son, born October 10, 1823; died October 10, 1823; ii. Caleb, born December 14, 1824; died December 22, 1874, unmarried; iii. Thomas Goodwin, born January 5, 1827; married Virginia Safford; iv. Mary Waugh, born December 23, 1829; married Mathias Moyer Waud; v. Littleton Goodwin, born March 14, 1831; died February 23, 1866, unmarried; vi. Elizabeth Doswell, born April 15, 1833; died July 2, 1834; vii. William Heber, born July 30, 1835; died July 21, 1837; viii. Ann Maria, born March 31, 1839; married Floyd Neely; ix. Channing Moore, born October 15, 1843; resides at Parkersburg, W. Va.; unmarried; x. Clarine Elizabeth, born April 19, 1845; resides at Parkersburg; unmarried.

Littleton Goodwin (Littleton, Peter, James, Peter, James), born

---

*Resides at Indian Town, Orange county, Va.

October 5, 1807, at "Oakley," was married, November 22, 1827, to Caroline A. H. Chiles, born June 24, 1806, a daughter of Samuel and Martha (Bell) Chiles. By occupation he was a planter. They resided in Louisa county, Va. Littleton Goodwin died August 12, 1852. Caroline A. H. (Chiles) Goodwin died April 6, 1871. Children: i. Mary Ellen, born August 25, 1828; married William F. T. Garnett; ii. Martha Bell, born November 10, 1829; died February 27, 1831; iii. Samuel Chiles, born September 22, 1831; married Margaret Ann Pollard; iv. Elizabeth Doswell, born March 19, 1833; died January 4, 1834; v. Ann Maria, born April 5, 1834; died February 13, 1853; vi. Littleton, born September 17, 1835; married Elizabeth Bell Chiles; vii. John Thomas, born April 17, 1837; married Mary Frances Abrahams; viii. William W., born October 31, 1838; died October 30, 1864, unmarried; ix. Caroline A. H., born December 14, 1839; died June 30, 1855, unmarried; x. Magnus Hardcastle, born February 4, 1852, perhaps 1840; died July 21, 1871, unmarried; xi. Robert Bruce, born October 18, 1842; died June 1, 1845.

Mary Ellen Goodwin (Littleton, Littleton, Peter, James, Peter, James), born August 25, 1828, was married August 24, 1848, to William F. F. Garnett. *Garnett* children: i. James Mosca, died in infancy; ii. Mary Louisa, died in infancy; iii. Ann; iv. Julia; v. Edith; vi. Rosa; vii. Caroline.

Samuel Chiles Goodwin (Littleton, Littleton, Peter, James, Peter, James), born September 22, 1831, was married, December 26, 1851, by Rev. Archibald Dick, to Margaret Ann Pollard, born October 9, 1834, in Caroline county, Va., a daughter of George Butler and Frances (Bridges) Pollard. They resided near Penola post-office, Va. No children.

Littleton Goodwin (Littleton, Littleton, Peter, James, Peter, James) was born September 17, 1835; was married October 30, 1856, to Elizabeth Bell Chiles. Littleton Goodwin died during the late war. He and his wife were cousins. Child: Mary Bell.

John Thomas Goodwin (Littleton, Littleton, Peter, James, Peter, James) was born April 17, 1837; was married in 1859, to Mary Frances Abrahams. John Thomas Goodwin died February 12, 1863. Children: i. Elizabeth, died ——; ii. Thomas.

John Thomas Goodwin (Littleton, Peter, James, Peter, James) was born June 8, 1818, at "Oakley," Caroline county; was married December 19, 1838, at Fredericksburg, by Rev. Edward McGuire, to Ann Elizabeth Goodwin, who was born April 27, 1818, in Fredericksburg, a daughter of Col. William Peter and Caroline (Heiskell) Goodwin,[6] Thomas,[5] Peter,[4] James,[3] Peter,[2] James.[1] By occupation he was a farmer, in politics a Democrat, and in religion an Episcopalian. They resided on the "Oakley" farm, in Caroline county, Va. Children: i. Caroline Heiskel, born April, 1841, resides in Berryville, Va., unmarried; ii. Littleton Clarence, born September 1, 1843, died unmarried; iii. William Peter, born November 19, 1845, married Mary Byrd Goodwin; iv. Elizabeth Glassell, died in infancy; v. Sarah Byrd, born February 8, 1850, married William J. Lacy; vi. Evelina Lewis, born September 11, 1852, married Prof. Bartelot F. Davies and d. s. p.; vii. John Thomas, died in infancy.

William Peter Goodwin (John Thomas, Littleton, Peter, James, Peter, James) was born November 19, 1847, at "Oakley"; was married November 21, 1871, at Rose Hill, Va., by Rev. William Green, to Mary Byrd Goodwin, who was born November 18, 1854, at Rose Hill, Spottsylvania county, a daughter of William Macy Byrd and Nancy (Holliday) Goodwin,[7] William Peter,[6] Thomas,[5] Peter,[4] James,[3] Peter,[2] James.[1] By occupation he was a farmer, in politics a Democrat, and in religion an Episcopalian. They resided on "Oakley" farm, Paige post-office (1897). William Peter Goodwin surrendered with Lee at Appomattox. Children: i. Elizabeth Hampton, born August 24, 1872; ii. Margaret Byrd, born July 5, 1874, married Mason Grant Scripture; iii. Mary Lewis, born March 22, 1876; iv. Annie J. Thomas, born December 10, 1878; v. Caroline Lacy, born February 20, 1880; vi. Everett Washington, born November 11, 1882; vii. Littleton Clarence, born May 4, 1885; viii. John Thomas, born March 29, 1889; ix. William Bryan, born October 29, 1891; x. Ruth Harwood, born July 17, 1894.

Sarah Byrd Goodwin (John Thomas, Littleton, Peter, James, Peter, James) was married to William J. Lacy. *Lacy* children: i. Clarence Davies; ii. Sterling Byrd; iii. Williams Jones.

Diana Dorothea Goodwin (Littleton, Peter, James, Peter, James) was born July 11, 1820, at "Oakley"; was married January 19, 1842, by Rev. —— Faulkner, to John Wingfield Goodwin, who was born February 6, 1818, in Hanover county, Va., a son of William Doswell and Mary Wingfield (Cosby) Goodwin. By occupation he was a farmer. Diana Dorothea (Goodwin) Goodwin died January 7, 1864. John Wingfield Goodwin died April 25, 1878. *Goodwin* children: i. William Littleton, born November 7, 1843, died June 8, 1868, unmarried; ii. Thomas Cosby, born March 21,

1846, resides in Reidsville, N. C.; iii. Elizabeth Doswell, born November 9, 1848, died February 20, 1849; iv. Nannie Washington, born March 19, 1850; v. Virginia, born March 6, 1853; vi. Mary, born December 1, 1854; vii. Edward, born September 16, 1856, died April 28, 1862; viii. John Walter, born November 22, 1859, resides in Hinton, W. Va.; ix. Charles Doratheus, born May 1, 1861.

Harwood Goodwin (Peter, James, Peter, James) was born September 3, 1775, at "Oakley," Caroline county, Va.; was married 1798, in Caroline county, Va., to Sarah Minor, who was born August 5, 1775, in Caroline county, Va., a daughter of John and Elizabeth (Cosby) Minor. (He was steward for General Nelson.) By occupation he was a farmer, in politics a Democrat, and in religion an Episcopalian. They resided at Topping Castle, Caroline county, Louisa county, and Orange county, Va. Sarah (Minor) Goodwin died September 19, 1852, in Louisa county; Harwood Goodwin died August, 1859, in Orange county.

My grandfather, Harwood Goodwin, was one of the most original characters I ever knew. He had no confidence in anything professional. Perfectly truthful himself, his word was as good as his bond. There were very few in whom he had any faith, though, to their credit be it said, in the other two members of his household, his wife and invalid daughter, he reposed implicit confidence. He was certainly an incongruous mixture of opposites. He was perfectly honest and just in all his dealings. His moral character was unimpeachable. Charitable in deed, he was uncharitable in word; harsh in speech, considerate and tender in action; severely critical of any deviation from the path of rectitude, yet always ready to help the transgressor. Perfectly honorable, an Israelite in whom there was no guile, and yet an unbeliever who feared not God nor respected man. His consideration for the females of his family was very beautiful. His wife was a cripple, his daughter an invalid of many years' standing. To save them from all annoyance and to minister to their slightest wants was the object and end of his existence. Never did I see self so completely laid aside; every wish was gratified that he ever heard them express. His daughter died first, and then his devotion centered itself on his wife. For years it seemed as if she might be spared as long as he was, but a sudden attack of apoplexy carried her off, and thenceforward his occupation was gone; he had nothing to live for. Her work-basket he kept by him, in it a cork-soled shoe that assisted her lameness; while her last words he constantly repeated, "Lay me down." He told me people thought he was in his dotage, but that though his memory might fail, he never wished to forget the last words he heard her speak. He died in 1860.

TO THE MEMORY OF HARWOOD GOODWIN.

"The friend of God, man's friend aright,
Stern enemy of lies,
Has gone to place his record bright
Before adoring skies.

"His keen blue eye of lightning flash,
Oft rent the bigot's veil,
And gave the flimsy web as trash
To every passing gale.

"Dull canting soul, thy tongue becurb,
For him thou needst not weep;
Be still, and dare not to disturb
The moral giant's sleep.

"Sleep on, thou rarity of earth,
Deep silence round thee reign,
Till sounds omnipotent in birth
Wake thee to life again."

Children: i. John Minor, born February 2, 1799, married Eliza T. Stevens; ii. Elizabeth Hawse, born March, 1800, married Dr. Joseph Winston Pendleton; iii. Mary Tompkins, born 1803, died unmarried.

Dr. John Minor Goodwin (Harwood, Peter, James, Peter, James) was born February 2, 1799, in Louisa county, Va.: was married November 23, 1824, in Orange county, Va., by Rev. Jeremiah Chandler, to Eliza Thompson Stevens, who was born December 24, 1801, in Orange county, Va, a daughter of Capt. William and Margaret (Mills) Stevens. (He was captain in the war of 1812.) By occupation he was a physician, in politics a Whig, and in religion a Baptist. They resided in Orange county, Va. Children: i. John Woolfolk, born September 27, 1825; married Caroline Decker and died *sine prole;* ii. Margaret Mills, born December 22, 1827; married Dr. David Pannill; iii. Sarah Minor, born May 4, 1830; married Dr. W. T. Woolfolk; iv. William Harwood, born May 31, 1832; married first, Belle Renick, second, Josephine Renick; v. Eliza Stevens, born August 21, 1835; unmarried; vi. Frederick Nathaniel, born 1837; died February, 1892, unmarried; vii. Julia Elizabeth Stanard, born March 16, 1840; unmarried; viii. Mary Virginia Terrill, born March 16, 1840; died August 6, 1888, unmarried; ix. Thomas Littleton, died from wound received in Confederate service; x. Eloise Pauline Eustace, born December 13, 1848; married Dr. W. Stevens.

Margaret Mills Goodwin (John Minor, Harwood, Peter, James, Peter, James) was born December 22, 1827, in Orange county, Va.; was married February 26, 1860, in Orange county, by Rev. James L. Powell, to Dr. David Pannill, who was born September 23, 1812, in Orange county, a son of George and Susan Harrison

Blackwell. By occupation he was a physician and farmer, in politics a Whig, and in religion a Methodist. They reside (1897) in Pine Top, Orange county. No children.

Elizabeth Hawes Goodwin (Harwood, Peter, James, Peter, James) was born March, 1800, in Louisa county, Va.; was married, 1818, at Louisa, Va., to Dr. Joseph Winston Pendleton, who was born 1797, in Louisa, Va., a son of Edmund and Winston Pendleton. By occupation he was a physician, in politics a Whig, and in religion a Christian. They resided in Louisa county. *Pendleton* children; i. John Harwood, died in infancy; ii. Sarah Littleton, died in infancy; iii. Sarah Littleton, died in infancy; iv. Joseph Winston, born 1826; married Margaret Ewing *; v. John Overton, born 1828; married Nannie Harris; vi. Mary Burnly, born 1831; married Prof. Charles I. Kemper †; vii. Elizabeth Hawse, born 1834; married Dr. John Anderson; viii. Louise Catherine, born 1836; married Dr. George Kimbrough; ix. other child, died in infancy.

Elizabeth Garland Goodwin (Peter, James, Peter, James) was born at Oakley; was married to Henry Coleman. *Coleman* children: i. Peter, died after graduating from University of Virginia; ii. son, died in infancy; iii. son, died in infancy.

Robert Goodwin (James, Peter, James) was born 1739; was married December 11, 1766, to Jane Tulloch, a daughter of Thomas and Barbara (Garland) Tulloch. By occupation he was a farmer. They resided in Louisa county. Robert Goodwin died May 12, 1789, in his fiftieth year. He served in the Revolutionary War, in which he received a wound. The descendants of Robert Goodwin claim to be the heirs, through Dr. Tulloch, to the Lady Jane Grant's countless millions. No copy of her will has been found by the compiler of these records, nor can he find that a Lady Jane Grant ever existed who was in any way related to the Goodwin or Tulloch family.

DEED.—Robert Goodwin, county of Louisa, parish of Trinity, to John Hogan, of same county and parish. Consideration fifteen pounds, one hundred acres.

Dated October 12, 1772. Admitted to record same day.

IN THE NAME OF GOD, AMEN. I, Robert Goodwin, of the county of Louisa, being in an ill state of health, but of perfect memory, in order to settle and

---

* Their daughter (Miss) Elizabeth Winston Pendleton resides in Wheeling, West Va.

† They reside in Lexington, Ky.

dispose of such estate, which has pleased Almighty God to bless me with, do make and ordain this my last will and testament in manner and form following, *imprimis:*

I lend to my tender and beloved wife, Jane Goodwin, during her natural life the tract of land I purchased of Major John Cratchfield, also the tract of land I purchased of Capt. Robert Barrett. I also lend her during her natural life my part of water mill. I likewise lend her all my household and kitchen furniture, and all the plantation tools where I now live. I also lend her $\frac{2}{3}$ of my slaves except twelve, namely, Ned, Squire, Jamey, Nancy, Moses, Reubin, Frank, David, Lewis, Esther, Silvey, and Paul.

I also give my beloved wife Jane my certificates of every kind to pay taxes with, and the balance of them, if any at her death, to be given or disposed of among my children as she thinks proper. I also lend her a pair of cart wheels, 25 head of cattle, 30 head of hogs, all my sheep, 2 work horses, and a riding horse. I also lend her my stall during her natural life.

Items: I give to my son Hugh that tract of land and that gold mine I purchased of Col. Wm. Johnson. I also give him one negro boy, Moses, and the black Cott, to him, his heirs and assigns forever.

Items: I give to my son Robert the tracts of land I purchased of Major John Cratchfield and Capt. Robert Barrett, which land I have lent to my wife during her natural life, also one negro boy named Frank, to him, his heirs and assigns forever.

Items: I give to my son John Chapman the tract of land that was given to me by my father, except 50 acres, being on the north side of the river; also I give my said son my part of the water mill at the death of my wife; also I give my said son one negro boy named Reubin, to him, his heirs and assigns forever.

Items: I give to son Archibald Tulloch 50 acres of land on the north side of Little River; it is a part of a tract given to me by my father. Also I give to my said son Archibald Tulloch 150 acres of land I purchased of Robert Garland; also I give my said son one negro boy named Ned, to him, his heirs and assigns forever. It is my will that if Robert Garland should refuse to make my son Archibald Tulloch a good and lawful right when required to the said 150 acres of land, then in that case I give to my said son Archibald Tulloch one hundred and ten pounds in lieu of this 150 acres of land; but if this Robert Garland should make my son Archibald Tulloch a good and lawful title to this 150 acres of land, then it is my will and desire that my executors do pay to the said Robert Garland one hundred and ten pounds.

Items: It is my will and desire to make all my sons as equal as I can, and to effect which I desire that the land, mills and moneys given to my sons Hugh, Robert, John Chapman and Archibald Tulloch be valued, and those whose lands, including mills and moneys, are most valuable shall pay to the others whose land, including mills and moneys, are least valuable, so much as the judgment of men shall be just and right to make their estate given them as nearly equal as possible.

Items: I give to my daughter Elizabeth Garland Coleman four negroes, viz.: Susie, Jane and her child Nancy, and Poll, to her heirs forever.

Items: I give to my daughter Mary two negroes, viz.: Esther and David, and one hundred and ten pounds, to be paid to her when she comes of age or marries; to her heirs and assigns forever.

Items: I give to my daughter Barbara two negroes, viz.: Silvey and Lewis, and also one hundred and ten pounds, to be paid to her when she comes of age or marries; to her assigns forever.

Items: It is my will and desire that, if in the judgment of disinterested men I have given my daughter Coleman before and by this will more than I have given my daughters Mary and Barbara, in that case my desire is that my daughters, Mary and Barbara, do have in that division of my estate as much more than my daughter Coleman, as they have been supposed to have had less given them by this will.

Items: It is my will and desire that all the rest of my estate, both real and personal not heretofore given by this will, be equally divided among my seven (7) children, viz.: Hugh, Robert, John Chapman, Archibald Tulloch, Elizabeth Garland Coleman, Mary and Barbara.

Items: It is my will and desire that the balance of the stock of any kind, and utensils not lent to my wife, be sold to pay off a part of the money.

Items: It is my will and desire that the negroes lent to my wife, at her death be equally divided among my said seven children, Hugh, Robert, John Chapman, Archibald Tulloch, Elizabeth G. Coleman, Mary and Barbara, or their heirs lawfully begotten.

Lastly, I do constitute and appoint my beloved wife, Jane Goodwin, executrix, Mr. Spencer Coleman and my son Hugh, executors to this my last will and testament, in confirmation whereof I have hereunto fixed my hand and seal this 9th day of May, one thousand seven hundred and eighty-nine (1789).

Sealed, Signed, ROBERT GOODWIN (seal).

Published and delivered in the presence of Robert Barrett, Andrew Todd, Jr., Francis Lipscomb, at a court for Louisa county, June 8, 1789. This will was this day in open court proved by the oath of Robert Barrett, Andrew Todd and Francis Lipscomb, and by the court is ordered to be recorded. Liberty is reserved to the executrix and executors therein named to qualify as executors and executrix to this said will when they shall think fit, and at a court held for Louisa connty July 13, 1789, Jane Goodwin, executrix, and Spencer Coleman and Hugh Goodwin, executors of Robert Goodwin, deceased, with their securities, entered into and acknowledged their bond for their deed, administration of the estate of this said deceased and performance of his will, and on motion certificate is granted then for obtaining a probate in due form.

Children: i. Elizabeth Garland, born May 2, 1768; married Spencer Coleman; ii. Hugh, born February 27, 1770; married Elizabeth Blades; iii. Mary, born September 28, 1772; married Joseph Graves; iv. Barbara, born November, 18, 1774; married William Coghill; v. Robert, born August 10, 1777; married Judith Tyler; vi. John Chapman, born November 6, 1779; married Anna Rhodes Thompson; vii. Mildred, born June 9, 1782; died September 11, 1784; viii. Archibald Tulloch, born November 30, 1785; married Candace Sandridge.

Elizabeth Garland Goodwin (Robert, James, Peter, James) was born May 4, 1768, in Louisa county, Va.; was married in Louisa county, Va., to Spencer Coleman, who was born in Pine Forest, Spottsylvania county, Va., a son of John and Nicie (Hawes) Coleman.[3] She was a daughter of Samuel and —— (Spencer) Hawes. By occupation he was a farmer, in politics a Democrat, and in religion a Baptist. They resided in Pine Forest, Va. Elizabeth Garland (Goodwin) Coleman died. Spencer Coleman married twice, but had no children by his second marriage. *Coleman* children: i. Robert, married Caroline Harris; ii. Jane, married D. DeJarnette; iii. Huldah, married Daniel DeJarnette; iv. Lucinda, married Henry Tyler; v. Spencer, married Rebecca Diggs; *vi. Elizabeth G., married Elliott DeJarnette; vii. Nicie Ann, married Hugh Goodwin.

Hugh Goodwin (Robert, James, Peter, James) was born February 27, 1770, in Louisa county, Va.; was married December 22, 1789, in Spottsylvania county, Va., to Elizabeth Blades. By occupation he was a farmer, and in politics a Democrat. They resided in Spottsylvania county, Va. Children: i. William, born January 21, (25) 1791, married Frances Jane Goodwin; ii. Jane, born June 30, 1793, married Rev. William Hiter; iii. Nicie Hawes, born July 22, 1797, married Benjamin Boxley; iv. Hugh, born December 21, 1800, married Nicie Ann Coleman; v. Elizabeth, born March 29, 1803, died in infancy; vi. Robert, born July 29, 1804, died in infancy; vii. Mary Ann, born August 14, 1808, married William P. Anderson; viii. Frances, born September 18, 1810, died in infancy; ix. Barbara Garland, born August 2, 1812, married 1st, Henry Booten; 2ndly, Capt. —— Jones; 3rdly, Joshua Tinsley; x. Nancy, born October 28, 1815, died in infancy.

Dr. William Goodwin (Hugh, Robert, James, Peter, James) was born January 21 (25), 1791, in Spottsylvania county, Va.; was married May 8, 1823, to Frances Jane Goodwin, who was born June 7, 1805, near Frederick's Hall, Va., a daughter of John Chapman and Anna Rhodes (Thompson) Goodwin,[5] Robert,[4] James,[3] Peter,[2] James.[1] By occupation he was a farmer and physician, and in politics a Democrat. Dr. William Goodwin served through the war of 1812. Children: i. Frances Ann, married Dr. K. M. Francesco; ii. John Thompson; iii. William Hugh, born September 22, 1829, married Julia Ann Goodwin; iv. Robert; v. James.

---

* Mother of Dr. J. S. DeJarnette.

Frances Ann Goodwin (William, Hugh, Robert, James, Peter, James) was married to Dr. K. M. Francesco, a son of Peter Francesco (in the navy during the war of the Revolution).

William Hugh Goodwin (William, Hugh, Robert, James, Peter, James) was born September 22, 1829, in Louisa county, Va.; was married September 27, 1853, in Hanover county, Va., to Julia Ann Goodwin, who was born May 2, 1827, in Hanover county, Va., a daughter of William Doswell and Mary (Cosby) Goodwin,[5] John,[4] James,[3] Peter,[2] James.[1] By occupation he was a gold-miner (retired), and in politics a Democrat. They reside at Louisa C. H., Va. Mr. Goodwin was the only one of the Virginia Goodwins who could trace his lineage to the immigrant ancestor. He states that his father claimed to have the family record for eight hundred years, but the MS. was destroyed during the war. Children: i. Mary A., married Malcolm Hiter; ii. Frances Jane, married Thomas Winston; iii. William D.; iv. H. B.; v. John C.; vi. Julia M.; vii. Maria; viii. Amelia.

Jane Goodwin (Hugh, Robert, James, Peter, James) was born June 30, 1793; was married in Louisa county, Va., to Rev. William Hiter, who was born in Christian county, Ky., a son of James and Elizabeth (Young) Hiter. By occupation he was a minister, in politics a Democrat, and in religion a Baptist. They resided in Louisa county, Va. *Hiter* children: i. James, born 1813, married first, Lucy Marina Dickinson; second, Jemima Boxley; ii. William Young, born 1815, married Sarah Montague Daniel; iii. Elizabeth, born 1817, married Archibald Tulloch Goodwin; iv. Hugh Goodwin, born December 13, 1819, married Susan Harris.

Nicie Hawes Goodwin (Hugh, Robert, James, Peter, James) was born July 22, 1797, in Louisa county, Va.; was married December 23, 1819, in Louisa county, Va., by Rev. William Y. Hiter, to Benjamin Boxley, who was born June, 1794, in Louisa county, Va., a son of Spiller Boxley. By occupation he was a farmer, in politics a Democrat, and in religion a Baptist. They resided in Louisa county, Va. Benjamin Boxley died in 1822 of typhoid fever. Nicie Hawes (Goodwin) Boxley died January —, 1866. Their youngest child was born three weeks after the death of Benjamin. *Boxley* children: i. Mary Hawes, born September 10, 1820, married Dr. Charles Grandison Powell; ii. Elizabeth, born September 10, 1820, married James Robert Goodwin; iii. Benjamin, born 1822, died in infancy.

Hugh Goodwin (Hugh, Robert, James, Peter, James) was born

December 21, 1800; was married July 6, 1824, to Nicie Ann Coleman, a daughter of Spencer and Elizabeth Garland (Goodwin) Coleman. She was a daughter of Robert,[4] James,[3] Peter,[2] James.[1] They resided at White Walnut, Louisa county, Va. Hugh Goodwin twice represented his county in the State legislature. Children: i. Spencer Coleman, born May 4, 1825, died July 17, 1826; ii. Robert Coleman, born August 15, 1827, died November 21, 1844; iii. Huldah Ann, born July 22, 1829, married first, Dr. John Meredith; second, William Henry Harris; iv. William Hawes Blades, born July 17, 1831, married Mrs. Mary Little Harris; v. Hugh, born February 23, 1833, married Mary Allen Farley; vi. Andrew Jackson, born March 2, 1835, married Harriet Jones; vii. John Coleman Blades, born June 29, 1837, married Elizabeth Evalina Moody; viii. Coleman Spencer, born November 12, 1839, died May 15, 1862, in Confederate army; ix. Archibald Tulloch, born March 21, 1842, married Candace L. Barret; x. Elizabeth Blades, born April 22, 1844, unmarried; xi. Chapman Hiter, born September 29, 1846, unmarried.

Huldah Ann Goodwin (Hugh, Hugh, Robert, James, Peter, James) was born July 22, 1829, at White Walnut, Louisa county, Va., was married first, in Louisa county, Va., to Dr. John Meredith, Jr., who was born in Louisa county, Va., a son of Dr. John Meredith. Dr. John Meredith, Jr., was a very prominent physician, and at one time represented his county in the House of Delegates. He was a Democrat in politics, and a Disciple in religious belief. They resided in Louisa county, Va., where he died. She married, second, William Henry Harris, who was born in Albemarle county, a son of William B. Harris. They resided in Albemarle county. No children by first husband. *Harris* children: i. Nannie Eliza, married Robert W. Moffette; ii. Charles Edward, married Ida Rogers.

Dr. William Hawes Blades Goodwin (Hugh, Hugh, Robert, James, Peter, James) was born July 17, 1831, in White Walnut, Louisa county, Va., was married October 3, 1874, at Sheltonville, Ga., to Mrs. Mary (Little) Harris, a daughter of E. D. Little. By occupation he was a physician, in politics a Democrat. They resided in Doraville, Ga. He was a physician of considerable distinction. He died September 14, 1885, in Doraville, and is buried in the Presbyterian churchyard. He graduated in Philadelphia, took a complete course of study in Europe, and was professor of chemistry and anatomy in several colleges in the South. (No children).

Hugh Goodwin (Hugh, Hugh, Robert, James, Peter, James) was born February 23, 1833, in White Walnut, Louisa county, Va., was married August 13, 1884, at Hutto, Texas, by John W. Pearson, to Mary Allen Farley, who was born March 9, 1861, in Trinity county, Texas, a daughter of William H., and Lucy (Hargrove) Farley. By occupation he was a farmer, in politics a Democrat, and in religion a Cumberland Presbyterian. They reside in Hutto Texas. Children: i. Lucy Coleman, born July 23, 1885; ii. Hulda Blades, born February 21, 1887; iii. Hugh, born November 30, 1888, died February 5, 1890; iv. William F., born September 8, 1890; v. Spencer C., born August 26, 1893.

Andrew Jackson Goodwin (Hugh, Hugh, Robert, James, Peter, James) was born March 2, 1835, in White Walnut, Louisa county, Va.; was married, 1856, in Louisa county, Va., by Rev. Lindsay Coleman, to Harriet Jones, who was born 1831 in Louisa county, Va., a daughter of Gabriel and ——— (Winston) Jones. By occupation he was a farmer, in politics a Democrat. They resided in Louisa county, Va., where he died May 9, 1892. No children.

John Coleman Blades Goodwin (Hugh, Hugh, Robert, James, Peter, James) was born June 29, 1837, in White Walnut, Louisa county, Va.; was married March 13, 1864, at Petersburg, Va., by Rev. Churchill J. Gibson, to Elizabeth Evalina Moody, who was born January 30, 1841, in City Point, Prince George county, Va., a daughter of George Edward and Elizabeth Ann (Wood) Moody. By occupation he was a farmer, in politics a Republican, and in religion an Episcopalian. They resided in Cuckoo, Louisa county, Va Children: i. Nicie Coleman, born January 25, 1868, married Joseph S. Goodwin; ii. Martha Aurelia, born April 24, 1872; iii. William Edward Shands, born September 27, 1874.

Nicie Coleman Goodwin (John Coleman Blades, Hugh, Hugh, Robert, James, Peter, James) was born January 25, 1868; was married to Joseph S. Goodwin, a son of John and Sarah A. (Dickinson) Goodwin (Archibald Tulloch, Robert, James, Peter, James). Nicie Coleman (Goodwin) Goodwin died March 11, 1888. *Goodwin* children (names not furnished).

Archibald Tulloch Goodwin (Hugh, Hugh, Robert, James, Peter, James) was born March 24, 1842, in White Walnut, Louisa county, Va.; was married July 17, 1867, in Louisa county, Va., by Mr. Bledsoe, to Candace Lamenda Barret, who was born in Louisa county, Va., a daughter of William Chiswell and Mary (Goodwin) Barrett; she was a daughter of Archibald Tulloch (Robert, James,

Peter, Robert.) By occupation he was a farmer, in politics a Democrat, and in religion a Disciple. They resided in Louisa county, Va. Children: i. Mary Elizabeth, born January 20, 1870; ii. Daniel Coleman, born May 7, 1873; iii. Hulda Ann, born May, 1875.

Mary Ann Goodwin (Hugh, Robert, James, Peter, James) was born August 14, 1808, in Louisa county, Va.; was married April 13, 1825, in Louisa county, Va., by Rev. William Y. Hiter, to William P. Anderson, who was born 1802 in Louisa county, Va., a son of Mathew and Martha (Tanner) Anderson. By occupation he was a farmer, in politics a Democrat, and in religion a Baptist. They resided in Louisa county, Va. *Anderson* children: i. Elizabeth, born 1826, married A. K. Bowles; ii. Mathew, born 1827, married Ella Kimbrough; iii. Nicie, born 1830; iv. William Goodwin, born 1832, married B. Anderson; v. Martha Jane, born 1834, married Charles G. Dickinson.

Mary Goodwin (Robert, James, Peter, James), born September 28, 1772, in Louisa county, Va., was married, October 26, 1790, in Spottsylvania county, Va., by Absalom Waller, to Joseph Graves, born July 10, 1760, in Spottsylvania county, Va., a son of Thomas and Frances (Coleman) Graves. By occupation he was a planter, in politics a Democrat, and in religion a Baptist. They resided at the "Red House," Spottsylvania county, Va, where Mary (Goodwin) Graves died, January 11, 1815. Joseph Graves died June 6, 1826, in Fayette county, Ky. *Graves* children: i. Eliza Tulloch, born December 18, 1791; married Jesse Key; ii. Frances Coleman, born October 26, 1793; married Joseph Graves Goodwin; iii. Mary Jane, born January 14, 1796; married Lloyd King Goodwin; iv. Adeline, born April 15, 1798; married James Cartwright; v. George L., born March 7, 1800; died unmarried; vi. Barbara Garland, born September 4, 1802; married Joseph Chinn; vii. Eleanor Burnly, born November 28, 1804; married Buford Early Allen;* viii. Elizabeth Chapman, born January 28, 1806; married Samuel L. Coleman; ix. Joseph, born March 1, 1809; married Margaret Hays; x. Benjamin R., born April 19, 1813; married Jane R. Hughes.

Barbara Goodwin (Robert, James, Peter, James), born November 18, 1774, was married to William Coghill, born in 1754, a son of Frederick and —— (Hawes) Coghill. Barbara (Goodwin) Cog-

* Their daughter, Mrs. Adeline Allen Graves, resides in Lexington, Ky.

hill died March 15, 1794. *Coghill* child: William Goodwin, born March 4, 1794; married —— Samuel; died 1832.

Robert Goodwin (Robert, James, Peter, James), born August 10, 1777, near Frederick's Hall, Louisa county, Va., was married, October 11, 1804, at Frederick's Hall, to Judith Tyler. By occupation he was a farmer. They resided in Louisa county. Children: i. George Tyler, born November 3, 1805; ii. Robert Woodson, born November 13, 1807; married Martha Waddy; iii. Elizabeth, born January 25, 1810; married Alfred M. Goodwin; iv. Semple, born December 20, 1811; married Sarah Waddy; v. Ann T., born March 3, 1814; vi. Henry H., born July 1, 1817; vii. Judith, born August 26, 1819; viii. Sarah C., born March 15, 1823.

Robert Woodson Goodwin (Robert, Robert, James, Peter, James), born November 13, 1807, in Spottsylvania county, Va., was married, July 22, 1842, in Louisa county, Va., by Rev. H. Frazer, to Martha Waddy, born October 5, 1825, in Louisa county, Va., a daughter of Garland Thompson and Martha (Patsy) (Chisholm) Waddy. In religion he was a Baptist. They resided in South Carolina and in Louisa county, Va. Children: i. Julia Dabney, born August 21, 1843; married George A. W. Kuper; ii. Martha Woodson, born October 26, 1844; married Hawes F. Powell; iii. Garland Waddy, born July 27, 1846; iv. Nannie, born December 17, 1847; v. Robert, born January 1, 1850; married Nora Mason.

Elizabeth Goodwin (Robert, Robert, James, Peter, James), born January 25, 1810, in Louisa county, Va., was married, March 1, 1832, in Louisa county, Va., by Rev. —— Billingsley, to Alfred Muren Goodwin, born 1807, in Louisa county, a son of Archibald Tulloch and Candace (Sandridge) Goodwin. By occupation he was a farmer, in politics a Democrat, and in religion a Baptist. They resided in Louisa county, Va. Alfred Muren Goodwin died July 25, 1867. Elizabeth (Goodwin) Goodwin died May 10, 1877. *Goodwin* children: i. Ann Tyler, born 1833; ii. Joseph S., born 1834; iii. Elizabeth Jane; iv. Archibald Tulloch, born July 13, 1837; unmarried; v. Josephine, born December 23 1840; married Robert W. Woolfolk; vi. Louise Virginia, born September 5, 1842; vii. Alfred Muren, born January 12, 1845; married Elizabeth Boxley; viii. John Tyler, born September 13, 1847; married Florence Denkle; ix. Judith Catherine, born October 29, 1857; married James H. Denkle; x. Jane Grant, born March 6, 1853; married Robert W. Zimmerman.

Semple Goodwin (Robert, Robert, James, Peter, James), born

December 20, 1811, in Louisa county, Va., was married, December 12, 1839, in Louisa county, Va., by Allen Mansfield, to Sarah D. Waddy, born September 9, 1820, in Louisa county, Va. By occupation he was a farmer, in politics a Democrat, and in religion a Disciple. They resided near Frederick's Hall, Va. Semple Goodwin died June 5, 1887. Children: i. Anthony T., born January 17, 1842; ii. Semple S., born May 20, 1847; iii. Richard T., born May 29, 1849; iv. Amanda Lee, born September 25, 1860; v. Judith, born July 10, 1863.

John Chapman Goodwin (Robert, James, Peter, James) was born November 10, 1779, near Frederick's Hall, Louisa county, Va.; was married December 20, 1803, near Frederick's Hall, Va., by Absalom Waller, to Anna Rhodes Thompson, who was born December 26, 1783, in Louisa county, Va., a daughter of David and —— (Quarles) Thompson. By occupation he was a farmer, in politics an old line Whig, and in religion a Baptist. They resided on "Oaksby" farm, about three miles from Frederick's Hall, Va. John Chapman Goodwin served in the war of 1812, and received a wound in the leg. He died December 13, 1845; Anna Rhodes (Thompson) Goodwin died August 11, 1865.

I, John C. Goodwin, of the county of Louisa and State of Virginia, do hereby make this my last will and testament in the manner and form following, that is to say:

I desire that my beloved wife, Anna R. Goodwin, have possession during her natural life of the land on which I now reside, lying together on the south side of Little River, and likewise the Colby tract of land which I purchased of David Bulloch; and to have like possession of what slaves she may think proper, except those she may dispose of in the allotment hereinafter mentioned. It is my desire that my said wife have possession of what money I may die possessed after paying my just debts; also my entire stock of horses, hogs, sheep, cattle, crops, plantation, utensils, household and kitchen furniture.

I give to my daughter, Frances I., the following slaves, to-wit: Billy, age thirty-five years; Hannah, thirty; Mariah, sixteen; Matilda, fourteen; Martin, twelve; Pleasant, eight; Delphin, five; Peter, three.

I give to my son, William T., the following slaves, to-wit: Mitchell, age twenty years; Nancy, eighteen; Silvia, fourteen; Daniel, eleven; Katy, two, and Dorcas, a child which has fallen to my grandson, Edmond Pendleton Goodwin; and inasmuch as he, by the death of his father, fell heir to a larger portion of property than I shall be able to give my own children, I have, therefore, thought proper not to give him anything more.

I have deeded to my son, John C. Goodwin, the tract of land on which he resides, valued at $2,400, and the following slaves: Elijah, age twenty years; Caroline, eighteen; Abram, ten; Susan, eighteen months old; Scipio, fifty-nine, and Lucy, fifty-one.

I give to my daughter, Mary Ann, the following slaves, to-wit: Henry, age eighteen years; Patsey, thirty; Lucy, twenty; Polly, thirteen; Washington, eleven; Rachel, thirteen; Eliza, six, and Janie, one.

I have deeded to my son, James R., the tract of land on which he resides, valued at $2,400, and the following slaves, to-wit: Lewis, age fifty years; Fanny, thirty-five; Frederick, nineteen; Mary, eleven; Addison, ten.

It is my will and desire that each of my two youngest daughters, Mildred B. and Maria E., when they become of age or marry, shall, out of the slaves which I leave my wife in possession of, have an allotment of the same description as my two daughters already married; and if said allotment cannot be made out of each of said shares, I desire it shall be made up to them in money, sufficient to make out an allotment of the same description, that is to say: They are to have enough money out of my estate to purchase a like description of property. It is also my desire that each of said daughters shall have the amount of $200 in stock and household furniture.

It is my desire that my son, Charles Q., shall have the tract of land which I purchased of Samuel A. Soles, and enough of the Hart tract to make it equal to the lands of my two sons, John C. Goodwin and James R., and likewise an allotment of negroes of the same description of each of theirs, and if such cannot be made out of those in my wife's possession, I wish him to have sufficient money out of my estate to purchase such, and $200 in stock and furniture.

The balance of my land on the north side of Little River, after making out an allotment to my son, Charles Q., I desire to be sold; and whereas I estimate that the allotment to each of my said sons is worth $900 more than that to each of my daughters, I desire the proceeds of said land to be applied as to make them equal. If there should be any more than enough to make these equal, I wish it equally divided between all of the above named children, and if not enough, I wish it made up from the sale of such perishable property as my wife can spare, or by money on hand.

At the death of my wife, I wish all the property and money she may die possessed of to be equally divided among the above named children now living.

It is also my wish that my beloved wife have like possession of the two small pieces of land which I purchased of William H. Howe and Dunmore Harris as she has of the lands mentioned above.

In witness whereof, I have hereunto set my hand and seal, the 13th day of August, 1841. JNO. C. GOODWIN [seal].

Solomon A. Guy,

Wm. W. Anderson.

I give to my son, Charles Q. Goodwin, the Sole tract and the Hart tract of land, to make his tract equal with his brothers. JNO. C. GOODWIN.

Also Robinson, Henry, Sinthy, Patsey, and two children, Fannie and Scot.

March 3, 1845.

I give to my daughter Ellen, Cloe and her two youngest children; also Betty, John, Elizabeth, and Lucy. JNO. C. GOODWIN.

Children: i. Frances Jane, born June 7, 1805, married Dr. William Goodwin; ii. William Thompson, born June 21, 1807, married Elizabeth Pendleton; iii. John Chapman Garland, born October

12, 1810, married, first, Amanda Herndon; secondly, Elizabeth May Gilbert; iv. Louisa Anne, born August 2, 1814, died unmarried; v. Mary Ann, born August 27, 1815, married Rev. Samuel Meredith; vi. James Robert, born June 24, 1818, married Elizabeth Boxley; vii. Mildred Barbara, born February 16, 1821, married Ferdinand Jones; viii. Charles Quarles, born May 4, 1824, married Sarah Jane Swift; ix. Maria Ellen, born November 4, 1826, married Nathaniel William Harris.

Frances Jane Goodwin (John Chapman, Robert, James, Peter, James) was born June 7, 1805; was married May 8, 1823, to Dr. William Goodwin, who was born January 21, 1791, in Spottsylvania county, Va., a son of Hugh and Elizabeth (Blades) Goodwin,[5] Robert,[4] James,[3] Peter,[2] James.[1] By occupation he was a farmer and physician, in politics a Democrat. *Goodwin* children: i. Frances Ann, married Dr. K. M. Francesco; ii. John Thompson; iii. William Hugh, married Julia Ann Goodwin; iv. Robert; v. James.

William Thompson Goodwin (John Chapman, Robert, James, Peter, James) was born June 21, 1807, in "Oaksby"; was married in March, near Frederick's Hall, by Parson Hiter, to Elizabeth Pendleton, who was born at Cuckoo, Louisa county, Va., a daughter of Col. Edmund and Unity Yancy (Kimbrough) Pendleton. By occupation he was a farmer, in politics a Whig. They resided at "Oak Hall" farm, Louisa county, Va.

IN THE NAME OF GOD, AMEN. I, William T. Goodwin, being of sound mind and good health, and calling to mind the uncertainty of life, do dispose of my worldly estate in the following manner. *Imprimis:*

The land on which I live reverts to my father, together with the slaves he gave me, viz.: Michael, Daniel, Nancy, and her increase. I also give my father my riding horse, Sambo. I give to my mother my silver lever watch as a memorial of me. My gold chain and buttons I leave to my son as a memento. I leave my son Edward Pendleton every specie of land or property that came by his mother; also my boy Isaac, likewise every other specie of property except what I shall bequeath for other purposes. I give my brother James my brace of pistols; my brother Charles Quarles I give my gun; my brother John I give thirty dollars, my sister Frances I give thirty, Ann fifteen, Mildred ten, Ellen ten dollars, to be laid out in something useful as a memorial of me. I give and bequeath to poor William W. Howe the sum of one hundred dollars in order that his family may live more comfortably. This is my last will and testament, revoking all others. Written with my own hand this the 13th day of September, 1832. WILLIAM T. GOODWIN.

In Louisa county court, October 14, 1833, a paper purporting to be the last will and testament of William T. Goodwin, deceased, was established in court, and William and John Goodwin appeared in court and renounced all interest they had in said will, and it appearing to the satisfaction of the court by the oath of said William and John Goodwin that the whole of said paper, writing, together with the signature thereto, was wholly written by the own hand of the said William T. Goodwin, it is ordered that the same be recorded.

In Louisa county court, November 11, 1833, on motion of John C. Goodwin, who made oath as the law directs, and, together with Edward Pendleton, his security, entered into and acknowledged a bond in the penalty of ten thousand dollars, conditioned according to law, and certificate is granted him for obtaining letters of administration with the will annexed of William T. Goodwin, deceased, in due form. Test: JOHN HUNTER, C. L. C.

Child: Edmund Pendleton, born December 2, 1830, married Lucy Ann Chiles.

Edmund Pendleton Goodwin (William Thompson, John Chapman, Robert, James, Peter, James) was born December 2, 1830, on "Oak Hall" farm, Louisa county, Va.; was married November 25, 1852, at "Cool Springs" farm, Louisa county, Va., by Rev. Martin P. Sumner, to Lucy Ann Chiles, who was born January 16, 1834, in "Woodlawn," Louisa county, Va., a daughter of Fendol and Susanna Randolph (West) Chiles. By occupation he was a physician, in politics a Whig, and in religion an Episcopalian. He attended the University of Virginia, and was graduated with the highest honors from Jefferson Medical College, Philadelphia, and acted as surgeon at Heningston Hospital, Richmond, Va., during the Civil War. He resided in Louisa county, where he died July 29, 1869. Children: i. Weir Randolph, born September 2, 1853, married, first, Lily Marshal Murray, second, Virginia Claybrook Chiles; ii. Rosa Elizabeth Pendleton, born August 3, 1855: iii. Lucy Fenola, born March 22, 1857; iv. Anna Rhodes, born October 18, 1859, resides at Louisa C. H.; v. Edmund Pendleton, born June 4, 1862, married Beulah Lee Maddox; vi. Thompson West, born October 30, 1864, resides in Roanoke; vii. Fendol, born October 30, 1864, died June 17, 1865.

Weir Randolph Goodwin (Edmund Pendleton, William Thompson, John Chapman, Robert, James, Peter, James) was born September 2, 1853, at "Cool Springs" farm Louisa county, Va.; was married, first, September 15, 1886, at Charlottesville, by Rev. James O. Moss, to Lily Marshal Murray, who was born May 20, 1853, at Louisa C. H., a daughter of Henry William and Mildred Marshall (Hunter) Murray, and died May 30, 1888, *sine prole.* He was married, second, October 7, 1895, at Louisa, by Rev. Richard Bagby to Virginia Claybrook Chiles, who was born February 2, 1869, at Sunnyside, Louisa county, a daughter of Henry and

Isabella Potter (Hunter) Chiles. By occupation he was a railroad employee, in politics a Democrat, and in religion a Baptist. He resided in Roanoke, and (1897) Boscobel, Louisa county. Child by second wife: i. Virginia Randolph, born August 4, 1896.

Edmund Pendleton Goodwin (Edmund Pendleton, William Thompson, John Chapman, Robert, James, Peter, James) was born June 4, 1862; was married June 6, 1883, at Parkersburg, W. Va. by Rev. F. B. Carroll, to Beulah Lee Maddox, who was born March 15, 1863, at Parkersburg, a daughter of William P. and Olivia R. (Hopkins) Maddox. By occupation he was chief train despatcher, in politics a Democrat, and in religion an Episcopalian. They resided in Richmond, Va. Children: i. Inez Lexington, born April 19, 1884; ii. William Prince, born August 31, 1888; iii. Edmund Pendleton, born August 31, 1888, died June 19, 1889; iv. Beulah Lee, born June 13, 1890; v. Lucy Randolph, born January 27, 1892.

John Chapman Garland Goodwin (John Chapman, Robert, James, Peter, James) was born October 12, 1810, in —— Va.; was married, first, December 21, 1840, in —— Ky., to Amanda Herndon, born March 29, 1822, at —— Ky. He was married, second, September 7, 1871, in ——, Mo., by Rev. Wm. Pugh, to Elizabeth May Gilbert, who was born February 14, 1843, in Berkley county, W. Va., a daughter of Bernard and Mary Jane (Myers) Gilbert. By occupation he was a merchant and farmer, in politics a Democrat, and in religion an Episcopalian. He resided in Louisa county, Va., until 1844, when he removed to Cooper county, Mo., where he died in 1883. His widow resides in Kansas City, Mo. Children by first wife: i. Elizabeth H., born November 12, 1841; ii. John Herndon, born August 7, 1843, married Frances Gentry; iii. William T., born March 23, 1845; iv. Scott Taylor, born April 18, 1847, married Lucy J. Ellis; v. William H., born August 8, 1849; vi. Charles T., born April 17, 1851, unmarried, resides at Vermont, Cooper county, Mo.; vii. Mary Ann, born June 3, 1853; viii. Josephine T., born February 11, 1855; ix. Eugene E., born March 24, 1857; x. Cornelia Amanda, born August 4, 1859, married Thomas Nelson Birch; xi. Mary Jane, born November 18, 1861, married John F. Vick. Children by second wife: i. Henry Garland, born September 1, 1872, died in infancy; ii. Frederick Chapman, born November 5, 1874, unmarried, resides in Kansas City, Mo.

John Herndon Goodwin (John Chapman Garland, John Chapman, Robert, James, Peter, James) was born August 7, 1843, in

Louisa county, Va.; was married December 28, 1876, near Bunceton, Mo., by Rev. B. G. Tutt, to Fanny Gentry, who was born February 7, 1859, in Winchester, Ky., a daughter of Nelson and Fanny (Elkins) Gentry. He was a banker and farmer, a Democrat, and member of the M. E. Church, South. They reside (1897) on their farm near Bunceton. Children: i. Gentry, born August, 1879; ii. Wallace Wyan, born March 16, 1881.

Scott Taylor Goodwin (John Chapman Garland, John Chapman, Robert, James, Peter, James) was born April 18, 1847, in Vermont, Mo.; was married August, 1871, at Kansas City, by Dr. Campbell, to Lucy J. Ellis, who was born in 1843, in Cooper county, Mo., a daughter of Thomas and Cynthia (Ferguson) Ellis. He was a farmer, and a Democrat. They resided in Bunceton, Mo. Scott Taylor Goodwin was murdered in October, 1876. Children: i. Eugene S. Herndon, born May, 1873; ii. John Lester, born 1875.

Mary Ann Goodwin (John Chapman, Robert, James, Peter, James) was born August 27, 1815; was married to Rev. Samuel Meredith. *Meredith* children: i. John; ii. Sarah; iii. James; iv. Victoria; v. Ellen; vi. Lewis E.; vii. Charles Quarles.

James Robert Goodwin (John Chapman, Robert, James, Peter, James) was born June 24, 1818, in Louisa county, Va.; was married December 28, 1837, in Louisa county, Va., by Rev. William Y. Hiter, to Elizabeth Boxley, who was born September 10, 1820, a daughter of Benjamin and Nicie Hawes (Goodwin) Boxley. She was a daughter of Hugh,[5] Robert,[4] James,[3] Peter,[2] James.[1] By occupation he was a farmer and tobacco manufacturer, in politics a Whig, and in religion a Christian. They resided in Louisa county, Va. James Robert Goodwin died January 2, 1870. Elizabeth (Boxley) Goodwin died February 12, 1883. Children: i. Nicie Ann, born November 14, 1838, died in infancy; ii. Mary Ellen, born September 30, 1840, married Dr. D. E. Byrd; iii. Benjamin Chapman, born January 18, 1843, married Margaret Moon; iv. James Hugh, born May 16, 1845, married first, Norah Garnett; second, Ella Hutt; v. Elizabeth Hawse, born July 12, 1847, married Philip B. Hiden; John Morgan, born July 8, 1850, married Elizabeth I. Impy; vii. Nannie Bertram, born August 1, 1853, married Dr. Joseph W. Baker.

Mary Ellen Goodwin (James, Robert, John Chapman, Robert, James, Peter, James) was born September 30, 1840, in Louisa county; was married June 10, 1867, at "Oak Hall," Louisa county, by Elder L. N. Cutler, to Dr. D. Ellis Byrd, who was born November 10, 1840, in Colleton District, S. C., a son of Thomas and Rosa (Davidson) Byrd. By occupation he was a physician, in politics a Democrat, and in religion a Christian. They resided at Marvell, Ark., removing from Virginia in 1870. Dr. Byrd died January 25, 1888. His widow resides in Marvell. *Byrd* children: i. Mary Ellis, born April 5, 1875, married Whitfield D. Wall.

Dr. Benjamin Chapman Goodwin (James Robert, John Chapman, Robert, James, Peter, James) was born January 18, 1843, in Louisa county, Va.; was married January 6, 1892, in Buckingham county, Va., by William Hall, to Margaret Moon, who was born September 12, 1863, a daughter of Schuyler B., and Elizabeth (Thompkins) Moon. By occupation he was a physician, in politics a Democrat. They resided in Marvell, Phillips county, Ark., in 1894, removing to Long Creek post-office, Louisa county, Va. Child: Benjamin Chapman, born August 18, 1893.

James Hugh Goodwin (James Robert, John Chapman, Robert, James, Peter, James) was born May 16, 1845; was married first, to Elnorah Garnett. He was married, second, to Ella Hutt, and resides in Rapidan, Culpeper county, Va. Children by first wife (names not furnished).

John Morgan Goodwin (James Robert, John Chapman, Robert, James, Peter, James) was born January 4, 1850, in Louisa county; was married January 7, 1885, at Marvell, Ark., by Elder James McGuffey, to Elizabeth I. Impey, who was born October 21, 1860, in Carlyle, Ill., a daughter of Joseph and Mary Ann (DeAlton) Impey. By occupation he was a real-estate dealer and notary, in politics a Democrat, and in religion a Christian. They resided (1897) in Marvell, Ark. Children: i. Mary E., born January 25, 1887; ii. James Impey, born April 25, 1895.

Mildred Barbara Goodwin (John Chapman, Robert, James, Peter, James) was born February 16, 1821, in Louisa county; was married September 22, 1841, in Louisa county, by Rev. William Y. Hiter, to Ferdinand Jones, who was born April 11, 1820, in Louisa county, a son of Charles S., and Sarah K. (Cowherd) Jones. By occupation he was a farmer, in politics a Whig. They resided in Orange county, where he died February 14, 1873. His wife died August 21, 1891, in Wytheville. *Jones* children: i. Annie Sarah, born January 29, 1846, married John James Audubon Powell*;

* They reside in Wytheville.

ii. John Charles, born April 25, 1849, died July 1, 1854; iii. Ferdinand, born July 18, 1857, died September 13, 1863.

Charles Quarles Goodwin (John Chapman, Robert, James, Peter, James), born May 4, 1824, was married to Sarah Jane Swift. Children: i. Manlius T.; ii. Charles Quarles; iii. John Clifton; iv. Anna Bell; v. Gertrude M.; vi. George Frederick; vii. Maria Birch; viii. David Harris.

Maria Ellen Goodwin (John Chapman, Robert, James, Peter, James), born November 4, 1826, was married to Nathaniel William Harris. *Harris* children: i. Frederick; ii. Flora; iii. Nathaniel C., resides at Frederick's Hall, Va.; iv. John Goodwin; v. Ellen L.; vi. Eliza; vii. Rosa; viii. Waller Overton; ix. Henry Lee; x. David Lewis.

Archibald Tulloch Goodwin (Robert, James, Peter, James), born Sunday morning, November 30, 1785, in Louisa county, Va.; was married, September 19, 1805, in Louisa county, Va., to Candace Sandridge, a daughter of Joseph Sandridge, born in Louisa county, Va. They resided in Louisa county, Va., where he died, October 2, 1845.

RELEASE.—Robert Garland, of Louisa county, to Archibald Tulloch Goodwin, in consideration of 110 pounds paid by Spencer Coleman, executor of Robert Goodwin, deceased. Dated June 8, 1789; admitted to record September 14, 1789.

Children: i. Alfred Muren, born June 21, 1807; married Elizabeth Goodwin; ii. Joseph, born August 1, 1809; died December 12, 1833, unmarried; iii. Thomas Tulloch, born November 25, 1810; married, 1st, Winifred Boxley; 2nd, Mary Chase; iv. Ralph S., born June 3, 1812; married Mary Boxley; v. Archibald Tulloch, born March 14, 1814; married —— Hiter; vi. Robert, born January 5, 1816; married Susan Ann Woolfolk; vii. Jane Grant, born September 8, 1817; died April 2, 1842; viii. Addison Galen, born February 20, 1819; married Maria Hawes Coleman; ix. John, born August 17, 1820; married, 1st, Sarah A. Dickinson; 2nd, Fanny Dabney; x. Mary, born May 15, 1823; married William Chiswell Barrett; xi. Lafayette, born March 28, 1825; died September 3, 1826; xii. Candace, born July 29, 1829; died January 7, 1830.

Alfred Muren Goodwin (Archibald Tulloch, Robert, James, Peter, James) was born June 21, 1807, in Louisa county, Va.; was married to Elizabeth Goodwin, born January 25, 1810, in Louisa county, Va., a daughter of Robert and Judith (Tyler) Goodwin

(Robert, James, Peter, James). By occupation he was a farmer, in politics a Democrat, and in religion a Baptist. They resided in Louisa county, Va. Alfred Muren Goodwin died July 25, 1867. Elizabeth (Goodwin) Goodwin died May 10, 1877. Children: i. Ann Tyler, born 1833; ii. Joseph S., born 1834; iii. Elizabeth Jane; iv. Archibald Tulloch, born July 13, 1837; unmarried; v. Josephine, born December 23, 1840; married Robert W. Woolfolk; vi. Louisa Virginia, born September 5, 1842; vii. Alfred Muren, born January 12, 1845; married Elizabeth Boxley; viii. John Tyler, born September 13, 1847; married Florence Denkle; ix. Judith Catherine, born October 29, 1851; married James H. Denkle; x. Jane Grant, born March 6, 1853; married Robert W. Zimmerman.

Thomas Tulloch Goodwin (Archibald Tulloch, Robert, James, Peter, James), born November 25, 1810, was married, first, to Winifred Boxley. He was married, second, to Mary Chase, of Independence, Texas. He resided in Louisa county, Va., until 1857, when he removed to Burleson county, Texas, where he died in 1872. Children by first wife: i. Laura S.; ii. Archibald Tulloch; iii. Thomas Tulloch; iv. Annie I.; v. Winifred S. Children by second wife: vi. Mary C.; vii. Ralph.

Ralph S. Goodwin (Archibald Tulloch, Robert, James, Peter, James), born June 13, 1812, was married to Mary Boxley. Ralph S. Goodwin died August 13, 1840. Mary (Boxley) Goodwin married, second, Jabez Massie. Children: i. J. B., married Frankie Lipscomb; ii. Candace, married —— Rosson; iii. Winifred, married —— Dickinson; iv. Mary (Mollie), married —— Jenkins.

J. B. Goodwin (Ralph S., Archibald Tulloch, Robert, James, Peter, James) married Frankie Lipscomb. They reside in Oakland, Va. Children: i. Jack; ii. William; iii. Caroline; v. Ethel.

Archibald Tulloch Goodwin (Archibald Tulloch, Robert, James, Peter, James) was born March 14, 1814; was married to Miss —— Hiter. Archibald Tulloch Goodwin died August 12, 1885. Children: i. William H.; ii. James S.; iii. Edward A.; iv. Elizabeth Y.; v. Nicie C.; vi. Hugh.

Robert Goodwin (Archibald Tulloch, Robert, James, Peter, James) was born January 5, 1816, in Louisa county, Va.; was married in Louisa county, by Rev. Mr. Hiter, to Susan Ann Woolfolk, who was born January 31, 1823, in Louisa county, Va., a daughter of William and Clara (Ellis) Woolfolk. By occupation he was a farmer, in politics a Whig, and in religion a Baptist. They resided in Louisa county, Va. Children: i. Mary Elizabeth, born September 17, 1839, married W. T. Sneed; ii. William Woolfolk, born June 27, 1841, married Elizabeth Sandridge Goodwin; iii. Jane Candace, born November 3, 1843, married Joseph Smith Jackson; iv. Clara Ellis, born February 12, 1845, married John Lafayette Sneed.

Mary Elizabeth Goodwin (Archibald Tulloch, Robert, James, Peter, James) was born September 17, 1839, in Louisa county, Va.; was married November 3, 1866, at Gordonsville, Orange county, Va., by Rev. Dr. Charles Quarles, to W. T. Sneed, who was born May 5, 1845, in Louisa county, Va., a son of Littleton Waller and Elizabeth Hurt (Woolfolk) Sneed. By occupation he was a merchant, in politics a Democrat, and in religion a Methodist. They reside in Gordonsville, Va. *Sneed* children: i. Bettie Woolfolk, born March 13, 1868, died February 8, 1874; ii. Susan Ellis, born January 5, 1871, died August 1, 1871; iii. Littleton Robert, born June 13, 1873, died February 28, 1893; iv. William Stapleton, born May 6, 1875; v. Jennie Claire, born June 11, 1877; vi. Mary Goodwin, born April 27, 1879; vii. John Lafayette Thweat, born April 1, 1882.

William Woolfolk Goodwin (Robert, Archibald Tulloch, Robert, James, Peter, James) was born June 27, 1841, in Louisa county, Va.; was married February 10, 1880, in Caroline county, Va., by Dr. John Wesley Williams, to Elizabeth Sandridge Goodwin, who was born September 19, 1855, in Louisa county, Va., a daughter of Addison Galen and Mariah Hawes (Coleman) Goodwin. By occupation he was a farmer and merchant, in politics a Democrat. They resided near Penola post-office, Caroline county, Va., in 1896. William Woolfolk Goodwin served in the late Civil War as a private in the Confederate army. Child: Maria George, born August 28, 1889.

Jane Candace Goodwin (Robert, Archibald Tulloch, Robert, James, Peter, James) was born November 3, 1843, in Louisa county, Va.; was married November 27, 1867, in Louisa county, Va., by Rev. Dr. Charles Quarles, to Joseph Smith Jackson, born April 18, 1838, in Orange county, Va., a son of Joseph Smith and Mary A. (Howard) Jackson. By occupation he was a farmer, in politics a Democrat, and in religion a Christian. They resided in Orange county, Va. Joseph Smith Jackson was a soldier in the late Civil War in "Stonewall" Jackson's command. No children.

Clara Ellis Goodwin (Robert, Archibald Tulloch, Robert,

James, Peter, James) was born February 12, 1845, in Louisa county, Va ; was married December 1, 1874, in Louisa county, Va., by Rev. James O. Moss, to John Lafayette Sneed, who was born January 12, 1848, in Gordonsville, Va., a son of Littleton Waller and Elizabeth Hurt (Woolfolk) Sneed. By occupation he was a merchant, in politics a Democrat, and in religion a Methodist. They resided in Gordonsville, Va., where Clara Ellis (Goodwin) Sneed died July 10, 1893. *Sneed* children: i. William Henry, born December 4, 1875; ii. John Leigh, born May 31, 1877; iii. James Woolfolk, born February 1, 1881; iv. Ellis Hurt, born February 10, 1883.

Addison Galen Goodwin (Archibald Tulloch, Robert, James, Peter, James) was born February 20, 1819, in Louisa county, Va.; was married September 17, 1844, in Caroline county, Va., by James Bagby, to Maria Hawes Coleman, who was born March 19, 1822, in Caroline county, Va., a daughter of Hawes and Maria (Harris) Coleman,[4] Jr. (John,[3]———,[2] ———.[1]) They resided near Penola post-office, Caroline county, Va. Addison Galen Goodwin served in the Confederate army. He was comptroller of revenue for ten years, and justice of the peace. Children: i. Virginia H., born June 22, 1845; ii. Marcellus, born January 31, 1847; iii. Ellen C., born September 1, 1849; iv. Elizabeth Sandridge, born September, 19, 1855, married William Woolfolk Goodwin; v. John G., born October 12, 1859.

John Goodwin (Archibald Tulloch, Robert, James, Peter, James) was born August 17, 1820, in Louisa county, Va.; was married first to Sarah A. Dickinson, who was born February, 1824, in Caroline county, Va., a daughter of John and Jane H. (Dickinson) Dickinson. John Dickinson was a prominent lawyer of Caroline county, Va. His wife was of Chestnut Valley, Caroline county. Sarah A. (Dickinson) Goodwin died in ———, 1864, in Texas. John Goodwin was married, second, in 1867, to Fanny Dabney, born in Virginia. He resided in Louisa county, Va., removing in 1857 to Burleson county, Texas, where he died in 1870. Children by first wife: i. Jane D., married Rev. I. N. May; ii. Helen; iii. Henry C.; iv. Florence; v. John T.; vi. Joseph S., married Nicie Coleman Goodwin; vii. Alfred M.; viii. William D.; ix. Sarah A.; x. Edgar C.; xi. Jefferson D.; xii. Lucie L. Child by second wife: Fannie B., married Rev. C. S. Dickinson.

Jane D. Goodwin (John, Archibald Tulloch, Robert, James, Peter, James) was married August, 1867, to Rev. I. N. May. They reside in Oakland, Va. *May* children: Names not furnished.

Mary Goodwin (Archibald Tulloch, Robert, James, Peter, James) was born May 15, 1823; was married to William Chiswell Barrett. Mary (Goodwin) Barrett died May 10, 1881. *Barrett* children: i Nannie; ii. Candace; iii. William; iv. Elizabeth; v. Maud; vi. Kate; vii. Jane G.; viii. Chiswell.

James Goodwin (James, Peter, James) was born in York county, Va.; was married to Margaret ———. Children: i. Rachel, born March 9, 1780; ii. James, born May 29, 1782.

DEED.—James Goodwin, of York county and Charles parish, of the one part, and Charles Smith, of the county of Louisa and parish of Trinity. Consideration, 262 pounds 10 shillings.
Dated February 24, 1772. Admitted September 14, 1772.

Diana Goodwin (James, Peter, James) was married to ——— Bailey. *Bailey* children: i. Wilson; ii. Elizabeth.

Elizabeth Goodwin (James, Peter, James) was married to Robert Blackwell. An entry in the Bible of her father, James Goodwin, says, "Elizabeth Blackwell went from Crab Neck November 15, 1765."

Martin Goodwin (James) was born in York county, Va.; was married to Barbara ———. They resided in York county, Va. Martin's will was proved May 16, 1718. He had "Elizabeth and other children." Barbara (———) Goodwin, in 1724, was the wife of John Power. Children: i. Elizabeth; ii. Martin (?), married Elizabeth ———.

Martin Goodwin (probably, Martin, James) was married to Elizabeth ———. They resided in Elizabeth City county, Va. The will of Martin Goodwin, dated June 21, 1749, mentions in addition to wife and children "my good friend, Merritt Moore, of York county." Merritt's aunt, Elizabeth Moore, was wife of Capt. John Goodwin,[2] brother of Martin,[2] and Merritt and this Martin were both of the third generation. Martin,[3] the son of Robert,[2] died, leaving his mother, Anne, as heir, so that he was evidently unmarried. Neither John nor Peter had a son Martin. Of Mathew, nothing is known. Martin, the fifth son of Major James, had a daughter Elizabeth "and other children." It would appear that this Martin was one of the "other children." Children: i. James, untraced; ii. Martin, untraced; iii. Elizabeth, untraced; iv. Robert, untraced.

APPENDIX.

APPENDIX A.

The Goodwins of Brookville, Indiana.

From his earliest recollection the writer had understood that he belonged to the F. F. V.'s, but when about ten years ago he attempted to grow a family tree he found it impossible to verify the claim. Resorting to the oldest living member of the family, Mrs. Mary (Goodwin) Marlatt, born 1809, and residing in Brookville, he found her unable to give the place of her father's birth, but she did know that his father was Thomas Goodwin, Sen., and that her father had brothers and sisters. Of these she had seen one when she was a small child who had come on horseback with a young son to visit her father. The name of the brother or of his son was James. She remembered only one question asked by the brother, and that was, how his brother, her father, had so soon spent the inheritance received from his father's estate. An appeal has been made to every Goodwin whose name and address could be secured for his own family data, hoping in this way to find eventually some of the descendants of the brothers, but so far without success. At the same time an attempt has been made to trace the descendants of all immigrant Goodwins past the year 1767, hoping to find record of a Thomas born in 1767, the son of Thomas, Sen. This also has so far failed of results. In the meantime the search continues, and all the data obtained is carefully preserved. From this collection is taken what appears here relating to the Goodwins of Virginia. It is perhaps needless to say that any information relating to the ancestry of Thomas of 1767 will be most gratefully received, and all other Goodwin data will be carefully preserved and prepared for publication, if sent to John S. Goodwin, 304 The Temple, Chicago.

Thomas Goodwin, born about 1730–1740; was married twice, but had no children by his second wife. By occupation he was a farmer and slave-owner, and in religion a Quaker. He resided probably in New Jersey, Pennsylvania, Maryland, or Virginia.

His granddaughter, Mrs. Marlatt, thinks he resided in Maryland and removed to Pennsylvania after his second marriage, as Catherine Rees, wife of Thomas, Jr., knew her husband's father and step-mother but not his own mother. He was a man of property and of education. His estate was probated, but it is not yet known where. The most plausible theory at this time is that some of the sons or grandsons of Major James Goodwin went north from York county into Westmoreland county, and then across into Maryland and north into Pennsylvania, and were the ancestors of Thomas. Children: i. Thomas, born April 27, 1767; married Catherine Rees: ii. James (?), married, and had at least one son living in 1815–'20.

Thomas Goodwin (Thomas), born April 27, 1767; was married about 1788 to Catherine Rees, born October 7, 1767, a daughter of David and Lydia (—) Rees, who were born in Wales. By occupation he was a farmer and inn-keeper, and in politics a Whig. But little is known of his residence before his marriage. He was a stern, uncommunicative man, well educated for a pioneer, writing a very perfect hand, a great reader, and much given to solitude and forest hunting. Whether there was a family estrangement is not known, but he was a man in whom the milk of human kindness had soured. He held himself aloof from his neighbors, and kept in advance of the wave of immigration. He was married about 1788, and Lancaster, Penn., seems to have been the place of marriage or else the birth-place of his wife, who was a Philadelphia (?) "school marm" before marriage and taught for a number of years after marriage. She often spoke of having seen Washington when she was a child. She had brothers, Hezekiah and David, and sisters, Lydia and Lucretia (married Mr. Alexander and had son, Samuel), and also other sisters, from whom she inherited silver with monograms A. F. and I. H. D. or I. D. H. She had a brother and a brother-in-law killed in the Revolutionary War. Wherever this Rees family lived at the time of her marriage was the home of Thomas Goodwin at that time. After marriage they went along what was afterwards known as the Old National Road to Old Fort, now Brownsville, Fayette county, Pa. They remained there for several years and then removed to Cincinnati. Thence they went to near Dayton, Ohio, returning to Franklin, Ohio, where they resided until about 1830. At this place Thomas' brother visited him before 1820, and one of his father's former slaves lived near and often worked for the family.

Leaving Franklin they settled in Brookville, Ind., where their eldest son Samuel had gone in 1816, and remained there until their deaths. Catherine (Rees) Goodwin died July 5, 1844, and Thomas Goodwin, Jr., died May 5, 1848. Children: i. Samuel, born April 12, 1789; married, 1st, Eunice Pearson; 2d, Mrs. Eleanor (Wiles) Moon; ii. Hezekiah Rees, born November 19, 1791; married Lydia Ligett; iii. William, born June 1, 1795; drowned on trip to New Orleans, 1815; iv. James, born October 22, 1797; died unmarried; v. Lydia, born August 9, 1800; killed by fall from horse in 1815; vi. Elizabeth, born November 9, 1806; married George Kepler; vii. Mary (Polly), born April 30, 1809; married James Marlatt.

Samuel Goodwin (Thomas, Thomas), born April 12, 1789, in Old Fort, now Brownsville, Fayette county, Pa.; was married, 1st, at Lebanon, Ohio, to Eunice Pearson, born in 1796, and died in Lebanon in 1814. Samuel Goodwin was married, 2nd, March 19, 1815, at Lebanon to Mrs. Eleanor (Wiles) Moon, who was born October 24, 1789, in Baltimore, Md., a daughter of John and Eleanor (McKinley) Wiles. She was born while her mother was on a visit from Pennsylvania to "her people." Her mother's parents were Rodger and Eleanor (Shaw) McKinley, who, with his father, James McKinley, born 1708 in Ireland, afterwards settled near Lebanon, Ohio, where James McKinley died in 1812, aged 104 years. The next year after their marriage Samuel and Eleanor settled in Brookville, Ind., where they remained the rest of their lives. They resided in the town, but owned farm lands adjoining. Mr. Goodwin was also a tanner, and made a voyage or two to New Orleans. They were strong Methodists, and their home was always open to the travelling preacher. When the Methodists were preparing to establish the Indiana Asbury (now De Pauw) University at Greencastle, Samuel Goodwin purchased the first perpetual scholarship sold and sent the first student from out of town. He gave every son a college education, and two of them became presidents of universities afterward, while his wife's nephew, Dr. J. P. D. John, was, until his recent resignation, for many years president of De Pauw. Samuel Goodwin died June 26, 1851. Eleanor (Wiles) Goodwin died May 18, 1873. Children by second wife: i. Eunice, born July 20, 1817; died September 6, 1817; ii. Thomas Aiken, born November 2, 1818; married Content Lucretia Craft; iii. John Reeves, born July 15, 1820; married Rachel Goudie; iv. Mary, born August 7,

1822; died July 31, 1339, unmarried; v. Eleanor, born May 13, 1824; died November 30, 1843, unmarried; vi. Martha Wiles, born March 4, 1826; married Wilson Morrow; vii. Samuel Augustus, born July 11, 1828; died March 17, 1829; viii. Samuel George, born February 21, 1830; resides at Indianapolis, Ind., unmarried; ix. William Rees, born July 7, 1832; married, 1st, Sue A. Keely; 2nd, Mrs. Mary (McAdams) Smith; x. Robert James, born January 29, 1834; died July 2, 1884, unmarried, brevet brigadier-general in Civil War.

Rev. Thomas Aiken Goodwin, D. D. (Samuel, Thomas, Thomas), born November 2, 1818, in Brookville, Ind.; was married September 13, 1842, at Rising Sun, Ind., to Content Lucretia Craft, born February 26, 1823, a daughter of Caleb A. and Elizabeth (Williams) Craft. (See Craft genealogy, where name is incorrectly given as Gordain). By occupation he was a teacher, editor, and minister, in politics a Republican, and in religion a Methodist. They have resided in Rising Sun, Brookville, and in Indianapolis, Ind., for about forty years. They celebrated their golden wedding in 1892. Thomas A. Goodwin was the first student from out of town at the Indiana Asbury University and valedictorian of the first class, 1840. He was president of the Brookville College, and editor of the *Brookville American.* He is well known in church circles, and has written a number of books relating to church polity. Children: i. Charles, born January 13, 1849; died, March 8, 1847; ii. Mary, born June 22, 1847; died May 31, 1856; iii. Martha, born July 18, 1850; died October 3, 1872; iv. Ella, born June 5, 1853; died February 22, 1859; v. Myra Ada, born July 22, 1856; married Rev. Samuel Plantz, D. D.; vi. Caroline Augusta, born June 7, 1859; married Edwin Eugene Rexford; vii. Edwin Morrow, born October 6, 1862; married Mabel Caroline Newcomb; viii. Alice Flora, born January 1, 1865; married Ozro DeLacy Weaver.

Myra Ada Goodwin (Thomas Aiken, Samuel, Thomas, Thomas), born July 22, 1856, in Brookville, Ind.; was married September 8, 1885, at Indianapolis, by Rev. J. Alabaster, to Rev. Samuel Plantz, D. D., born June 13, 1859, in Johnstown, N. Y., a son of James and Elsie (Stoller) Plantz. By occupation he was a teacher and minister, in politics a Prohibitionist, and in religion a Methodist. They resided in Detroit, Mich., removing in 1895 to Appleton, Wis., where Dr. Plantz is president of Lawrence University. Mrs. Myra (Goodwin) Plantz has been for years a contributor to the religious periodicals, and has acquired a wide reputation as a poet and platform speaker. She was before marriage an instructor in the Indiana Asbury University. After marriage they resided for a year in Berlin, where Mrs. Plantz studied in the university. *Plantz* children: i. Elsie Content, born January 12, 1890; ii. Florence John, born March 26, 1893.

Caroline Augusta Goodwin (Thomas Aiken, Samuel, Thomas, Thomas), born June 7, 1859, in Indianapolis; was married April 12, 1881, at Indianapolis, by Dr. Henry J. Talbott, to Edwin Eugene Rexford, born December 9, 1856, in Piqua, Ohio, a son of Eugene Motier and Ann Elizabeth (Ferguson) Rexford. By occupation he was a bank officer, in politics a Republican, and in religion a Methodist. They reside in Indianapolis. Caroline was the first woman notary public commissioned in Indiana. *Rexford* children: i. Edna May, born December 25, 1882; ii. Eugene Goodwin, born August 13, 1884.

Edwin Morrow Goodwin (Thomas Aiken, Samuel, Thomas, Thomas), born October 6, 1862, in Indianapolis; was married May 8, 1884, at Indianapolis, by Rev. H. M. Morey, to Mabel Caroline Newcomb, born July 11, 1862, in Indianapolis, a daughter of Horatio Cooley and Eliza (Pabody) Newcomb. By occupation he is general agent of the Accident Department of the Ætna Life Insurance Company for New York, in politics a Republican, and in religion a Methodist. They resided in Indianapolis and Terre Haute, returning to Indianapolis, and removed (1895) to Buffalo, N. Y. Children: i. Alice Emma, born March 5, 1887; died March 28, 1893; ii. Helen Newcomb, born November 7, 1890; iii. Thomas Arthur, born November 2, 1893.

Alice Flora Goodwin (Thomas Aiken, Samuel, Thomas, Thomas), born January 1, 1865, in Indianapolis; was married September 13, 1887, at Indianapolis, by Rev. Samuel Plantz, D. D., to Ozro DeLacy Weaver, born November 26, 1857, in Wayne county, Ind., a son of Jesse and Martha (Howell) Weaver. By occupation he was a member of the Indianapolis Board of Trade, in politics a Republican. They reside in Indianapolis. *Weaver* child: i. Louise Content, born January 11, 1893.

Dr. John Reeves Goodwin (Samuel, Thomas, Thomas), born July 15, 1820, in Brookville; was married July 30, 1846, at Brookville, by Rev. Thomas Aiken Goodwin, D. D., to Rachel Goudie, born December 28, 1826, in Brookville township, a daughter of Joseph and Pamela (Clarkson) Goudie. By occupation he was a physician and banker, in politics a Republican, and in religion a Methodist. They resided in Brookville until Dr. Goodwin was appointed to a position in the Department of the Interior under President Grant, when they removed to Washington, returning to Brookville, where Dr. Goodwin died in May, 1880. His widow resides in Brookville. He was graduated from the Indiana Asbury University in the class of '45, and was a trustee of the University at the time of his death, and endowed a chair in the University. Children: i. Charles Francis, born November 6, 1849; married Martha Shirk; ii. Joseph Goudie, born March 19, 1852; died August 9, 1852; iii. Edward R., born January 31, 1860; died February 16, 1861.

Charles Francis Goodwin (John Reeves, Samuel, Thomas, Thomas), born November 6, 1849, in Brookville township; was married November 17, 1874, at residence of wife's parents in Springfield township, by Rev. J. L. Roop, to Martha Shirk, born October 16, 1854, in Springfield township, a daughter of Andrew and Sarah (Wright) Shirk. By occupation he was a banker, in politics a Republican, and in religion a Methodist. They resided in Brookville, where Mr. Goodwin's business interests were very great. He contributed both time and money to the compiling of the Goodwin records. His sudden death Sunday afternoon, January 12, 1896, came like a public calamity. By request of the mayor all business-houses were closed and business suspended the day of his burial. He was universally loved and respected. His daughter, Mary, was graduated in June, 1897, from the De Pauw University, where he succeeded his father as trustee, and from which he was graduated in 1871. His son, John, enters the same College in 1897. Children: i. Mary McKee, born January 24, 1876; ii. John Pemberton, born February 26, 1880.

Martha Wiles Goodwin (Samuel, Thomas, Thomas), born March 4, 1826, in Brookville; was married September 8, 1852, at Brookville by Dr. Enoch G. Wood to Wilson Morrow, who was born October 11, 1823, in Rush county, Ind., a son of Charles Wesley and Elizabeth (Wilson) Morrow. By occupation he was a lawyer, in politics a Republican, and in religion a Methodist. They resided in Brookville, removing at the close of the war to Indianapolis. Mrs. Morrow was the "Lady Bountiful" of the family, her husband's position permitting her hospitable disposition to be exercised without stint. Beloved by all, a patient sufferer for a year, Aunt Mattie, as she was known to all, died in Indianapolis, April 10,

1896. *Adopted* child: i. Mollie, married Ernest W. Matthews.

Rev. William Rees Goodwin, D. D. (Samuel, Thomas, Thomas), born July 7, 1832, in Brookville; was married 1st, August 5, 1856, at Brookville, by Rev. S. T. Gillet, to Susan Ann Keely, born April 4, 1838, in Mt. Carmel, Ill., a daughter of Rev. John Wesley and Elizabeth (Fisher) Keely[5] (John,[4] John,[3] Sebastian,[2] Michael[1]), and died at Lincoln, Ill., Sept. 29, 1868. Dr. Goodwin was married 2nd, June 24, 1869, at St. Louis, Mo., by Rev. B. F. Crary, D. D., to Mrs. Mary (McAdams) Smith. By occupation he is a teacher and minister, in politics a Prohibitionist, and in religion a Methodist. They reside (1897) near Los Angeles, Cal. Dr. Goodwin was graduated from the Indiana Asbury University in 1856; was president of the Brookville College; Professor of Belles Lettres in the Illinois Wesleyan University; twenty-five years a member of the Illinois Conference; delegate to the General Conference; five years a member of the Rock River Conference and stationed at Chicago. He is one of the best-known contributors to the periodicals of the Methodist Church. Children by first wife: i. John Samuel, born March 16, 1858; married Mary Elizabeth Forbes; ii. George Keely Holliday, born April 29, 1861; died April 13, 1862; iii. William Ransdall, born August 19, 1863; married Mrs. Mary Eva (Putman) Hazlett; iv. Frank Morrow, born April 14, 1868; died May 6, 1869. Child by second wife: v. Eleanor, born May 25, 1870; married Dr. Charles H. Whitman.

John Samuel Goodwin (William Rees, Samuel, Thomas, Thomas), born March 16, 1858, in Edinburg, Ind.; was married October 7, 1880, at Danville, Ill., by Rev. William Rees Goodwin, D. D., to Mary Elizabeth Forbes, born June 9, 1858, in Danville, a daughter of Thomas Richard and Anna Eliza (Robinson) Forbes[7] (Thomas Chester,[6] Benjamin,[5] Elijah,[4] Joseph,[3] John,[2] James Forbes[1], of Hartford, Conn.). By occupation he is a lawyer, and in religion a Methodist. Mr. Goodwin was graduated from the Indiana Asbury University in 1877, the valedictorian of his class. He resided in Beloit, Kansas, from 1878 to 1888; was appointed judge in April, 1879; spent some time abroad in 1885–'86; resided in Danville, Ill., until January, 1891, and in Chicago thereafter. He is law partner of General John C. Black, ex-Commissioner of Pensions and at present United States District Attorney. He is interested very extensively in the breeding of registered Aberdeen-Angus cattle. He is the compiler of the genealogy of the Goodwins of Virginia. Child: i. Anna, born December 15, 1886.

William Ransdall Goodwin (William Rees, Samuel, Thomas, Thomas), born August 19, 1863, in the Brookville College building, his father being president of the College and residing with his family in the College apartments; was married November 3, 1892, at Quincy, Ill., by Rev. William Rees Goodwin, D. D., to Mrs. Mary Eva (Putman) Hazlett, born May 24, 1864, in Mt. Sterling, Ill., a daughter of John and Sarah (Stone) Putman. By occupation he is one of the editors and publishers of the *Breeders' Gazette*, in politics Independent, and in religion a Methodist. Since graduation from the Indiana Asbury University in 1883, he resided in Beloit, Kansas, and Kansas City, Mo., until 1885, and since then in Chicago. He is secretary of the Chicago Equestrian Day Association, incorporated, and a director in the National Saddle-Horse Breeders' Association. He has a national reputation as an expert judge of live-stock and a critical reporter of horse-shows and live-stock expositions. *No* children.

Eleanor Goodwin (William Rees, Samuel, Thomas, Thomas), born May 25, 1870, in Champaign, Ill.; was married January 11, 1893, at 520 Englewood avenue, Chicago, by Rev. William Rees Goodwin, D. D., to Dr. Charles H. Whitman. (See Whitman Genealogy). By occupation he was a physician, in politics a Republican. They resided in Chicago until 1894, when they removed to Los Angeles, Cal. Mrs. Whitman has won a wide reputation as a brilliant performer on the piano-forte. *No* children.

Hezekiah Rees Goodwin (Thomas, Thomas), born November 19, 1791, in Old Fort, Fayette county, Penn.; was married to Lydia Ligett. They resided near Franklin, Ohio. Hezekiah Rees Goodwin died in 1826 at Natchez, Miss., while on a trip to New Orleans. Lydia (Ligett) Goodwin died July 18, 1839. Children: i. Mary Ann, born August 14, 1814; married George Bunton Hall; ii. Ellen, born May 3, 1817; married William Ogdon Bradstreet.

Mary Ann Goodwin (Hezekiah Rees, Thomas, Thomas), born August 14, 1814, near Franklin, Ohio; was married August 4, 1831, near Franklin to George Bunton Hall, born September 30, 1810, in Virginia. They resided in Rising Sun, Ind. George Bunton Hall died January 2, 1872, at Winchester, Ohio. Mary Ann (Goodwin) Hall died November 24, 1885, at Rising Sun. *Hall* children: i. Smith C., born May 8, 1832; died May 8, 1832;

ii. Lydia Ann, born September 28, 1833; died May 10, 1836; iii. Francis Mead, born February 13, 1836; married Esther Huffins; iv. Elizabeth Eleanor, born September 10, 1838; married Joseph W. Swallow; v. Nancy Lutitia, born May 26, 1841; married Thomas Jefferson Tibbals; vi. Mathias Rees, born November 18, 1843; married Mary Matilda Jones; vii. James Tate, born November 22, 1846; married Hattie Elston Howard; viii. Clarinda, born July 18, 1849; died July 6, 1851; ix. Harriet S., born July 15, 1854; died October 13, 1857.

Ellen Goodwin (Hezekiah Rees, Thomas, Thomas), born May 3, 1817, in Rising Sun, Ind.; was married January 1, 1835, to William Ogdon Bradstreet. They resided in Miamisburg, Ohio, where Ellen (Goodwin) Bradstreet died November 13, 1891. *Bradstreet* children: i. Samuel Ellis; ii. Milton Henry; iii. Thomas Goodwin; iv. Willis Rees.

Elizabeth Goodwin (Thomas, Thomas), born November 3, 1806, near Franklin, Ohio; was married September, 1825, at her home near Franklin, to George Kepler, born July 3, 1790, in Frederick county, Md., a son of George and —— (Mooler) Kepler. By occupation he was a merchant tailor, in politics a Whig and Republican, and in religion a Methodist. They resided in Dayton, Ohio, where Elizabeth died in January, 1889. *Kepler* children: i. Thomas, born May 8, 1826; ii. Catherine, born November 29, 1828; iii. Samuel, born December 9, 1830; iv. Jesse, born March 16, 1832; v. Eleanor, born November 29, 1834; vi. Mary, born June 5, 1836; vii. Francis, born February 25, 1839; viii. Owen, born March 6, 1840; died February 17, 1844.

Mary (Polly) Goodwin (Thomas, Thomas), born April 30, 1809, near Franklin, Ohio; was married May 7, 1829, at her home near Franklin, to James Marlatt, born September 30, 1806, near Martinsburg, W. Va., a son of —— and Jane (——) Marlatt. By occupation he was a carpenter and builder. They resided in Franklin, Ohio, until about 1830, and since then in Brookville, Ind., where James Marlatt died. Aunt Polly, as she is known to the family, resides with her daughter, Mary, sound in mind and strong of body, although in her 89th year.* *Marlatt* children: i. Samuel Goodwin,† born December 14, 1830; married

* "Aunt Polly" entered into rest August 24, 1897. A faithful friend, a kind and sympathetic neighbor, she was a perfect type of the pioneer women of the early West. She was the last of her day and generation.

† Resides in Richmond, Ind.

Hester A. Miller; ii. Jane, born December 6, 1833; married Nathan D. Lee; iii. Hezekiah Rees, born January 7, 1838; married Caroline Ketchum; iv. Mary, born June 8, 1840; resides at Brockville, Ind; v. Charles E.., born August 12, 1842; married Helen J. Huston; vi. William P., born March 73, 3845; married Hannah Moorman; vii. James P., born December 12, 1847; died June 29, 1849; viii. James, born March 17, 1852; died April 5, 1876.

APPENDIX B.

THE GOODWINS OF WASHINGTON COUNTY, INDIANA.

This family followed, as nearly as now known, the exact route taken by the GOODWINS OF BROOKVILLE, but no relationship could be traced by the older members of the family.

Aaron Goodwin was born 1753, in Virginia. He resided, until a young man, in Virginia, removing to the Cumberland Valley, Md., where he married, 1st, Susannah Leasure, and in 1790, with his wife and family, went along the old National Road to Old Fort, now Brownsville, Fayette Co., Pa., and then by flatboats to Maysville, Ky. They afterwards settled at Hinkston station, Ky., where Susannah (Leasure) Goodwin died. Some of their children remained in Kentucky with their mother's people, but others went with Aaron to Champaign Co., Ohio, where, in 1803, he married, 2ndly, Mary Chapman, a daughter of Elijah and Achsah (Burden) Chapman, who had removed to Ohio from Virginia "at a very early day." Aaron Goodwin removed from Kentucky on account of his prejudice against slavery. In 1809 he went with his family to Illinois, finishing his journey at a point about twelve miles east of St. Louis. Deciding, in 1812, to return to Ohio, he stopped, on his return journey, twelve miles north of Princeton, Indiana. Being pleased with the appearance of the country, and winter approaching, he took possession of an abandoned log house, where he remained with his family through the winter, and he then settled half-a-mile north of Washington, Ind., where he remained until his death, which occurred October 26, 1828. He was a teacher and a farmer. His birthplace is given by one grandson as Hartford, Conn., but he seems not to have belonged to that family.

Children by first wife: i. William; ii. Jeremiah, untraced; iii. Aaron Leasure, born 1778; married, 1st, Margaret McCully; 2ndly,

Mrs. Ann (———) Redd; iv. Enoch, untraced; v. Thomas, untraced; vi. Ruth, untraced. Children by second wife: vii. Benjamin, born August 17, 1804; married Drucilla Davis; viii. Elijah, born January 16, 1807; married Jane Moore Davis; ix. Moses, left descendants, untraced; x. Lourana, born February 22, 1812; married Arthur Johnson; xi. Achsah, born 1819; married Washington Crabtree; xii. James, untraced.

William Goodwin (Aaron) resided in Mason or Fleming Co., Kentucky. Children: i. Enoch, born 1807; ii. William, untraced; iii. Theopolis, untraced; iv. Edward, untraced; v. Elizabeth, untraced; vi. Rebecca, untraced.

Enoch Goodwin (William, Aaron), born in 1807 in Mason or Fleming Co., Ky., resided in Curtisville, Ind., where his son, Leander, resides (1897). No further information given. Child: i. Leander.

Aaron Leasure Goodwin (Aaron), born in 1778, in Maryland or Virginia, was married, in 1806, at Pittsburg, Pa., to Margaret McCully, born near Belfast, Ireland, a daughter of William McCully. Aaron Leasure Goodwin married, 2ndly, Mrs. Ann (——) Redd. He was a farmer, a Democrat, and a Methodist. He resided in Pittsburg, Pa., Elizabethtown, Ohio, Washington, Ind., and Vevay, Ind., at which last-named place he died. Children by first wife: i. Jane, married, 1st, J. L. Whitehead; 2ndly, N. D. Marchand; ii. Mary Ann, married John Waller; iii. Matilda, married N. D. Marchand; iv. William McCully, born June 15, 1818; married Marietta Wilbur; v. James A., died 1842; vi. Ruth Hendricks, married John Allen; vii. Aaron Leasure, died 1870; viii. John McCully, born January 26, 1826; married Nannie J. Pool; ix. Laura C., married Dr. C. Williams. Child by second wife: x. Matilda, married Squire Hulley.

William McCully (McCullough) *Goodwin* (Aaron Leasure, Aaron), born June 15, 1818, in Daviess Co., Ind., was married, June 13, 1841, at Leavenworth, Indiana, to Marietta Wilbur, born August 8, 1822, in Leavenworth, Ind., a daughter of William Wilbur. By occupation he was a saddler, in politics a Democrat, and in religion an Universalist. They resided in Mississippi Co., Mo., 1842–'59; Leavenworth, Ind., 1859–'67; Cave in Rock, Ill., 1867–1886. Marietta (Wilbur) Goodwin died May 9, 1874, at Cave in Rock; William McCullough Goodwin died April 7, 1886, at Anna, Ill. Children: i. John Jefferson, born August 14, 1842; married Norah C. Mitchell; ii. William S., born November 25, 1844; died

February 10, 1862; iii. Catherine Laura, born December 23, 1847; married John H. Caldwell; iv. Jacob Aaron, born March 31, 1851; died September 19, 1851; v. James Robert, born June 18, 1853; married Alice M. Cook; vi. Millard Fillmore, born January 23, 1857; died December 17, 1881; vii. Joseph Benjamin, born October 9, 1859; died in infancy.

James Robert Goodwin (William McCully, Aaron Leasure, Aaron), born June 18, 1853, in Mississippi Co., Mo.; was married, January 5, 1876, in Crittenden Co., Ky., by Rev. Thomas Moore, to Alice M. Cook, born March 8, 1858, in Crittenden Co., Ky., a daughter of L. E. and P. A. (Walker) Cook. By occupation he was a manufacturer of clothing, in politics a Democrat. He resided in Missouri until he was six years old, then in Crawford Co., Ind., until thirteen years of age; in Harden Co., Ill., until twenty-six years of age; and since then in Evansville, Ind. Children: i. James Raymond, born November 4, 1876; ii. Walter Cook, born July 23, 1879; iii. Percy, born September 9, 1881; iv. Grace, born October 17, 1883.

John McCully Goodwin (Aaron Leasure, Aaron), born January 26, 1826, in Washington, Indiana, was married, December 23, 1857, at Sardis, Ohio, by Rev. A. D. McCormack, to Nannie J. Pool, born September 25, 1840, in Belmont Co., Ohio, a daughter of Philip and Ann Maria (Caldwell) Pool. By occupation he was a merchant and farmer, in politics a Democrat, and in religion a Methodist. They resided in Belmont Co. and Sardis, Ohio (1897). Children: i. George Philip, born September 25, 1858; married Mary A. Scharf; ii. Laura Jane, born July 31, 1860; married George Case; iii. John Pool, born September 30, 1862; married Flora M. Talbott; iv. William McCully, born July 27, 1867; married Rachel Burton.

Benjamin Goodwin (Aaron), born August 17, 1804, in Urbana, Champaign Co., Ohio, was married in 1824, at Washington, Ind., by Abner Davis, to Drucilla Davis, born November 25, 1804, in Maysville, Mason Co., Ky., a daughter of Levi Davis. By occupation he was a farmer and politician. They resided near Washington, Ind. He held a number of political offices, from constable to representative. He died in 1877. Children: i. George Washington; ii. Anderson; iii. Levi; iv. Mary Ellen, born October 30, 1836; married John W. Wainman; v. Elijah; vi. Alfred Davis; vii. Moses Aaron; viii. Matilda Jane; ix. Jeremiah, born April 7, 1848; married Margaret Jane Barber; x. Leatha Ann, born July 7, 1853; married Charles Rodarmel.

Jeremiah Goodwin (Benjamin, Aaron), born April 7, 1848, near Washington, Ind., was married December 8, 1875, at Cumback, Ind., by Tilman Willis, to Margaret Jane Barber, born April 10, 1853, near Cumback, Ind., a daughter of Samuel and Eleanor (Horrall) Barber. By occupation he was a farmer, and in politics a Populist. They resided (1897) in Cumback, Ind. Children: i. Ora Ellen, born April 15, 1877; ii. Samuel Benjamin, born April 7, 1879; iii. Lionel Edgar, born October 26, 1880; iv. James Weaver, born January 21, 1883; died young; v. Ulla Belva, born February 20, 1885; vi. Joseph Thomas, born October 27, 1887; vii. John Roy, born January 11, 1890; viii. Hollis Roy, born March 25, 1893.

Rev. Elijah Goodwin (Aaron), born January 16, 1807, in Champaign Co., Ohio, was married August 5, 1828, in Gibson Co., Ind., to Jane Moore Davis, born July 16, 1805, in Tennessee, a daughter of David and Eleanor (Moore) Davis. By occupation he was a minister, and in religion a Christian. They resided in Indianapolis, Ind. Rev. Elijah Goodwin was one of the most noted divines in the Christian Church. Jane Moore (Davis) Goodwin died February 16, 1863, in Indianapolis; Rev. Elijah Goodwin died October 7, 1879, in Cleveland, Ohio. Children: i. Mary Eleanor, born September 20, 1829; died August 25, 1845; ii. Sarah Ann, born April 5, 1831; married Elijah Washington Knapp; iii. Melissa Jane, born October 22, 1833; married James Jefferson Reed; iv. Elizabeth, born August 26, 1836; died November 10, 1838; v. Aaron Davis, born January 22, 1839; married Emma Dale; vi. Friend Chapman, born November 13, 1841; died April 22, 1861; vii. Zeno, born April 10, 1844; died April 28, 1848; viii. Angelo Quincey, born March 31, 1847; married Louisa Jayne; ix. Moses; x. Joses, born April 28, 1850; died April 30, 1850.

Sarah Ann Goodwin (Elijah, Aaron), born April 5, 1831, in Gibson Co., Ind., was married October 15, 1848, at Bloomington, Ind., by Rev. James M. Mathis, to Elijah Washington Knapp, born April 15, 1825, in Jennings Co., Ind., a son of Amos and Mary (Butler) Knapp. They resided (1897) in Irvington, Ind. *Knapp* children: i. Ovid Butler, born August 12, 1848; married Jennie McNeal; ii. Elijah Goodwin, born November 2, 1851; died December 17, 1867; iii. Friend Chapman, born January 31, 1854; married Lutie Moore; iv. Alvin Scott, born October 4, 1856; married Katie Holman Carry; v. Daniel Franklin, born February 2, 1860; died March 20, 1867; vi. William Wallace, born July 18, 1862; married Margretta Tebbott; vii. Laura Melissa, born February 25, 1866; resides at Irvington, Ind.; unmarried; viii. Almira Emma, born May 31, 1875; died September 9, 1876.

Angelo Quincey Goodwin (Elijah, Aaron), born March 31, 1847, in Mt. Vernon, Ind., was married to Louisa Jayne. They resided (1897) in Indianapolis, Ind. Children: not furnished.

Aaron Davis Goodwin (Elijah, Aaron), born January 22, 1839, was married to Emma Dale. Aaron Davis Goodwin died June 10, 1891. Children: one son and three daughters.

APPENDIX C.

THE GOODWINS OF FAYETTE COUNTY, PENNSYLVANIA.

The same road was travelled by the brothers Joseph and John as had been taken by Thomas and Aaron, but they remained in Pennsylvania and Virginia, now West Virginia. They had doubtless started west from Baltimore, or from a neighboring county, but seem not to have been related to the John Goodwin from Montgomery county, Md. (Appendix F.)

John Goodwin was born in Ireland, as were his sons, if the statement of a grandson is to be relied upon. It seems more probable that the sons were born in America, and perhaps their father before them. It is suggested that a complete record of the family of this John Goodwin may show the names of William, James and Thomas in addition to those here given, and that the entire family is of a Virginia-Maryland origin. Children: i. Joseph, born ———; married Martha Greenlee; ii. John.

Joseph Goodwin (John) was born ———, in Maryland (?); was married to Martha Greenlee, who was born in Sussex county, Del. By occupation he was a farmer. They resided in Spring Hill Furnace, Fayette county, Penn., between 1790 and 1800. Their son William is said to have "gone back" to Baltimore, or near there, to work on a public building, and was killed by a fall. In a letter dated March 12, 1893, written by Joseph, Jr., to Mr. John S. Goodwin, the following statements were made: "My father came from Ireland. Your father had *six* brothers, if you are one of *John* Goodwin's boys. I am the only one now living, and am the seventh son. Your grandfather was born at Spring Hill Furnace (if you are a grandson of John)." This is the only time John's name is given as a son of Joseph by any of Joseph's descendants. Others dispute there having been a son John, but his brother Joseph should know, and without him Joseph would not be the "seventh son." Children: i. Daniel, born July 22, 1799, married Martha Coale; ii. Robert, born ——; iii. Samuel, born ——, married Nellie Warman; iv. William, born ——, killed in Baltimore, unmarried; v. John (untraced); vi. Jacob, born ——; vii. Joseph, born ——, married Ruth Richards; viii. Mary, born ——, married Robert Beattie.

Daniel Goodwin (Joseph, John) was born July 22, 1799, in Fayette county, Penn.; was married in 1825 at Uniontown to Martha Coale, who was born in 1799 in Fayette county, a daughter of John Coale. By occupation he was a shoemaker, in politics a Whig and in religion a Methodist. They resided in Smithfield, Pa. Children: i. John Coale, born February 25, 1827, married Nancy A. Meeker; ii. William T., born June 16, 1829, married Drusilla West; iii. Joseph Thomas, born August 9, 1831, married, first, Sarah R. Williams; second, Cora E. Knight; iv. Daniel Sturgeon, born July 5, 1836, married Mary Phillips.

John Coale Goodwin (Daniel, Joseph, John) was born February 25, 1827, in Fayette county, Pa.; was married September 12, 1854, at Hamilton, Ohio, by Rev. Mr. Pierson, to Nancy A. Meeker, who was born October 30, 1830, in St. Charles, Butler county, Ohio, a daughter of Michael and Margaret (Harris) Meeker. He was a merchant, in politics a Republican. They resided in Mechanicsburg, Ind. He died December 12, 1870. Children: i. Samuel Houston, born December 15, 1854, died May 20, 1879, unmarried; ii. Charles Sumner, born December 14, 1856, married Lizzie E. Swain; iii. John William, born September 15, 1860, married Lucy McCormack; iv. Infant, born February 15, 1865; v. Thomas Arthur, born September 22, 1867, married Georgiana Howard.

Charles Sumner Goodwin (John Coale, Daniel, Joseph, John) was born December 14, 1856, in Mechanicsburg, Ind.; was married to Lizzie E. Swain. They resided in Mechanicsburg. Charles Sumner Goodwin died January 31, 1876. His widow and child reside in Newcastle, Ind. Child: i. Georgia LaMott.

John William Goodwin (John Coale, Daniel, Joseph, John) was born September 15, 1860, in Mechanicsburg, Ind; was married in 1881 at Mechanicsburg, by C. W. Wood, to Lucy McCormack, who was born November 17, 1865, in Cadiz, Ind., a daughter of James and Minerva (Wyatt) McCormack. By occupation he was a merchant, in politics independent and in religion an Adventist. They reside, 1897, in Mechanicsburg. Children: i. Blanche, born March 23, 1882; ii. Laurence, born February 14, 1884.

Thomas Arthur Goodwin (John Coale, Daniel, Joseph, John) was born September 22, 1867, in Mechanicsburg, Ind; was married to Georgiana Howard. They reside, 1897, in Mechanicsburg. Children: i. Charles; ii. Lucile.

Joseph Thomas Goodwin (Daniel, Joseph, John) was born August 9, 1831, in Smithfield, Pa; was married, first, October 25, 1859, at Niles, Mich., by A. J. Eldred, to Sarah R. Williams, who was born August 31, 1841, in Niles, where she died February 24, 1879. He resided in Smithfield until 1855, when he removed to Niles, Mich. He enlisted as 1st sergeant Company K, Eleventh Michigan Cavalry, and was promoted to lieutenant Company A, Eighth Michigan Cavalry. After the death of his wife he removed to Webster City, South Dakota, in 1884, where he married, second, November 8, 1886, Cora E. Knight. His occupation was salesman, and in politics a Democrat. He was elected county commissioner in 1885, and county treasurer in 1888–'90 and '92. Children by first wife; i. Cora A., born November 9, 1860; ii. Gertrude E., born April 21, 1869, died December, 1869 Children by second wife: iii. George Earle, born August 25, 1887; iv. Leslie Thomas, born January 30, 1894.

Joseph Goodwin (Joseph, John) was born in Spring Hill Furnace, Pa.; was married to Ruth Richards. They resided in Smithfield, Pa., where Joseph Goodwin died about 1893. Children: i. ———; ii. ———; iii. ———; iv. John R., born January 2, 1842, married Nancy Hibbs; v. James R., born February 2, 1845, married Sarah J. Sweeney.

James R. Goodwin (Joseph, Joseph, John) was born February 2, 1845, in Oldframe, Pa.; was married March, 1866, at Ruble, Pa., by Squire Hunter, to Sarah J. Sweeney. By occupation he was a farmer, in politics a Democrat and in religion a Presbyterian. They reside, 1897, near Fairchance, Pa. Children: i. Anna R., born August 27, 1867; ii. James R., born October 30, 1868, married Anna F. Dunne; iii. Joseph, born ———, died ———; iv. Sarah Ella, born ———, married C. C. Bowers; v. Charles Porter, born May 16, 1872.

John Goodwin (John) was born in Ireland or Maryland. By occupation he was a farmer. He resided "over the line" from Smithfield, Pa., in West Virginia. Children: i. Joseph, born 1800, married, first, Margaret Griffith; second, Sarah (———) Reed; ii. John; iii. Daniel.

Joseph Goodwin (John, John) was born in 1800; was married, first, to Margaret Griffith, a daughter of Captain Griffith. Joseph married, second, Mrs. Sarah (———) Reed. By occupation he was a farmer. They resided near Smithfield, Pa., where he died. Children, twelve in all: i. Thomas, born June 19, 1825; married Susanna Adams; ii. Benjamin F., born June 29, 1827, married Emily Britt.

Benjamin F. Goodwin (Joseph, John, John) was born June 29, 1827, in Bruceton Mills, West Virginia; was married November 25, 1847, at New Geneva, Pa., by Rev. H. O. Rosboro, to Emily Britt, who was born September 1, 1833, in Uniontown, Pa., a daughter of Robert and Asenath (Greenlee) Britt. By occupation he was a farmer, in politics a Democrat and in religion a Presbyterian. They reside, 1897, near Fairchance, Fayette county, Pa. Children: i. Mollie M., born August 14, 1857; married W. F. Morgan; ii. Charles R., born April 21, 1859, married Hattie E. Bowers; iii. Walter M., born September 2, 1860; married, first, Jennie Coffman; second, Eunice Woolsey; iv. Clara M., born December 16, 1864, married A. J. Hicks; v. Franklin Pierce, born July 10, 1868; married Lucetta Franks; vi. Britt R., born February 6, 1872; vii. Centennial B., born July 20, 1876; viii. Norval B., born February 28, 1880.

John Goodwin (John, John) was a farmer. He resided in Preston county, West Virginia. Child: i. John, born April, 17, 1830; married, first, Martha Beattie; second, Mrs. ——— Titcher.

John Goodwin (John, John, John) was born April 13, 1830, in Preston county, West Virginia; was married, first, 1873, at Uniontown, Pa., by Rev. Dr. Bowman, to Martha Beattie; and second, February 20, 1894, by Rev. Mr. Friend, in Preston county, to Mrs. Titcher. By occupation he was a farmer, in politics a Republican and in religion a Baptist. He resides, 1897, in Preston county, West Virginia. Child by first marriage; i. William, born August 4, 1875.

APPENDIX D.

THE GOODWINS OF WHEELING, WEST VIRGINIA, AND THE GOODWINES OF WARREN COUNTY, INDIANA.

THE history of John Goodwin, who must have been born before 1740, is wholly unknown to his descendants until after his marriage. "He came to Kentucky from Virginia" is the sum total of their knowledge. He may have been a descendant of Major James Goodwin, but it is well to note these things: THOMAS GOODWIN, the ancestor of the GOODWINS OF CHESTER COUNTY, PENNSYLVANIA, had immigrated by 1708. He was accompanied by his son, Thomas, Jr., born 1694. This son married in 1729, and had seven children, the first being John, and the second, Thomas, *tertius*. This third Thomas married, and moved over into Virginia, but returned to Chester county, Pa. John, the first son of Thomas, Jr., married Naomi Potter in 1759, and became lost to his family. We may suppose that Naomi died, and that John married, second, a Miss Heddie, of German nationality, and moved through York county to the western part of the State, and across the line into (West) Virginia. A Seth Goodwin was a son of this John of Wheeling, and a Seth Goodwin of "German parentage" (that is, his mother, Heddie, was a German?) lived in York county, Pa. (See Appendix E.)*

The name was changed to "Goodwine" by James, son of John, and it is written "Goodin" by the descendants of another son, not now known which, who accompanied John to Bardstown, Kentucky.

John Goodwin, born before 1740, was married to Miss Heddie. By occupation he was a farmer. They resided near Wheeling, W. Va., and removed to near Bardstown, Ky., where they died. Some of their children remained in Virginia, coming west at a later date. Children: i. William; ii. Abner; iii. John; iv. Thomas; v. Seth (see Appendix E); vi. Heddie; vii. James, born April 20, 1780; married, first, Elizabeth Snyder; second, Mrs. Sarah (Shoemaker) Logan; viii. Lydia, married Isaac Birch; ix. Martha, died unmarried; x. Obadiah (?).

William Goodwin (John) resided near Wheeling, W. Va. He removed to Indiana after his father went to Kentucky, and settled near Lebanon, Boone county, Indiana, where he died, leaving descendants. No reply has been received to any letter sent them.

* This conjecture was submitted to Dr. William H. Egle, Harrisburg, Pa., State Librarian, and a noted genealogist, and he very materially strengthens the supposition that the Seth of York county was son of John Goodwin of Wheeling, W. Va., by answering that the Heddie family is an old York county, Pa., family, of German descent, and that two of the sons, of about the age of the wife of John Goodwin, moved west to around Wheeling, W. Va. It should also be noted that a Moses Goodwin was executor of the will of a Benjamin Taylor in York county in 1753. What relation, if any, he was to this John Goodwin is not known.

Abner Goodwin (John) was born in Virginia. By occupation he was a farmer. He resided near Wheeling until, perhaps, about 1835, when he removed to Ohio, and later to Indiana, finally settling near Greencastle, Putnam county, Ind., where he died about 1848. Children: i. Francis, born September 24, 1799; married Sarah Gratehouse; ii. William, untraced; iii. John, untraced; iv. Nathan, untraced; v. Alexander; vi. James, resided and died in Peru, Indiana.

Francis Goodwin (Abner, John), born September 24, 1799, in Virginia, was married, April 15, 1819, to Sarah Gratehouse, born October 29, 1800. By occupation he was a farmer. They resided near Wheeling, removing to Blanchester, Ohio, and about 1844 settled near Clinton Falls, Putnam county, Ind., where he died March 12, 1871. Sarah (Gratehouse) Goodwin died April 30, 1878. (For descendants of this branch see Sharpless genealogy.) Children: i. Jane, born April 30, 1820; married Thomas Holland; ii. Zadock, born September 27, 1822; resides in Nebraska; iii. William, born February 16, 1825; resides in Kansas; iv. Rachel, born May 2, 1827; v. Michael, born March 16, 1830; resides in Council Bluffs, Iowa; vi. Emmaline, born September 28, 1832; vii. Lydia Ann, born May 13, 1837; died July 22, 1864; viii. Elizabeth, born May 13, 1839; ix. Eliza, born May 22, 1842; x. James Thomas, born June 20, 1845; resides in Council Bluffs, Iowa.

Alexander Goodwin (Abner, John) was born in Virginia. By occupation he was a farmer. They resided in Bedford, Taylor county, Iowa, where Alexander died in 1879. (No response to inquiries.) Children: i. Jemima, born May, 1819; married William Lewis; ii. Jane, married ——— Busey; iii. Martha, married William Webb; iv. Polly, married ——— Lewis; v. Lydia, married ——— Farlow; vi. Sarah, married ——— Newgent; vii. Amanda, married ——— Houck; viii. Nancy C., married ——— Shepard; ix. Seth, married, and left descendants, untraced.

James Goodwine (John), born April 20, 1780, in Virginia; was married, first, in 1807, in Kentucky, to Elizabeth Snyder, "a German woman." He married, second, Mrs. Sarah (Shoemaker) Logan, in Jackson county, Ind. She was born in 1788, in Virginia, a daughter of John Shoemaker, a Revolutionary soldier, and died in 1872, in Warren county, Ind. James Goodwine accompanied his parents from near Wheeling, Va., to Bardstown, Ky. After marriage he removed to Jackson county, Ind., then to Brown county, and again, to Bartholomew, and finally, to Warren county. He was in the wars of 1812 and 1822. He was a farmer, stockman, and shipper. He became very wealthy, and owned thousands of acres of land at his death, in 1851. He changed the spelling of his name by adding a final "e," done by reason of dispute. Some of his brothers omitted the "w." Children by first wife: i. Elizabeth, born 1808; married James Quick; ii. Thomas, born August 10, 1810; married Eliza A. Baird; iii. James, born June 19, 1812; married Sophia Buckles; iv. Indiana, born October 16, 1814; married Wesley Clark; v. Martha, born 1816; married Richard Lyon; vi. Harrison, born 1818; married Isabell Charlton; vii. John Washington, born 1822; married, first, Jane Charlton; second, Arminda (Sperry) Dare. Child by second wife: viii. Abner, born July 10, 1826; married Barbara Pence.

Thomas Goodwine (James, John) was born August 10, 1810, in Bardstown, Ky.; was married in 1834, in Warren county, Ind., to Eliza Ann Baird, who was born March 1, 1819, at Clarksburg, Ross county, O., a daughter of James and Elizabeth (Clark) Baird. By occupation he was a farmer, in politics a Whig, and in religion a Protestant. He resided in Bardstown, Ky., until he was five years of age, and then with his father's family lived in Jackson, Brown, Bartholomew, and Warren counties, Ind. He died in 1872 near West Lebanon. His son John Clark has assisted greatly in collecting the family data. Children: i. James Snyder, born 1836, married Mary Miller; ii. John Clark, born 1838, resides at Birmingham, Ala., unmarried; iii. Wesley, born 1841, died unmarried; iv. William Wallace, born 1843, died unmarried; v. Rosa, married William V. Farr; vi. Elizabeth, died unmarried; vii. Jane, died unmarried; viii. Thomas, married C. C. Page; ix. Julian, unmarried; x. Scott, born 1860, unmarried.

James Goodwine (James, John) was born June 19, 1812; was married to Sophia Buckles. By occupation he was a farmer. They resided near West Lebanon, Ind. Children: i. Mary Jane; ii. John Quincy; iii. William Harrison; iv. Frank; v. James; vi. Washington; vii. Louisa; viii. Christina; ix. Indiana; x. Marion; xi. Horace Greely; xii. Fremont.

John Washington Goodwine (James, John) was born December 22, 1822, at Columbus, Ind.; was married, first, June, 1845, in Warren county, by John Pugh, justice of the peace, to Jane Charlton, born in 1821, in East Tennessee, a daughter of Thomas and Jane (Glass) Charlton, and who died August 26, 1871. He was married, second, to Mrs. Arminda (Sperry) Dare, born December 24, 1842, a daughter of Erastus and Ruth (Rees) Sperry. By occupation he was a farmer, stock-breeder and feeder, and in politics a Republican. He resided (1897) in Potomac, Ill., and is a very noted man in his part of the State. Children by first wife: i. Marion, born August 26, 1846, married Susan Selsor; ii. John, born December 2, 1848, married, first, Mary H. Alexander; second, Ledora A. Lane; iii. James, born May 19, 1851, married Minerva King; iv. Mary Jane, born December 17, 1853, married J. M. Tillotson; v. Fremont, born November 16, 1858, died December 1, 1862. Children by second wife: vi. Martha, born September 6, 1872, married D. M. Juvinall; vii. Helen, born October 16, 1874, married D. E. Juvinall; viii. Dora, born March 3, 1877, married F. Chapman; ix. Grant Washington, born August 7, 1879.

John Goodwine (John Washington, James, John) was born December 2, 1848, in Vermilion county, Ill.; was married, first, December 22, 1870, at Danville, Ill., by Samuel Stansbury, justice of the peace, to Mary K. Alexander, who was born in Vermilion county, a daughter of John C. and Esther (Holtsclaw) Alexander, and died October 29, 1872. He was married, second, May 14, 1874, at Danville, by Judge R. W. Hanford, to Lidora Alice Lane, who was born September 22, 1855, at McArthur, O., a daughter of Royal H. and Mary (Brewer) Lane. By occupation he was a farmer, stock-breeder and feeder, and in politics a Republican. He resided (1897) at Potomac, Ill. Child by first wife: i. Anna, born July 19, 1872, married L. D. Lane. Children by second wife: ii. Daughter, born August 31, 1875, died at birth; iii. John Washington, born November 20, 1877; iv. Wilber Harrison, born October 13, 1879; v. Nora Elsie, born July 13, 1882, died February 6, 1890; vi. Ulysses Sidney, born February 11, 1884; vii. Cora, born December 31, 1885; viii. Villa, born December 3, 1887, died February 2, 1890; ix. Everett, born November 4, 1889; x. Vesta, born January 12, 1892; xi. Wayne, born May 12, 1895.

Abner Goodwine (James, John) was born July 10, 1826, in Bartholomew county, Ind.; was married October 30, 1851, in Warren county, Ind., by Mac. Shepard, to Barbara J. Pence, who was born October 19, 1830, in Bartholomew county, a daughter of George and Mary (Swisher) Pence. By occupation he was a farmer, and in politics a Republican. They resided near Rossville, Ill., (1897) post-office, the farm being in Jordan Tp., Warren county, Ind. Children: i. George, born July 11, 1852, died February 16, 1853;

ii. Mary C., born October 16, 1853, married William R. Hemebright; iii. Newton C., born March 17, 1855, married Elizabeth A. Briggs; iv. Bell, born November 3, 1856, died December 4, 1873; v. Sarah E., born November 23, 1858, married Joseph R. Wonegardner; vi. Clara V., born February 11, 1861, married John H. Crawford; vii. Frank S., born January 16, 1863, married Alice Dice; viii. Olive, born February 28, 1865, married Isaac Newton Heaton; ix. Nora, born June 27, 1867, married Alvin A. Pugh; x. Cora, born June 27, 1867, married Martin F. Briggs; xi. Leola, born April 8, 1870, unmarried; xii. Harry M., born September 27, 1874, unmarried.*

APPENDIX E.

THE GOODWINS OF YORK COUNTY, PENNSYLVANIA.

Whatever the ancestry of JOHN GOODWIN, Appendix D, it seems very probable that his son Seth is the Seth of "German descent" who lived in York county, and that it will be found that the wife of John, Miss Heddie, was of German descent, or, perhaps, born in Germany.

Seth Goodwin was born of "German parentage;" was married and resided in York county, Pa., where he and his wife died, near Little York. Children: i. John, born 1796, married Sally Gardner; ii. William, untraced.

John Goodwin (Seth) was born in 1796, in York county, Pa.; was married in 1819, in Washington county, to Sally Gardner, who was born in 1799, in Washington county. By occupation he was a farmer. They resided in Washington and Greene county, Pa. Sally (Gardner) Goodwin died in Greene county in 1843. Children: i. Andrew Jackson, born February 2, 1817, married Eliza Sargent; ii. Daniel, born April 3, 1820, resides at Wind Ridge, Greene county; iii. William, born 1822, married Nancy Wilson; iv. Polly; v. Seth F. C., born 1828, resides at Rutan, Greene county; vi. Elizabeth; vii. Sarah; viii. Delila; ix. John T., born July 31, 1840, resides at Waynesburg, Pa.

---

* A John Goodwin and his brother came to West Lebanon, Ind., about 1840, and settled near their "cousin," James Goodwine. John married Rebecca ——— in Warren county, and both he and his brother removed about 1850.

APPENDIX F.

The Goodwins of Harrison County, West Virginia.

The Pension Office records show that John Goodwin was born in 1762 in Montgomery county, Md., and enlisted from Harrison county, Va., in 1778, aged sixteen. He is said to have had a younger brother Edward, who lived in Harrison county; and it is also asserted that Zadock Goodwin, who married Mary Winters, was not a son of this John. These facts indicate that several brothers, some very young, were living in Harrison county in 1778, and presumably their parents had come with them from Montgomery county, Md. They seem not to have been related to the John and Joseph, Appendix C.

John Goodwin was born, 1762, in Montgomery county, Md.; was married to Elizabeth Webb. By occupation he was a farmer. They resided in Harrison county, W. Va. He enlisted from Harrison county in 1778, and served in Capt. William Lother's company of Virginia in 1778–'80, and in Capt. Joseph Gregory's company until 1782. He was pensioned in 1833, then residing in Harrison county. Children: i. Zadock, married Mary Winters; ii. John, born January 30, 1799, married Sarah Bartlett; iii. William, married Nancy McDonald; iv. George, married, first Ingalby Bartlett; second, Surrepta Lang; third, Helen Vandegraft; v. Elizabeth, married Miner Clevenger; vi. Margaret, married Humphrey Faris; vii. Zepporah, married Samuel Chidister; viii. Comfort, married Samuel Cleavinger; ix. Nancy, married John Bartlett; x. Tabitha, married Solomon Frum; xi. Mary, married Moses Husted; xii. Sarah, unmarried.

Zadock Goodwin (John) was married October 15, 1818, at Middleville, Harrison county, by Jesse H. Goss, to Mary Winters, who was born October 10, 1803, in Harrison county, a daughter of Matthias and Martha (Johnson) Winters. By occupation he was a farmer, in politics a Democrat, and in religion a Baptist. They resided on Beards Run until in 1852, removing in the spring of the year to Lewis county, and in the fall of the same year they moved to Jackson county, where he died June 1, 1855. She died October 21, 1879. Children: i. Matthias W., born March 2, 1820, married Amanda Britton; ii. John E., born January 14, 1822, married, first, Mary Curry; second, Mrs. Erli Stone; iii. Emily Adaline, born August 8, 1824, married John Kayser; iv. Martha M., born

July 20, 1826, married Thomas Maddox; v. Webb Granville, born May 3, 1828, married Sarah Cleavenger; vi. Joseph J., born July 4, 1830, married Edith Cookman; vii. Sarah Ann, born February 18, 1833, died in infancy or early childhood; viii. William L., born June 22, 1834, married Barbara Casto; ix. Elizabeth A., born July 14, 1837, died before she was ten years; x. Martin Van Buren, born January 8, 1840, married, first, a Miss Greene; second, a Miss Maddox; xi. James W., born March 13, 1842, died when about twelve or thirteen; xii. Hiram, born June 3, 1844, married Ann Eliza Holt; xiii. George W., born February 21, 1847, married Sarah Cookman. (The above were given by Webb Goodwin, of Barbour county, W. Va. There is not a particle of doubt as to the grandfather of the above children. Zed's father's name was John Goodwin.)

John Goodwin (John) was born January 30, 1799, in Virginia; was married June 2, 1825, to Sarah Bartlett, who was born February 12, 1809, a daughter of Eppa and Rebecca (Barnes) Bartlett. By occupation he was a farmer and teacher, in politics a Republican, and in religion a Methodist. They resided in Harrison county. Sarah (Bartlett) Goodwin died September 3, 1874, in Harrison county, W. Va. John Goodwin died July 28, 1880, in Harrison county. Children: i. Rebecca, born May 2, 1827, unmarried; ii. Elizabeth T., born November 14, 1829, married Alfred St. Clair; iii. Nancy J., born March 8, 1831, married Elias Lawson; iv. Mary, born October 20, 1832, married Nathan L. Bartlett; v. Sarah, born June 15, 1834, married James Bartlett; vi. James W., born February 21, 1836, unmarried; vii. Comfort, born July 9, 1838, married W. L. Shields; viii. Edith, born February 21, 1841, unmarried; ix. Eppa D., born June 19, 1843, married Marrietta Lang; x. Zepporah, born November 19, 1848, unmarried; xi. Granville, born October 10, 1849, married Mary Wiseman; xii. Franklin Sylvanus, born January 17, 1852, killed October 20, 1871, by fall in mines.

Eppa D. Goodwin (John, John) was born June 19, 1843, in Harrison county, W. Va.; was married November 15, 1866, in Harrison county, by Rev. Mr. Day, to Marrietta Lang, who was born September 13, 1846, in Harrison county, a daughter of Lemuel and Surrepta (Bartlett) Lang. By occupation he was a farmer, in politics a Republican, and in religion a Methodist Protestant. They reside at Bridgeport, W. Va. (1897). Elmer Forrest Goodwin is a member of the class of '98 W. V. U. and is prominent in Y. M. C. A. work. Children: i. Cleophas M., born September 25, 1867, died; ii. Elmer Forrest, born May 4, 1869; iii. James Edward, born August 23, 1872; iv. William Virgil, born April 2, 1878; v. Gail Jacob, born February 14, 1884.

Granville Goodwin (John, John) was born October 10, 1849, in Harrison county; was married February 5, 1878, at Bridgeport, W. Va., by Rev. Mr. Murray, to Mary Wiseman, who was born October 14, 1861, in Bridgeport, a daughter of Zachariah and Louise (Haley) Wiseman. By occupation he was a farmer, in politics a Republican, and in religion a Methodist Protestant. They resided near Tyrconnell Mines, W. Va., where he died October 20, 1883. Children: i. Jessie Maud, born December 26, 1878, married Virgil E. Frum; ii. Daisy Virginia, born May 7, 1881; iii. Flora May, born October 21, 1882.

William Goodwin (John) was married to Nancy McDonald. Children: i. Tabitha, married John Lancaster; ii. Elizabeth, married Sidney Horner; iii. Judson, died in Illinois, unmarried; iv. James N., married Mary Fitzhugh; v. Henrietta, married James Crim; vi. John, married Rachel Corder; vii. Zadock, unmarried; viii. Matthew, married L. Lawson.

George Goodwin (John) was married first to Ingalby Bartlett, and second to Surrepta Lang, and third to Helen Vandegraft. Children by first wife: i. Samuel S., born December 26, 1835, married, first, Jane Harrison; second, Malinda Coll; ii. Benjamin F., born August 20, 1837, married Margaret Ross; iii. John T., born September, 1839, married, first, Margaret Lancaster; second, Margaret Shields; third, Elizabeth Estlich; iv. L. Elmore, born 1841, died unmarried; v. William S., born 1843, married Sarah Clelland; vi. L. Meb, born January 9, 1845, married, first, Salina Dean; second, Edna M. Dawson; vii. Marshall S., born 1847, married Susan Greene; viii. Martha V., born 1849, married James W. Morris.

Edward Goodwin was born probably in Montgomery county, Maryland; was married to Taney ——. By occupation he was a farmer. They resided near Simpson, Taylor county, W. Va., on Buck's Run, where Edward died. Their daughter Margaret died at the same place. Children: i. James; ii. Gabriel, born about 1810, married, first, Sarah Wyckoff; second, Rachel Whithair; iii. Margaret.

James Goodwin (Edward) was born in Taylor county, W. Va., and died near West Union, Doddridge county. Children: i. Richard, untraced; ii. Edward, untraced.

Gabriel Goodwin (Edward) was born about 1810 near Simpson, Taylor county, W. Va.; was married, first, in 1841, at Simpson, to Sarah Wyckoff, who was born in Hampshire county, W. Va., a daughter of William and Mary (Shillingburg) Wyckoff. He married, second, Rachel Whithair. By occupation he was a farmer, in politics a Republican and in religion a Baptist. He resided in Taylor county, where he died about 1882 from injuries received by a fall. Mrs. Rachel (Whithair) Goodwin resides (1897) near Simpson. Children by first wife: i. James L., born August 16, 1842, married, first, Philena A. Robinson; second, Dora B. Selney; ii. Emanuel; iii. Timeon (Timothy); iv. Fannie. Children by second wife: v. Almira; vi. Granville; vii. David L.; viii. Grant, resides in Wheeling, W. Va.

James L. Goodwin (Gabriel, Edward) was born August 16, 1842, in Taylor county, W. Va.; was married in 1872 at Pruntytown, by Rev. Mr. Barnett, to Philena A. Robinson, who was born December 1, 1849, near Triconnell, W. Va., a daughter of ——— and Elizabeth (Snider) Robinson. She died in 1874. He married, second, Dora B. Selney. By occupation he was a farmer, in politics a Republican and in religion a Baptist. He resided in Marion county, W. Va., and near Peoria, Ill. Children by first wife: i. Okey, born January 30, 1873, resides in Flemington, W. Va.; ii. child died in infancy. Children by second wife: iii. Parke, born 1879; iv. Milley, born 1881; v. Iva, born 1883.

APPENDIX G.

THE GOODWINS OF ST. MARY'S COUNTY, MARYLAND.

This family, starting from St. Mary's county, opposite Westmoreland county, Va., has passed into Northern Maryland, Northeastern Virginia, and then westward into the Central States.

It is suggested that it may be a part of the descendants of Major James Goodwin, who owned land in Westmoreland county.

Thomas Goodwin resided in St. Mary's county, and possibly in Calvert county, Md. Accompanied by his eldest son, name unknown, he sailed for England about 1786, and both were lost at sea. It is a family tradition that Thomas was going to look after some property interests, and that a Bartholomew Goodwin was perhaps an ancestor. Children: i. Son, lost at sea; ii. John, born 1773; married Elizabeth Adams; iii. Charles, married Elizabeth

Dowell; iv. Thomas, married Virginia ———; v. William, born 1784, married Ann Carter.

John Goodwin (Thomas) was born 1773, in St. Mary's county, Md.; was married 1803, at her home in Frederick county, Va., to Elizabeth Adams, who was born 1788, a daughter of Gowen Adams. By occupation he was a farmer, in politics a Whig. They resided on their farm in Frederick county, Va., on the Shenandoah River, removing to Prince William county and to Fauquier county, and in 1829 went west to Clark county, Ohio, where they remained for five years, going from there to McLean county, Ill., where John died about 1844, and was buried at Funk's Grove. At the time of their marriage Gowen Adams kept a hotel between Brentsville and Dumfries. John Goodwin served in the war of 1812. He was a stern, reserved man, of retiring disposition, and never talked with his children about his ancestry. Elizabeth (Adams) Goodwin died in LaFayette county, Mo., in 1864. Children: i. James, born January 9, 1804; married, first, Elizabeth Jane Corder; second, Evaline Corder (cousin); third, Martha Marshall; ii. Nancy, married Samuel Murphy; iii. William, died unmarried; iv. Thomas, died unmarried; v. Maria, born September 18, 1812, married John Reed Miller; vi. Eliza, married Thompson Miller; vii. Amanda, married William Baker; viii. Mary, died in childhood; ix. John, married Nancy A. Sheller; x. Martha, married John Stubblefield; xi. Katherine, married Samuel Collins; xii. Sarah, married John or Lewis Harrison; xiii. Jeremiah, born February 18, 1826, married, first, Martha Mock; second, Mrs. S. E. (Henley) Pendleton.

James Goodwin (John, Thomas) was born January 9, 1804, in Prince William county, Va.; was married January 29, 1827, in Rappahannock county, Va., by Rev. Lewis Connor, to Elizabeth Corder, who was born in 1812, in Fauquier county, Va., a daughter of Judge Vincent and Elizabeth (Smoot) Corder. By occupation he was a merchant, in politics a Whig and Democrat, and in religion a Presbyterian. They resided in Rappahannock county, removing to Missouri in 1839. James Goodwin was first lieutenant in the Virginia militia. He contributed much data, and was in 1895 living in Waverly, Mo. He married, second, Evaline Corder, cousin to his first wife; and third, Martha Marshall. Children by first wife: i. John Thomas, born January 27, 1829; married Amanda Goggin; ii. George E., born 1831; married Catherine Burns; iii. Eliza J., born 1833, married Judge Gilmore Hays; iv. Elizabeth, born 1835; unmarried; v. Joseph W. (James ?), born 1837; married Lucy Corder. Children by second wife: vi. Martin; vii. Calvin, died; viii. Mary, died; ix. Martha, married Perry Catron; x. Henry. Children by third wife: xi. Frank; xii. Alice; xiii. Jennie, died; xiv. Joseph; xv. Birdie; xvi. Albert.

Nancy Goodwin (John, Thomas) was married to Samuel Murphy. *Murphy* children: i. Mathew; ii. George, died; iii. John, died; iv. Isaac, died; v. Charles; vi. Mary, died; vii. Eliza; viii. Samuel; ix. William, resides at McLean, Ill.; x. Jeremiah, died.

Maria Goodwin (John, Thomas) was born September 18, 1812, in Farquier county, Va.; was married December 19, 1833, at New Carlisle, Clark county, Ohio, by Rev. Mr. Dike, to John Reed Miller, who was born May 30, 1811, near Enon, Clark county, a son of Daniel and Elizabeth (Reed) Miller. By occupation he was a merchant and nurseryman, in politics a Whig and Republican, and in religion a Congregationalist. They resided at Enon and Springfield, Ohio, and Sedalia, Mo. John Reed Miller was postmaster at Enon about 1838. He died at Sedalia January 22, 1881. Mrs. Maria (Goodwin) Miller resides in Gainesville, Texas, with her daughter, Mrs. Fletcher, and has materially contributed to the compilation of these records. *Miller* children: i. Philena Elizabeth, born December 20, 1834; married Joseph Roper Swan; ii. Albert Thompson, born June 3, 1840; married Rebecca Jane Driscoll; iii. Martha Jane, born September 16, 1843; married Horace B. Fletcher; iv. Horace Mann, born September 18, 1853; unmarried.

Eliza Goodwin (John, Thomas) was married to Thompson Miller, who was a son of Daniel and Elizabeth (Reed) Miller. *Miller* children: i. Mary Jane, married Melyn Shellabarger; * ii. Maria, married Henry Weinland. †

Amanda Goodwin (John, James) was married to William Baker. She resided at 2716 E. 9th Street, Kansas City, Mo., in 1896. *Baker* child: i. Annie, married William Starr.

John Adams Goodwin (John, Thomas) was born December 23, 1822, in Fauquier county, Va.; was married June 3, 1847, at Clark county, Ohio, by Rev. M. Baker, to Nancy Ann Sheller, who was born November 6, 1829, in Mad River township, Clark county, a daughter of Adam and Mary (Heastend) Sheller. By occupation he was a nurseryman and hotel keeper, in politics a Republican and in religion a Christian. They resided in Dayton, Ohio, where John A. died in 1865. Mrs. Nancy Ann (Sheller) Goodwin resides

* He resides in Enon, Ohio. † They reside in Springfield, Ohio.

in West Liberty, Ohio. Children: i. Orrin Sheller, born September 15, 1848, married Sallie E. Kennedy; ii. Anna Belle, born May 16, 1851, married Theodore F. Miller; iii. Edgar James, born June 14, 1853, died September 27, 1874; iv. Albert Miller, born February 11, 1857, died February 11, 1859; v. Marcia Willetta, born April 21, 1861, married Harold E. Knight; vi. Jessie, born May 21, 1863, died August 8, 1864.

Orrin Sheller Goodwin (John Adams, John, Thomas) was born September 15, 1848, in Enon, Ohio; was married November 7, 1872, at Bellefountaine, Ohio, by Rev. G. L. Kalb, to Sallie Eleanor Kennedy, who was born August 23, 1848, in Bellefountaine, a daughter of William G. and Mary Edwards (Patterson) Kennedy. By occupation he was a carriage manufacturer and printer, in politics a Republican and in religion a Presbyterian. They resided in Dayton and Bellefountaine, Ohio, and (1897) Chicago. Mr. O. S. Goodwin spent six years in Sacramento, Stockton and San Francisco, Cal. Children: i. Edgar James, born August 29, 1874; ii. Alda Kennedy, born February 7, 1879; iii. Mary Crooke, born October 23, 1881.

Anna Belle Goodwin (John Adams, John, Thomas) was born May 16, 1851, in Donelsville, Ohio; was married September 12, 1872, at Bellefountaine, by Thomas Branden, to Theodore Freilinghuysen Miller, who was born August 26, 1844, in Fredericksburg, Ohio, a son of John and Agnes (Serrels) Miller. By occupation he was a travelling salesman, in politics a Republican and in religion a Methodist. They reside, 1897, in West Liberty, Ohio. *Miller* children: i. Bessie Goodwin, born August 27, 1877; ii. Albert Theodore, born May 8, 1880; iii. Maud Helen, born July 11, 1882; iv. Nellie Field, born August 21, 1884; v. Anna Mildred, born March 5, 1887; vi. Harry Howard, born May 18, 1889.

Marcia Willetta Goodwin (John Adams, John, Thomas) was born April 21, 1861, in Clark county, Ohio; was married December 29, 1879, at Bellefountaine, Ohio, by W. I. Lawrence, to Harold Edward Knight, who was born July 17, 1837, in Logan county, Ohio, a son of Edward Henry and Maria Janette (Richards) Knight. By occupation he was a manufacturer, in politics a Republican and in religion a Presbyterian. They resided in Bellefountaine, Ohio, in 1897. *Knight* children: i. Bessie Eleanor, born November 8, 1880; ii. Florence Anna, born August 20, 1882; iii. Edward Henry, born August 8, 1884; iv. Harold Octarion, born July 14, 1891.

Martha Goodwin (John, Thomas) was married to John Stubblefield. *Stubblefield* children: i. Daniel, resides in Kingston, Mo.; ii. Robert, resides in Catawba, Mo.; iii. Stephen; iv. Mary; v. Richard.

Katherine Goodwin (John, Thomas) was married to Samuel Collins. *Collins* child: i. Elizabeth.

Sarah Goodwin (John, Thomas) was married to Lewis Harrison. *Harrison* children: i. William; ii. Daughter.

Jeremiah Goodwin (John, Thomas) was born February 18, 1826, in Fauquier county, Va.; was married, second, in 1891, at Independence, Jackson county, Mo., by Rev. Mr. Shackelford, to Mrs. S. E. (Henley) Pendleton, who was born, 1835, in Kentucky, a daughter of Captain Alonzo and Elizabeth (Bilt) Henley. By occupation he was a farmer, in politics a Democrat and in religion a Christian Scientist. They resided in Independence, Mo., in 1896. Jeremiah's first wife was Martha Mock. She and her family reside in Marshall, Mo. No response. One of the sons is known as Frank. Children by first wife: i. Clifford; ii. Oscar; iii. Fannie; iv. Sue; v. Annie; vi. Georgia; vii. John T.; viii. George; ix. Martin; x. Henry. No children by second wife.

Charles Goodwin (Thomas) was born in Maryland; was married to Elizabeth Dowell. By occupation he was a farmer. They resided in Fairfax county, Va. Charles Goodwin died in 1852. Children: i. Elizabeth, born February 24, 1796, married James W. Driscoll; ii. Sarah, married Walter McCuen; iii. Jane, married William Wright; iv. William, married Mary Chick; v. Thomas, born April 13, 1813, married Mary Wright; vi. James, married Annie Smallwood; vii. Ann F., born November 3, 1822, married William E. Goodwin.

Elizabeth Goodwin (Charles, Thomas) was born February 24, 1796, in Fairfax county, Va.; was married to James Watson Driscoll, who was born in Cork county, Ireland; a son of ——— and Mary (Watson) Driscoll. By occupation he was a stone-cutter, in politics a Democrat. They resided in New Baltimore, Fauquier county, Va. *Driscoll* children: i. James Watson, born January 17, 1823; ii. Sample Wellington, born May 21, 1825; iii. Mary Jane, born September 25, 1826, married Thomas Keys; iv. Margaret C., born September 5, 1828, married Albert Magruder; v. Sarah Frances, born December 18, 1831; vi. Charles Morgan, born April 8, 1835, married Alconda J. Powell; vii. Lucy, born February 22, 1839, married John L. Boyer.

William Goodwin (Charles, Thomas) was married to Mary Chick, a daughter of Charles and ——— (Clark) Chick. By occupation he was a farmer, in politics a Whig. Children: i. James, married J. Virginia Commings; ii. Mary Jane, married Thomas Dowell; iii. John R., born June 1, 1833, married Margaret Bridwell; iv. Charles R.

John R. Goodwin (William, Charles, Thomas) was born June 1, 1833; was married in 1858 at Stafford county, Va., by John Clark to Margaret Bridwell, who was born in 1842 in Stafford county, a daughter of Benjamin and Ann (Burroughs) Bridwell. They resided (1897) in Onvil, Stafford county. Children: i. Alfred, married Willie Goodwin; ii. Zenaida, born 1860, married Henry Wheeler; iii. Benjamin, born 1862; iv. John, born 1864; v. Margaret, born 1866, married Eugene Thornton; vi. Martha, born 1868; vii. Alonzo, born 1871; viii. Belle, born 1873; ix. William, born 1875; x. Goldie, born 1878; xi. Allan, born 1881; xii. Child, born 1884.

Thomas Goodwin (Charles, Thomas) was born April 13, 1813, in Prince William county; was married in 1837 at Prince William county by Jessie Whems to Mary Wright, who was born in 1811 in Prince William county, a daughter of John and Elizabeth (Randolph) Wright. By occupation he was a farmer, in politics a Democrat. They resided in Orlando, Va. Children: i. Hortensia, born February 11, 1838; ii. Marshall, born June 4, 1840; iii. George M., born December 12, 1843; iv. Octavia, born June 10, 1845; v. Lue B., born March 16, 1850, married B. M. Bridwell; vi. Emma, born December 16, 1852.

James Goodwin (Charles, Thomas) was married to Annie Smallwood. They resided in Liberty, Mo. (No response.) Left children.

Ann F. Goodwin (Charles, Thomas) was born November 3, 1822; was married to William E. Goodwin, who was born January 20, 1821; a son of Thomas and Virginia (———) Goodwin. By occupation he was a farmer. Children—see William E.

Thomas Goodwin (Thomas) was married to Virginia ——. By occupation he was a farmer. Thomas Goodwin died in 1822. Children: i. William E., born January 20, 1821, married Ann F. Goodwin; ii. Maria.

William E. Goodwin (Thomas, Thomas) was born January 20, 1821; was married December, 1843, to Ann F. Goodwin, who was born November 3, 1822; a daughter of Charles and Elizabeth

(Dowell) Goodwin. Children: i. Margaret C., born July 3, 1843; ii. Mary V., born October 30, 1846; iii. John T., born January 3, 1848, married Sarah Cannon; iv. Roberta E., born April 12, 1850; v. Rebecca J., born June 11, 1852; vi. James A., born February 15, 1854; vii. Emma E., born July 28, 1856; viii. Eppa H., born March 9, 1861; ix. William J., born November 7, 1864.

John T. Goodwin (William E., Thomas, Thomas), born January 3, 1848, was married, November 17, 1868, to Sarah Cannon, born March 7, 1844, a daughter of George and Sarah (——) Cannon. By occupation he was a hotel-keeper. They resided in Manassas, Va., in 1896. Children: i. Dora, born 1871; married John M. Snyder; ii. Walter E., born 1874; iii. Wade A., born 1877; iv. Henry I., born 1879.

William Goodwin (Thomas), born in 1784, in Prince William county, Va., was married, 1821, in Prince William county, to Ann Carter, born 1801, in Prince William county, a daughter of Robert G. Carter. By occupation he was a farmer, in politics a Democrat. They resided in Prince William county, Va. William Goodwin was a soldier in the war of 1812. He died 1861. Ann (Carter) Goodwin died June, 1885. Children: i. Mary Jane, born 1822; married Zebulon Sullivan; ii. William Thomas, born March 2, 1824; married Mary J. Burke; iii. Julia Ann, married Stephen Hammill; iv. Martha, born February 3; married William Taylor; v. Robert G., died aged twelve years; vi. Adelaide, born August 31; married Henry Duty; vii. Susan Virginia, born May 21, 1841; married James Henry Cranford; viii. John Henry, born October 3, 1843; married Rachel Atwell; ix. Sarah, born April 16, 1844; married John William Cranford.

William Thomas Goodwin (William, Thomas), born March 2, 1824, in Prince William county, Va., was married, February 5, 1877, at Clifton, Fairfax county, by Rev. B. P. Dulin, to Mary J. Burke, born April 15, 1848, in Fairfax county, a daughter of Frank and Mary E. (Taylor) Burke. By occupation he was a merchant, in politics a Republican, and in religion a Methodist. They resided in Clifton, Virginia, where Mary J. (Burke) Goodwin died March 5, 1884. William T. Goodwin resides, 1897, in Farr, Fairfax county, Va. No children.

John Henry Goodwin (William, Thomas), born October 3, in Brentsville, Va., was married at Leesburg, Va., by Rev. Dr. Head, to Rachel Atwell, born March 5, 1853, in Leesburg, a daughter of Ewell and Mary (Newton) Atwell. By occupation he was a merchant, in politics a Republican. They resided (1897) in Washington, D. C. John Henry Goodwin served in the Confederate army, and was wounded at the battle of Seven Pines. Children: i. William Ewell, born December 29, 1872; died October 6, 1873; ii. Edwin Dickerson, born June 21, 1874; iii. Irving Wilson, born October 29, 1875; iv. John Harrison, born December 17, 1878; v. William Rogers, born February 15, 1884; vi. Wilbur Young, born February 16, 1888; vii. Edith May, born October 25, 1891.

Susan Virginia Goodwin (William, Thomas), born May 22, 1841, in Prince William county, was married, March 22, 1867, at Occoquan, by J. L. Porter, to James Henry Cranford, born 1829, in Fairfax county, a son of James and Susan (Athey) Cranford. By occupation he was a farmer, in politics a Democrat, and in religion a Methodist. They resided (1897) in Lorton Valley, Va. James W. Cranford has contributed a very large amount of the family data. *Cranford* children: i. James William, born June 2, 1868; resides in Washington, D. C.; ii. Wesley Hammond, born March 4, 1870; iii. John, born September 8, 1872; died young; iv. Edward Beamer, born June 18, 1874; v. Ida Adelaide, born December 21, 1878; vi. Walter Wilson, born June 29, 1880; vii. Grace Elizabeth, born June 19, 1882.

APPENDIX H.

THE GOODWINS OF BOTETOURT AND TAZEWELL COUNTIES, VIRGINIA.

It is possible that the name of the earliest given ancestor may not be JOHN as stated, and it is suggested that the list of children may not be complete, and that Daniel, the ancestor mentioned in Appendix J, may have been another son. Daniel lived in Botetourt county, and his son John resided in Tazewell county. Thomas, the son of Micajah, resided in Tazewell county before his marriage and removed to Botetourt county.

Granting that John is the correct name, these facts appear: Thomas, second son of Micajah, was born in 1775; and we can approximate the birth of Micajah as 1740–'50, and that of his father John about 1710–'15. The only John of about that date appears to be the John Goodwin who married Jane, and had Robert in 1732, and Jane in 1735. This John was a brother to George Goodwin and, if our surmise is correct, had a son George. The names (Daniel, suggested as a son of this John, named a son

John) and dates harmonize with these suggestions. George and John Goodwin are sons of John and Mary (Elliott) Goodwin, supposed to be son of Robert, eldest son of Major James Goodwin. This line is, therefore, presented for consideration; the doubtful links in italics. See also Appendix Y.

MAJOR JAMES GOODWIN.[1]

Eldest son, Robert[2] married Anne ——.

ROBERT GOODWIN[2] (James) married Anne ——.

Children:

i. Martin,[3] died *sine prole.*
ii. *Robert.*[3]
iii. *John,*[3] married Mary Elliott.

John Goodwin[3] (*Robert,* James), married in 1705 to Mary Elliott.

Children:

i. George,[4] married, first, Jane Hazelwood; second, Elizabeth Warwick.
ii. John,[4] married Jane ——.

JOHN GOODWIN[4] (John, *Robert,* James), married Jane ——.

Children:

i. Robert,[5] born December 30, 1732–'33.
ii. Jane,[5] born February 27, 1735.
iii. *Daniel.*[5]
iv. *Micajah.*[5]
v. *John*[5].
vi. *Richard.*[5]
vii. *George.*[5]
viii. *Nelson.*[5]

Perhaps this John[4] and the following John[4] was the same man.

John Goodwin[4] was born in Virginia; was married and resided in that State. The name of the father and the list of children is given on the authority of Miss Emily Virginia Goodwin, of Louisville, Ky., (granddaughter of Micajah and of John). Children: i. Micajah, married Elizabeth Buford; ii. John, married Mary Johnston; iii. Richard (see Appendix X); iv. George, see Appendix I; v. Nelson.

Micajah Goodwin (John) was born in Virginia; was married in Amherst county, Va., to Elizabeth Buford, who was born in Amherst county. Micajah and Richard Goodwin, of Nelson, now Amherst county, were ordered into service in 1781, under John Pope, to join the army commanded by General LaFayette. (Copied from an old muster roll in Hardesty's *Encyclopædia.*) Children:

i. Cornelius, married Hannah Paxton; ii. Thomas, born 1775, married Martha Reed; iii. James, probably died unmarried*; iv. Virginia, died unmarried; v. Daughter, married Mitchell; vi. John Lipscomb Lynch, born 1793, married Mary E. Goodwin; vii. Daughter, married White.

Cornelius Goodwin (Micajah, John) was born in Virginia; was married to Hannah Paxton. Children: i. Mary; ii. James E., born 1803, married Lucy Woolfork Gibson; iii. Hugh; iv. Banckley.

James E. Goodwin (Cornelius, Micajah, John) was born in 1803 in Virginia; was married November 7, 1839, in Woodford county, Ky., to Lucy Woolfork Gibson, who was born August 8, 1816, in Woodford county, Ky., a daughter of William and Frances (Samuel) Gibson. James E. Goodwin was a farmer, a Democrat, and a Presbyterian. His wife died in 1851. He died in Woodford county in 1875. He had a gourd, carried by his grandfather Micajah through the Revolutionary War. It had name, date, and purpose cut on it. Mr. Goodwin presented it to the public library in Louisville, but it seems to have been stolen. Children: i. Fannie, born January 25, 1842, married B. W. Thompson, and resides in Versailles, Ky.; ii. Mary Hannah, born August 20, 1844; iii. Anne Belle, born 1846; iv. William, born 1851.

Thomas Goodwin (Micajah, John) was born in 1775 in Virginia; was married in 1803 to Martha Reed. By occupation he was a farmer, and in religion a Methodist. They resided near Saltpetre Cave postoffice, Botetourt county. Thomas Goodwin died about 1830, and his wife shortly thereafter. He is said to have lived in Tazewell county before his marriage. Children: i. John, born 1805, married Ellen Ritchie; ii. Mary, born 1818, married Edward Barry.

John Goodwin (Thomas, Micajah, John) was born in 1805, in Botetourt county; was married in 1826, in Botetourt county, to Ellen Ritchie, who was born in 1804, in Botetourt county, a daughter of Robert and Isabella (Ripley) Ritchie. By occupation he was a farmer, in politics a Republican, and in religion a Methodist. They resided near Saltpetre Cave postoffice, where John

*James Goodwin had a bounty claim or land warrant for one hundred and sixty acres of land near Little Rock, Ark. After his death his brother, John L. L., placed it in the hands of a man to take to Washington, and neither man nor claim was heard of afterward. The bounty was for services in some war, probably 1812.

Goodwin died June 21, 1871. His wife died May 10, 1875. Before the late war John Goodwin frequently corresponded with a Mr. Goodwin, a "cousin," who resided in Georgia. This Georgia branch has not been identified, and all trace seems lost for the present. See Appendix X. Children: i. Harriet; ii. Mary T.; iii. Wilbur F., married Lucy C. Payne; iv. Etta B., resides at Saltpetre Cave; unmarried.

Wilbur F. Goodwin (John, Thomas, Micajah, John) was born June 15, 1844, in Botetourt county; was married in 1868 in Botetourt county, by Rev. Andrew Hart, to Lucy C. Payne, who was born in 1842 in Alleghany county, Va., a daughter of Charles and Frances (Pitzer) Payne. By occupation he was a farmer, in politics a Democrat. They resided near Saltpetre Cave postoffice, Va. Children: i. Carrie B., born November, 1869; ii. Mary W., born May, 1876; iii. Wilbur P., born December, 1878; Ellen F., born April, 1881.

Mary Goodwin (Thomas, Micajah, John) was born 1818, in Botetourt county; was married in Botetourt county to Edward Barry. Thomas G. Barry, 553 North Meridian street, Indianapolis, Ind., is a son. No response.

John Lipscomb Lynch Goodwin (Micajah, John) was born in 1793, in Amherst county; was married, first, in Amherst county, to Mary E. Goodwin, a daughter of John and Mary (Johnston) Goodwin. He was married, second, to Martha Crews. He resided in Amherst county, where he died January 5, 1857. (Called John Lewis Goodwin by his son Dr. Edward.) Children by first wife: i. Gustavus Adolphus, unmarried; ii. James Edwin; iii. Thomas, died young; iv. Edward Johnston, born December 30, 1829; married, first, Sarah Barnett; second, Hester L. Wills; third, ———; v. Samuel Boyle, married Helen Sexton; vi. Mary Elizabeth, married George A. Harvey; vii. Emily Virginia, resides in Louisville, Ky.; unmarried. Child by second wife: viii. William Lewis.

Dr. Edward Johnston Goodwin (John Lipscomb Lynch, Micajah, John) was born December 30, 1828, in Amherst, Va.; was married, first, October, 1854, at Alleghany Springs, Va., to Sarah Barnett, a daughter of Joseph Barnett. Sarah (Barnett) Goodwin died in 1866. Dr. Goodwin was married, second, to Hester L. Wills, and third, to ———. He resides in Solitude, Posey county, Ind. He is a physician and mathematician. Children by first wife: i. Viola Minnesota, married Ezra Stevens; ii. John Breckenridge; iii. Ovello Manassa, married Clifford Thompson.

INDIANA'S SQUARED CIRCLE.

All about the Method Formally Approved in the Legislature. It Substitutes the Ratio 3.2 for the Time-Honored 3.1416—but Prudent People will be Likely to Stick to the Old Figures.

[*From the Indianapolis Journal.*]

Official recognition by one branch of the Indiana Legislature has been given *Dr. Edward Johnston Goodwin* for solving three geometrical problems which have puzzled the brains of mathematicians since the erection of the pyramids of Egypt, and which the French Academy of Science, in 1775, and the Royal Society of Great Britain, in 1776, both declared impossible of solution. The first and most important of these problems is what has been popularly termed for centuries the squaring of the circle, or, in science, the quadrature of the circle. The other two problems solved by Dr. Goodwin are known in mathematics as trisection of the angle and the duplication of the cube.

The solution of these problems is a matter of little interest to the average citizen, but to science the worth of these solutions cannot be estimated in money. To the development of astronomical science their value is incalculable. The mystery surrounding the supposed impossibility of these problems has ever inspired both cranks and mathematicians to unceasing toil in their search for the correct formulas. Squaring the circle has been a chimera as vague as perpetual motion, and it was because of the worry and waste of time in examining the many alleged solutions presented by would-be discoverers of the key to squaring the circle that the French and English societies, over a hundred years ago, decided that the problem was impossible, and refused to consider the subject further. This action was supposed to settle for all time the fact that the decimal 3.1416 plus (Pi), multiplied by the diameter of a circle, would give the circumference. It was always known that this decimal was not the correct multiple, but it was taken so nearly accurate that it would serve for all purposes, and the mathematicians let it go at that.

Dr. Goodwin discovered the formula for squaring the circle eight years ago, but not until the World's Fair did he make any effort to get his discovery before the world. He secured space in the Liberal Arts building for hanging his charts, and intended to be present and make his demonstration to those visiting the educational exhibit, but Selim H. Peabody, chief of the department, after granting the space, revoked his permit, and advised the author to present his solution to the mathematical journals. Dr. Goodwin then sent his solution to the *American Mathematical Journal*, the highest authority in this country, and the editor instantly accepted it and printed it in the September number, 1893, while the World's Fair was in progress. It attracted the attention of mathematicians the world over, the scientific journals at Paris at once communicating with the author for original contributions to their papers.

Dr. Goodwin has his formulas and laws derived from them copyrighted in the United States and in seven countries of Europe—England, Germany, Belgium, France, Austria, Italy, and Spain. During his visit to Washington he won the support of the professors at the National Astronomical Observatory, at the head of which is the celebrated Professor Hall, whose fame is secure with the discovery of the moons of Mars. Dr. Goodwin's demonstration was accepted by all at the observatory. The venerable author has a deskful of letters from mathematicians at the leading colleges in America, and better than all, a letter from his agent in London showing that his demonstration was presented to both Huxley and Tyndall, and endorsed by them before it was copyrighted.

The man who has thus shown the errors in the text-books from Euclid's time to Loomis is a *native of Virginia, where he was born near Lynchburg, December* 30, 1828. *A wealthy aunt sent him to school, and furnished the funds for a course at the Philadelphia Medical College.* For forty years he has been a practicing physician in the vicinity of *Solitude, Posey county, Ind.*, that densely rural part of the State referred to by the humorists as Hooppole Township. He is a most modest citizen, refusing all modern methods of advertising himself. He is six feet tall and his frame is strong and elastic, and his massive, angular head correctly suggests his rugged mathematical brain.

The laws for the quadrature of the circle discovered by Dr. Goodwin, which are copyrighted, and which he permits the use of for the first time in any newspaper, are as follows:

"To quadrate the circle is to find the side of a square whose perimeter equals that of the given circle; rectification of the circle requires to find a right line equal to the circumference of the given circle. The square on the line equal to the arc of 90 degrees fulfils both of the said requirements.

"It is impossible to quadrate the circle by taking the diameter as the linear unit, because the square root of the product of the diameter by the quadrant of the circumference produces the side of a square which equals 9 when the quadrant equals 8. It is not mathematically consistent that it should take the side of a square whose perimeter equals that of a greater circle to measure the space contained within the limits of a less circle. Were this true, it would require a piece of tire iron eighteen feet to bind a wagon wheel sixteen feet in circumference.

"This new measure of the circle has happily brought to life the ratio of the chord and arc of 90 degrees, which is as 7:8, and also the ratio of the diagonal and one side of a square, which is as 10:7. These two ratios show the numerical relation of diameter to circumference to be as $1\frac{1}{4}:4$.

"Authorities will please note that while the finite ratio ($1\frac{1}{4}:4$) represents the area of the circle to be more than the orthodox ratio, yet the ratio (3.1416) represents the area of a circle whose circumference equals 4 plus 2 per cent. greater than the finite ratio $1\frac{1}{4}:4$, as will be seen by comparing the terms of their respective proportions stated as follows: 1:3.20 :: 1.25:4—1:3.1416 :: 1.1732:4.

"It will be observed that the product of the extremes is equal to the product of the means in the first statement, while they fail to agree in the second proportion. Furthermore, the square on a line equal to the arc of 90 degrees shows very clearly that the ratio of the circle is the same in principle as that of the square. For example, if we multiply the perimeter of a square (the sum of its sides) by one-fourth of one side, the product equals the sum of two sides, by one-half of one side which equals the square on one side. Again, the number required to express the units of length in one-fourth of a right line is the square root of the number representing the squares of the linear unit bounded by it in the form of a square whose ratio is as 1:4.

"These properties of the ratio of the square apply to the circle without an exception, as is further sustained by the following formula to express the numerical measure of both circles and square: Let C represent the circumference of a circle whose quadrant is unity, Q½ the quadrant, and CQ2 will apply as the numerical measure of a circle and a square.

"The following facts may be set down as showing that the diameter is the wrong factor to employ as the line on which to measure in squares the linear unit. The square on the diameter is the mean proportional between the circle's circumference and the square circumscribing it. The square of the quadrant of the circumference is the mean proportional between the circle's inscribed square and the square on the diameter as the linear unit. Therefore, the product of the diameter by one side of the inscribed square produces a line that is greater than the circle's circumference; that is to say, by taking the diameter as the linear unit in computing the area of the square, we can make its area about 43 per cent. greater than the fact. This is because there is about 43 per cent. of the diagonal not represented four times in the square's perimeter. Another reason that the diameter should be discarded as the wrong factor to employ as the linear unit is because it fails to work both ways, and, therefore, is not mathematically trustworthy.

"For instance, the circle whose circumference equals 32, the diameter is 10.1856 plus, according to the ratio 1:3.1416 plus, and the area is 81.4848 plus. The square root of 81.4848 plus is 9.0265 plus. Now, let us multiply the diameter 10.1856 plus by the square root to see if the product equals 81.4848 plus, which it should do if the diameter is the proper lineal unit: 10.1856 by 9.0265 plus equals 91.9392 plus. It will be found by extracting the square root of 91.9392 plus and multiplying the diameter, 10.1856 plus, by it, and repeating the procedure often enough, the resultant will be the side of the square circumscribing the circle. The same result is obtained by employing the diagonal of a square as the linear unit, instead of one side.

"The fact that the square on a line equal to the arc of 90 degrees fulfils the requirements of both quadrature and rectification of the circle's circumference leaves no margin to doubt the validity of the quadrant of the circumference being the true factor to take as the linear unit in computing the area of a circle.

"The above data show very clearly that when the circle's area is computed on the diameter as the linear unit, it is one-fifth greater than the area of a square of equal perimeter. This is because there is 25 per cent. of the diameter not represented four times in the circumference. Therefore, the area of a circle is to the square on one-fourth of its circumference as the area of an equilateral rectangle is to the square on one side.

"We are now able to get the true finite dimensions of a circle by the exact ratio of $1\frac{1}{4}$:4, and have simply to divide the circumference by four and square the quotient to complete the area. Thus this new truth in mathematical progress carries us above and beyond the curious necessity of having to teach that the finite is one with the infinite, or that to one finite there is a multiplicity of infinites."

When the bill was recently introduced in the Indiana Legislature for the purpose of recognizing Dr. Goodwin's solution, it was taken as a huge joke by

Speaker Pettit, a graduate of Annapolis Naval Academy, and was referred to the Committee on Swamp Lands. Two days later Dr. Goodwin had a hearing before State Superintendent Geeting and the Educational Committee, who at once endorsed the solution, called up the bill, and it passed the House under a suspension of the rules, without a negative vote. Professors from Ann Arbor and Johns Hopkins have seen the demonstration, and declared it perfect.

Dr. Samuel Boyle Goodwin (John Lipscomb Lynch, Micajah, John) was married, 1860, to Helen V. Sexton. By occupation he was a physician. They resided in Rich Valley and Chatham Hill, Va. Dr. Samuel Boyle Goodwin died December, 1861. No children.

Mary Elizabeth Goodwin (John Lipscomb Lynch, Micajah, John) was born December 30, 1828, in Amherst county; was married November 6, 1867, in Campbell county, by Josiah Little, to George A. Harvey, a son of Richard and Katherine (Bowers) Harvey. By occupation he was a farmer, in politics a Democrat. They resided in Diuguid, Campbell county, Va. (Mt. Athos P. O.) *Harvey* children: i. John William, born September 1, 1869, married Sue Moore; ii. Mary Jones, born December 31, 1872.

John Goodwin (John) was born in Virginia; was married to Mary Johnston. They resided in Pittsylvania county, Va., until after the death of Col. Philip Johnston, brother to Mary (Johnston) Goodwin, from whom they received a large estate. They resided thereafter in Amherst county, in which county Col. Johnston had resided. John Goodwin is also called John H. Goodwin by a granddaughter. Children: i. Frances, married Greenville Reynolds: ii. Nancy, married Charles Raleigh; iii. Virginia, born 1800, married Hezekiah Jones; iv. John H., died unmarried; v. Mary E., married John L. L. Goodwin; vi. Philip, died unmarried; vii. Robert, married —— Minton; viii. Susan, married, first, William Minton; second, Stephen Diuguid.

Frances Goodwin (John, John) was born in Pittsylvania county, Va.; was married in Amherst county to Greenville Reynolds. By occupation he was a farmer, and in religion a Methodist. They resided in Botetourt county, Va. No children.*

Nancy Goodwin (John, John) was born in Pittsylvania county, Va.; was married to Charles Raleigh. They resided in Amherst county, removing to Arkansas, near Little Rock. *Raleigh* children: i. Fannie; ii. Permelia; iii. Mary Jane; iv. John; v. Alderson; vi. Charles; vii. Robert.

---

* Other statement is that Frances had children, and they and their children reside in Botetourt county. No response.

Virginia Goodwin (John, John) was born in 1800 in Pittsylvania county, Va.; was married in 1834 in Amherst county to Hezekiah Jones, who was born in 1795 in Nelson county, Va., a son of ——— and ——— (Lucas) Jones. By occupation he was a farmer, in politics a Democrat and in religion a Baptist. They resided in Nelson county, Va. No children.

Mary E. Goodwin (John, John) was born in Virginia; was married to John Lipscomb Lynch Goodwin, who was born in 1793 in Amherst county, a son of Micajah and Elizabeth (Buford) Goodwin. *Goodwin* children: i. Gustavus Adolphus, unmarried; ii. James Edwin; iii. Thomas, died young; iv. Edward Johnston, married, first, Sarah Barnett; second, Hester L. Wills; third, ———; v. Samuel Boyle, married Helen V. Sexton; vi. Mary Elizabeth, married George A. Harvey; vii. Emily Virginia, resides in Louisville, Ky., unmarried.

Robert Goodwin (John, John) was born in Pittsylvania county; was married in Campbell county to Miss Minton. They resided in Campbell county, removing to Tennessee. Child: i. Ann Elizabeth Minton,* born 1820, married William Toney.

Susan Goodwin (John, John) was born in Pittsylvania county; was married in Amherst county, to William Minton, who was born in Campbell county. She married, second, Stephen Diuguid. They resided in Campbell county, Va. No children.

APPENDIX I.

THE GOODWINS OF DAVIDSON COUNTY, TENNESSEE.

It will probably be definitely ascertained that George Goodwin, of Davidson county, Tenn., was George, son of John Goodwin, Appendix H.

George Goodwin was born August 31, 1753, in Virginia; was married to Polly Clark, who was born July 18, 1753, in Virginia. By occupation he was a farmer. They resided in Virginia until before 1800, when they settled in Davidson county, Tenn. Polly Goodwin died September 6, 1800; George Goodwin died April 22, 1808. Children: i. Nancy Alden, born February 27, 1780, married —— Smith; ii. John L., born September 9, 1782; iii. Sarah Webb, born December 10, 1783, married —— Thompson; iv. Polly Clark,

* She died in Nashville, leaving an only child, Marcus Breckenridge Toney, who resides in Nashville.

born October 15, 1786; v. Tabitha, born October 15, 1789, married —— Greer; vi. Lavinia, born February 20, 1791; vii. William Washington, born April 1, 1793, married Anne Blackman; viii. Jesse, born April 1, 1796; ix. George.

William Washington Goodwin (George) was born April 1, 1793, in Virginia; was married to Anne Blackman. By occupation he was a contractor. They resided near Nashville, in Davidson county, Tenn., where he died January 24, 1832; Anne (Blackman) Goodwin died April 19, 1835. Children: i. George Bennett, born February 28, 1821, married Louisa Henrietta Minter; ii. Susan Hays, born 1822, married John H. Ewin; iii. William Washington, born March 21, 1825, died unmarried; iv. Martha Anne, married E. G. Pearl; v. Elizabeth, married William Craighead.

George Bennett Goodwin (William Washington, George) was born February 28, 1821, in Nashville, Tenn; was married December 25, 1845, at Columbia, Tenn., by Dr. William H. Wharton, to Louisa Henrietta Minter, who was born November 22, 1822, in Columbia, Ky., a daughter of William and Elizabeth Green (Waggoner) Minter. By occupation he was a lawyer, in politics a Democrat, and in religion a Christian. They resided in Nashville, where he died March 7, 1892. Children: i. William Washington, born September 10, 1846, married Mary Blythe; ii. John Ewin, born July 26, 1848, married Louisa Buford; iii. George Minter, born July 23, 1850, resides at Nashville, unmarried; iv. Mary Theresa, born March 16, 1852, died young; v. Anne, born March 17, 1854, died in 1897, unmarried; vi. Louisa, born January 10, 1858, married William H. Stovall, and died *sine prole*; vii. Arthur, born July 13, 1860, unmarried; viii. Albert Fall, born December 19, 1862, unmarried; ix. Martha, born June, 1865, died young; x. Lamira, born August 4, 1867, unmarried.

William Washington Goodwin (George Bennett, William Washington, George) was born September 10, 1846, in Nashville, Tenn.; was married to Mary Blythe, of Missouri. By occupation he was a lawyer. They resided in 1897 in Memphis, Tenn. Children: i. Robert B.; ii. Anne; iii. Margaret.

John Ewin Goodwin (George Bennett, William Washington, George) was born July 26, 1848, near Nashville, Tenn.; was married October 20, 1868, at Buford, Tenn., to Louisa Buford, who was born October 20, 1848, in Buford, a daughter of Thomas and Mary Ann Elizabeth (Gordon) Buford. In politics he was a Democrat and in religion a Christian. They resided in 1897 in Nashville.

Children: i. Mary Louisa, born August 19, 1869; ii. Rose Fowler, born October 14, 1870; iii. Thomas Buford, born July 25, 1872; iv. George Bennett, born November 20, 1873; v. Helen Mar, born September 1, 1875; vi. Anne, born February 17, 1878; vii. Elizabeth Buford, born January 16, 1880; viii. William Minter, born October 31, 1881; ix. Alice Ewin, born November 2, 1884; x. Harold, born January 7, 1887.

APPENDIX J.

For discussion of the probable ancestry of Daniel Goodwin, of Botetourt county, see Appendix H.

Daniel Goodwin, born in Botetourt county, Va., was married to Elizabeth Moore. By occupation he was a farmer. They resided in Botetourt county, Va., but removed to Kentucky, where they died. Children: i. Samuel, untraced; ii. Thomas, untraced; iii. John, born 1770; married Nancy Barnes.

John Goodwin (Daniel), born in 1770, in Botetourt county, was married in 1799, in Botetourt county, to Nancy Barnes, born in 1783, in Tazewell county, Va., a daughter of Robert and Grace (Brown) Barnes. By occupation he was a farmer, in politics a Democrat, and in religion a Baptist. They resided in Tazewell county, Va. Samuel David Goodwin, son of David, adds a son Charles to this list, and gives Culpeper county, Va., as the birthplace of John, and gives John and Nancy (———) Barnes as the parents of Nancy (Barnes) Goodwin. Children: i. David, born May 8, 1800; married Mrs. Louisa (Cecil) Sample; ii. Robert, born May 19, 1802; married Isabella Pogue; iii. Elizabeth, born June 19, 1803; married John Sawyers; iv. Polly, born September 16, 1805; v. Margaret, born May, 1807; married Richard Belcher; vi. Grace, born May, 1809; married Thomas Higginbotham; vii. Sallie, born December, 1811; married Edward Wilson; viii. William, born November, 1813; married Mary Hurt; ix. Thomas Barnes, born December 13, 1818; married Mary Ann Hurt.

David Goodwin (John, Daniel), born May 8, 1800, in Tazewell county, Va., was married, in 1838, in Tazewell county, to Mrs. Louisa (Cecil) Sample, born in 1818, in Tazewell county, a daughter of Samuel and Rebecca (Smith) Cecil. By occupation he was a farmer, in politics a Democrat, and in religion a Methodist. They resided in Tazewell. David Goodwin died in Richmond,

Va. Child: Samuel David, born April 4, 1843; married Eliza Ann Pieratt.

Samuel David Goodwin (David, John, Daniel), born April 4, 1843, in Tazewell county, Va., was married, in 1866, at Ezel, Ky., by Elder Joseph Nickell, to Eliza Ann Pieratt, born in 1844, in Morgan county, a daughter of Eli and Gillie A. (Nickell) Pieratt. By occupation he was a teacher and farmer, in politics a Democrat, and in religion a Christian. They resided, 1897, in Ezel, Morgan county, Ky. Children: i. Olie Ann, born 1867; married Frank Sample; ii. Emma, born 1869; iii. Ellen Ann, born 1876; iv. Asa, born 1878; v. John, born 1882.

Robert Goodwin (John, Daniel), born May 19, 1802, in Tazewell county, Va., was married in Botetourt county, Va., to Isabella Pogue, born in Botetourt county, a daughter of William Pogue. By occupation he was a farmer, in politics a Democrat, and in religion a Baptist. They resided in Botetourt. Children: i. Nancy, married William McNabb; ii. Elizabeth, married Samuel Cecil;* iii. Robert, married ——— Turley.

Elizabeth Goodwin (John, Daniel), born June 19, 1803, in Tazewell county, Va., was married, in Tazewell county, to John Sawyer. By occupation he was a farmer, in politics a Democrat. They resided in Tazewell and in Kentucky. *Sawyer* children: i. Nancy, married William White; ii. William; iii. Susan, married ——— Peery; iv. John, born 1841; married F. A. Hurt; v. Alexander; vi. David, resides in Tazewell, Va.; vii. Sarah; viii. Margaret, married ——— Gibson.

Margaret Goodwin (John, Daniel), born May, 1807, in Tazewell county, Va., was married to Richard Belcher, born in Tazewell county. By occupation he was a farmer. They resided in Tazewell county, where Margaret died. Richard died in Missouri. *Belcher* child: i. Patton, unmarried.

Grace Goodwin (John, Daniel) was born May, 1809, in Tazewell county, Va.; was married in Tazewell county by David Young to Thomas Higginbotham, who was born in 1807 in Tazewell county, a son of Moses Higginbotham. By occupation he was a farmer, in politics a Democrat, and in religion a Methodist. They resided in Tazewell county. Grace died in Missouri. *Higginbotham* children: i. Zarilda (Surilda), born 1829, married Hiram Greer; ii. John, born 1831, unmarried; iii. William, born 1833, married —— Horton; iv. Elizabeth, born 1835, married Calvin Stamper; v. Jo-

*Edward Cecil resides at Hazlegreen, Kentucky.

seph, born 1837, unmarried; vi. Moses, born 1839, unmarried; vii. Oscar, born 1841, unmarried; viii. Robert, born 1843, unmarried.

Sallie Goodwin (John, Daniel) was born December, 1811, in Tazewell county, Va.; was married in 1832, in Tazewell county, by David Young to Edward Wilson, who was born in Tazewell county, a son of Hugh and ——— (Barnes) Wilson. By occupation he was a farmer, in politics a Democrat, and in religion a Methodist. They resided in Tazewell county, Va., where he died in 1863. Sallie (Goodwin) Wilson died in 1870. *Wilson* children: i. Hugh, born 1833, died in the war; ii. Nancy, born 1835, married ——— Currem; iii. John, born 1837, unmarried; iv. Charles, born 1839, married Cosby Moore.*

William Goodwin (John, Daniel) was born November, 1813, in Tazewell county, Va.; was married in 1851, in Russell county, Va., to Mary Hurt, who was born in 1836 in Russell county, Va., a daughter of James and ——— (Ewell) Hurt. By occupation he was a tanner, in politics a Democrat, and in religion a Methodist. They resided in Virginia and Kentucky. Children: i. Charles, born 1852, married Elizabeth Reed; ii. Susan, born 1854, married —— Lykins; † iii. Nancy Jane, born 1856, married —— Lykins; iv. William, born 1864, married —— Wills; v. Mary Frances, born 1866, married —— Stacy.

Thomas Barnes Goodwin (John, Daniel) was born December 13, 1818, in Tazewell county, Va.; was married June, 1849, in Russell county, Va., by Rev. David Yount to Mary Ann Hurt, who was born in 1827 in Washington county, Va., a daughter of Vincen and ——— (Burke) Hurt. By occupation he was a farmer, in politics a Democrat, and in religion a Baptist. They resided in Russell county, Va., and Maysville, Ky. Children: i. Nancy Jane, born March 9, 1850, married Joseph Samples; ii. Silas Winton, born January 1, 1852; iii. John Vincen, born October 8, 1854; iv. Thomas Franklin, born May 1, 1856, married Mary V. Sawyers; v. Mary Catherine, married James Bell; vi. Sallie Wilson; vii. Martha Isabella, born April 20, 1866, married Samuel Feters.

Thomas Franklin Goodwin (Thomas Barnes, John, Daniel) was born May 1, 1856, in Morgan county, Ky.; was married July 3, 1877, at Camargo, Ky., by Rev. —— Southgate to Mary Virginia Sawyers, who was born in Wolf county, Ky., a daughter of John and Frances Ann (Hurt) Sawyers. By occupation he was a farmer, in politics a Democrat, and in religion a Baptist. They

* Resides Abb's Valley, Va. † She resides at Walnut Grove, Ky.

reside in Rectorville, Ky. Children: i. Della Lee, born August 24, 1878; ii. Silas John Thomas, born March 28, 1881; iii. Mary Elizabeth, born April 23, 1884; iv. Frances, born March 30, 1888; v. Katie May, born May 6, 1891; vi. Kavanaugh, born November 15, 1894; vii. Carrie Crocker, November 15, 1894.

APPENDIX K.

THE GOODWYNS OF DINWIDDIE COUNTY, VIRGINIA.

Two branches of this family have been found, one descending from Thomas Goodwyn, through his son Joseph. Joseph's son, Col. Peterson Goodwyn, is said to have used on his silver the same coat-of-arms as belonged to Major James Goodwin. This would indicate a connection with Major James, but the following should be noted: Joseph Goodwyn married Miss Peterson, of the Isle of Wight county family, and Col. Peterson Goodwyn's wife was also one of this family, and a blood relative. Joseph *Godwin* had land grants in Isle of Wight county in 1723 and 1746, and a Thomas *Godwin*, Jr., also had land grants in the same county in 1746. These Godwins were the descendants of Thomas Godwin and Richard Godwin, brothers, sons of Thomas (?) Godwin. Whether they are the Thomas and Joseph Goodwyn of Dinwiddie county remains to be determined.

The second branch of the Dinwiddie Goodwyns descends through Robert, said to have been a brother of Thomas; but as Robert and Joseph, son of Thomas, had grandchildren in 1776, Robert would be too young a man to be the brother to Thomas, Joseph's father. As some of the descendants of Joseph have given him a brother named Thomas, it perhaps will appear that Thomas, Sen., was the father of Joseph, Thomas and Robert, and that Thomas, Jr., was the father of Lieut. Dinwiddie Goodwyn. Both branches claim Lieut. Dinwiddie, and Capt. Armistead Goodwyn's grandson says that his grandfather, son of Robert, and Lieut. Dinwiddie were *first cousins*, and that Robert had a brother Thomas. Harwood Goodwin and John Goodwin had land grants in Dinwiddie county in 1759–'60, and they may have been other brothers of Joseph and Robert. It has been impossible to obtain replies from any of Robert Goodwyn's descendants, excepting two.

Capt. Robert Armistead Goodwyn says that he was brought up by his aunt Fannie, born in 1775, and she stated to him that her father,

Capt. Armistead, had told her that his grandfather Goodwyn had a Swiss woman for a wife, having bought her for 150 pounds of tobacco, and that she was possessed of considerable musical ability, which was very generally inherited by her descendants. The name of Robert's father, husband of the Swiss woman, she gave as Sir Francis Arthur Goodwin. Sir Francis Goodwin was in Virginia in 1620, and died in England about 1633, leaving a son, Arthur, who married, but left no male issue. Sir Francis had another son, but the male line of this family seems to be extinct. The date of Robert's birth was around 1725, nearly one hundred years after the death of Sir Francis.

Thomas Goodwyn was born in Virginia. He resided in Dinwiddie county, and is said to have been a grandson of Major James. (Mrs. Grigg's grandfather thinks so.) Thomas Goodwyn had land grants for 71 and 80 acres in Dinwiddie county, April 28, 1748. A Thomas Goodwin also had land grant of 100 acres in Sussex county, August 15, 1764. Harwood and John Goodwin had land grants in Dinwiddie county in 1759 and 1760. Children: i. Joseph, married ——— Peterson; ii. Thomas (perhaps); iii. Robert (perhaps); iv. Harwood (perhaps); vi. John (perhaps).

Joseph Goodwyn (Thomas) was born in Virginia; was married to Miss ——— Peterson, who was born in Isle of Wight county. By occupation he was a planter. They resided at "The Martins," in Dinwiddie county, the old home place still standing. Children: i. John* (disputed); ii. Joseph, married Mary Coleman; iii. Braddock, married Elizabeth Brown; iv. Esau, married S. Sturdivant; v. Peterson, married Elizabeth Peterson; vi. Burwell* (disputed), untraced. Peterson and Joseph, Jr., were twins.

John Goodwyn † (Joseph, Thomas) was born in Dinwiddie county, where he married, resided and died. Children; i. John, married Elizabeth Fowler; ii. Burwell, born in 1793; iii. Daughter, married ——— Rives; iv. Daughter, married ——— King.

John Goodwyn (John, Joseph, Thomas) was born in Dinwiddie county; was married to Elizabeth Fowler. By occupation he was a planter. They resided in Dinwiddie county. Children: i. Ann

---

* It is strongly denied that Joseph[2] was the father of John and Burwell. It is said that Joseph's *brother* was their father. That would indicate a John or Harwood.

† It is disputed that John and Burwell were sons of Joseph, and it is said they are sons of a brother of Joseph—perhaps of the John Goodwin who had land grant in Dinwiddie county.

Eliza, born March, 1823; unmarried; ii. Timoleon W., born June, 1825; unmarried; iii. Emma Virginia, born September 17, 1827; unmarried; iv. John William, born July 17, 1829; married Minerva S. Johnson.

John William Goodwyn (John, John, Joseph, Thomas) was born July 17, 1829, in Dinwiddie county, Va.; was married June 14, 1858, in Dinwiddie county, by Rev. C. J. Gibson, to Minerva Stith Johnson, who was born July 19, 1833, in Dinwiddie county, a daughter of Edward and Minerva Stith (Maclin) Johnson. By occupation he was a druggist, in politics a Whig and Democrat, and in religion an Episcopalian. They reside in Macon, Ga. (1897). Dr. Goodwyn served through the war with rank of Captain on the scientific corps of the mining department. Children: i. T. Gray, married Hattie Rogers; ii. John W.; iii. E. F. (dau.), married T. E. Artope.

Burwell Goodwyn (John, Joseph, Thomas) was born 1793 in Dinwiddie county; was married, and resided in Dinwiddie county. In 1896–'97, while repairing a house in Petersburg, which had belonged to a lawyer long since dead, but who had, in his life-time, managed the estate of a Robert Goodwyn, an Ancient History was found, on one page of which was written, "Burwell Goodwyn, born 1793." Children: i. Archer, resides at Ream's Station, Va.; ii. McClure.

Col. Joseph Goodwyn (Joseph, Thomas) was born in Dinwiddie county, Va.; was married in Dinwiddie county to Mary Coleman. By occupation he was a planter, in politics a Whig, and in religion an Episcopalian. They resided in Dinwiddie county, Va. Joseph Goodwyn was a Colonel in the Revolutionary War. Children: i. Mary, married John Gilliam; ii. William, married Harriet Williamson.

Mary Goodwyn (Joseph, Joseph, Thomas) was born in Dinwiddie county, Va.; was married in Dinwiddie county to John Gilliam, who was born in Brunswick county, Va. In religion he was an Episcopalian. They resided in Dinwiddie county, Va. *Gilliam* children: i. John, unmarried; ii. Joseph Peterson, unmarried; iii. Mary Eliza, married Robert Neblett; iv. Susan, married Edmund Fitzgerald; v. Bena, married J. A. Johnson; vi. Samuel Y., unmarried.

William Goodwyn (Joseph, Joseph, Thomas) was born in Dinwiddie county, Va.; was married to Harriet Williamson. By occupation he was a planter, in politics a Whig, and in religion an

Episcopalian. They resided in Dinwiddie county, Va. Child: i. Mary Ann, married John Dodson.

Braddock Goodwyn (Joseph, Thomas) was born in Dinwiddie county; was married to Elizabeth Brown. By occupation he was a planter, in politics a Whig. They resided in Dinwiddie. Children: i. Joseph; ii. Burwell, married Nancy or Anne Dance; iii. Monroe; iv. Thomas; v. Robert, unmarried; vi. William, unmarried; vii. Jane, unmarried; viii. Martha, unmarried; ix. Mary, married Patrick Roney; x. Elizabeth Ann, married Joel Studevant; xi. Amy, married Rev. Burwell S. Goodwyn; xii. Harriet, married ——— Coleman.

Joseph Goodwyn (Braddock, Joseph, Thomas) was born in Dinwiddie county. He resided in Dinwiddie county. Children: i. Thomas; ii. John.

Burwell Goodwyn (Braddock, Joseph, Thomas) was born in Dinwiddie county, Va.; was married in 1811, in Dinwiddie county, to Nancy or Anne Dance, who was born in Greenville county, Va., a daughter of Thomas and Sallie (Fisher) Dance. By occupation he was a farmer, and in politics a Whig. They resided in Dinwiddie county, Va. Hon. Burwell Goodwyn was for several terms a State senator. He died in Dinwiddie county, February, 1834. Nancy (Dance) Goodwyn died January 5, 1867, in Coweta county, Ga. Their residence is given also as Brunswick county, and Burwell is said to have died in this county. Children. i. Thomas Dance, born February 27, 1813, married Mary A. C. Griffin; ii. Braddock, married Eliza Dominick; iii. Napoleon B., died unmarried; iv. Maria Louisa, married, first, John Ledbetter; second, Marcus D. North; third, John J. Hunt; v. Anne Eliza, married, first, John M. Sims; second, Walter R. Pope; vi. Sarah Fisher, married John W. Powell; vii. James Fisher, married, first, Kittie Turner; second, Frances Puckit; viii. Henry Clay, married Lucy Bloodworth.

Thomas Dance Goodwyn (Burwell, Braddock, Joseph, Thomas) was born February 27, 1813, in Dinwiddie county, Va.; was married March 15, 1838, in Coweta county, Ga., to Mary A. C. Griffin, who was born November 14, 1817, in Henry county, Ga., a daughter of John and Sallie (Barnett) Griffin. By occupation he was a farmer, in politics a Whig, and in religion a Methodist. They resided in Dinwiddie county, Va., until 1840, when they removed to Coweta county, Ga., where he died September 24, 1866. Mrs. Goodwin resides (1897) in Newman, Ga. Children: i. John Burwell, born March 7, 1839, married Cattie Pope; ii. Thomas Dance, born April 12, 1841, married Elizabeth Baughn; iii. Virginia, born February 22, 1843, married John L. Bailey; iv. James Monroe, born December 16, 1845, died September 23, 1847; v. Mary Lucy, born September 24, 1848, married, first, Benjamin Gibson; second, —— Eddington; vi. William Henry, born September 27, 1850, married Mollie Davis; vii. Joseph Peterson, born July 9, 1852, married Mintie McVay; viii. Martha Amanda, born July 15, 1854, married James R. Ellis; ix. Woodson Hubbard, born October 13, 1856, married Anne Thompson; x. Ellen, born July 9, 1859, married Dr. George Wyche.

John Burwell Goodwyn (Thomas Dance, Burwell, Braddock, Joseph, Thomas) was born March 7, 1839, in Greensville county, Va.; was married May 27, 1869, in Meriweather county, Ga., by Robert F. Jones, to Cattie Pope, who was born November 5, 1849, in Meriweather county, a daughter of Walter R. and Catherine (Thrash) Pope. By occupation he was a farmer, civil engineer, and surveyor, in politics a Democrat, and in religion a Baptist. They resided at Newman, Coweta county, Ga. (1897). John Burwell Goodwyn was graduated from Mercer University in 1861; served through the war, and was member of the Legislature in 1884–'85. Children: i. Mary Etta, born March 21, 1870; ii. Walter Pope, born April 16, 1871, died November 13, 1894; iii. Henry Jackson, born January 14, 1874; iv. Ernest Codesman, born July 27, 1875; v. Alvan Freeman, born December 23, 1877; vi. John Bunyan, born November 15, 1880; vii. Bessie Kate, born July 22, 1885; viii. Annie Lou, born November 24, 1887; ix. Thomas, born October 25, 1891.

Monroe Goodwyn (Braddock, Joseph, Thomas) was married and had two children. Children: i. Arlene; ii. Ada Byron.

Thomas Goodwyn (Braddock, Joseph, Thomas) was born in Dinwiddie county. Child: i. Algernon.

Amy Goodwyn (Braddock, Joseph, Thomas) was married to Rev. Burwell S. Goodwyn. By occupation he was a minister, and in religion a Methodist. The ancestry of Rev. Burwell S. is not yet learned.

Esau Goodwyn (Joseph, Thomas) was born in Dinwiddie; was married to S. Sturdivant. By occupation he was a planter. They resided in Greensville county, Va. Children: * i. Keziah, married William Boisseau; ii. Martha, married John Pegram.

* It is asserted that Esau had no children. The two given here are on the authority of Dr. John William Goodwyn, of Macon, Ga.

Col. Peterson Goodwyn (Joseph, Thomas) was born about 1745 in Dinwiddie county, Va.; was married in Dinwiddie county, Va., to Elizabeth Peterson, who was born in Dinwiddie county, Va., a daughter of Peter and Lucy (Osborne) Peterson. By occupation he was a planter and lawyer, in politics a Whig and Democrat, and in religion an Episcopalian. They resided at "Sweden," Dinwiddie county, Va. Col. Peterson Goodwyn was for many years the representative for this county in the Virginia Legislature. In 1803 he was elected congressman, and continuously re-elected until his death, February 21, 1818, aged about 73. He was Colonel in the Revolutionary War, and a member of the Society of the Cincinnati. His wife died October, 1817. Children: i. Edward Osborne, born 1776, died unmarried; ii. Martha, married ——— McGruder; iii. Emma Epps, married Daniel E. Allen; iv. Lucy Ann K., died unmarried; v. Elizabeth, married Thomas Whitworth; vi. Peterson, born 1802, married Mary Campbell Powell; vii. Albert Thweat, married, first, Martha King; second, Amelia Meade.

Martha Goodwyn (Peterson, Joseph, Thomas) was born in Dinwiddie county, Va.; was married in Dinwiddie county to ——— McGruder. Mr. McGruder was a member of Congress. *McGruder* child: i. Adeline, married ——— Wyatt.

Emma Epps Goodwyn (Peterson, Joseph, Thomas) was born in Dinwiddie county, Va.; was married February 23, 1826, by Rev. Milton Thrift to Daniel C. Allen. They resided in Dinwiddie county. *Allen* child: i. Eliza Ann Epps, married Fletcher H. Archer.

Elizabeth Goodwyn (Peterson, Joseph, Thomas) was born in Dinwiddie county, Va.; was married January 10, 1833, in Dinwiddie county, Va., by Rev. Milton Thrift to Thomas Whitworth. They resided in Dinwiddie county. *Whitworth* child: i. Elizabeth, married Chamberlain Wilson.

Peterson Goodwyn (Peterson, Joseph, Thomas) was born 1802 in Dinwiddie county, Va.; was married August 22, 1822, at Petersburg, Va., by Rev. —— Syme to Mary Campbell Powell, who was born August 12, 1804, in Petersburg, Va., a daughter of Edward and Elizabeth (Williams) Powell. By occupation he was a planter, in politics a Whig, and in religion an Episcopalian. They resided in Greensville county, Va. Peterson Goodwyn died October 14, 1838, in Petersburg, Va. Mary Campbell (Powell) Goodwyn died April 17, 1882, in Petersburg. Children: i. Edward Albert, born

May 1, 1823, married Martha Clough Perkinson; ii. Elizabeth Harrison, born September 15, 1825, resides at Warrenton, N. C., unmarried; iii. Peterson, born September 5, 1827, killed in a duel, San Francisco; iv. Charles Frederick, born March 14, 1830, married S. Lacy Tuggle; v. Martha Ann Epps, born May 27, 1832, married James Collier; vi. Junius Alexander, born August 9, 1836, married Eugenia L. Feild.

Edward Albert Goodwyn (Peterson, Peterson, Joseph Thomas) was born May 1, 1823, in Dinwiddie county, Va.; was married August 10, 1843, in Amelia county, Va., by Rev. John Hobson to Martha Clough Perkinson, who was born July 5, 1828, in Amelia county, Va., a daughter of Matthew and Mary Cowan (Williams) Perkinson. By occupation he was a railroad officer, in politics a Whig and Republican, and in religion an Episcopalian. They reside in Petersburg, Va. From 1849 to 1852 Mr. Goodwyn served in the Virginia Legislature from Dinwiddie county. He was a member of the City Council of Petersburg a number of times after 1852, and president of the same for six years. He was Captain of Company E, Thirteenth Virginia Cavalry, General W. H. T. Lee's Division, in the late war. He has held the position of Master of Transportation on the A. M. & O., Railroad for forty years. Children: i. Matthew Peterson, born June 20, 1844, married Mary Parthenia Lewis; ii. Edward Albert, born July 24, 1846.

Matthew Peterson Goodwyn (Edward Albert, Peterson, Peterson, Joseph, Thomas) was born June 28, 1844, in Amelia county, Va.; was married April 23, 1863, in Dinwiddie county, Va., by Rev. William H. Platt to Mary Parthenia Lewis, who was born February 20, 1845, in Petersburg, Va., a daughter of Dr. Heartwell Heath and Alpha (Hawthorne) Lewis. By occupation he was a railroad official, freight agent, in politics a Democrat, and in religion an Episcopalian. They resided in Petersburg, Va. Matthew Peterson Goodwyn was a student of the Annapolis Naval Academy, leaving at the opening of the late war, he being then only sixteen years old, and returning home. He was first a member of the Lafayette Guards, subsequently a First Lieutenant, but afterward entered the Confederate Navy, and was on the Merrimac during its fight with the Monitor, and he was also in the fight with the Satelite and Reliance, for which service he gained honorable promotion. He died February 1, 1882, in Petersburg. Children: i. Lillie Wood, born October 12, 1865, married Edward W. Grigg; ii. Edward Albert, born December 20, 1867; iii. Jessie Hoge, born

January 20, 1870, married Robert B. Anderson; iv. Peterson Agee, born August 2, 1872, married Priscilla Chapman Fowler.

Lillie Wood Goodwyn (Matthew Peterson, Edward Albert, Peterson, Peterson, Joseph, Thomas) was born October 12, 1865, in Petersburg, Va.; was married October 18, 1887, at Petersburg, by Rev. C. R. Haines to Edward Williamson Grigg, who was born September 30, 1862, in Petersburg, Va., a son of Wesley and Augustina Frances Peyton (Wells) Grigg. He was an Episcopalian. They resided in Petersburg, Va., until April, 1892, when they removed to Winston, S. C., returning thereafter to Petersburg. Mrs. Grigg has contributed a very large portion of the data concerning the Goodwyns. *Grigg* children: i. Frank Peyton, born September 17, 1888, died July 9, 1889; ii. Martha Goodwyn, born May 6, 1890.

Jessie Hoge Goodwyn (Matthew Peterson, Edward Albert, Peterson, Peterson, Joseph, Thomas) was born January 20, 1870, in Petersburg, Va.; was married December 18, 1889, at Petersburg, by Rev. C. R. Haines to Robert Beverly Anderson, who was born November 3, 1863, in Dinwiddie county, Va., a son of Robert Mayo and Virginia (Stone) Anderson. He was an Episcopalian. They resided in Petersburg, Va. Robert Beverly Anderson died September 29, 1891, in Dinwiddie county. *Anderson* child: i. Jessie Hoge Goodwyn, born April 13, 1891.

Peterson Agee Goodwyn (Matthew Peterson, Edward Albert, Peterson, Peterson, Joseph, Thomas) was born August 2, 1872, in Dinwiddie county, Va.; was married June 20, 1895, at St. Thomas Episcopal Church, Abingdon, Va., to Priscilla Chapman Fowler, a daughter of J. C. Fowler. By occupation he was connected with the freight claim department, in politics a Democrat. They resided in Roanoke, Va.

Charles F. Goodwyn (Peterson, Peterson, Joseph, Thomas) was born 1829; was married to S. Lacy Tuggle. By occupation he was a lawyer. They resided in Nottoway C. H., Va.

Junius Alexander Goodwyn (Peterson, Peterson, Joseph, Thomas) was born August 9, 1836, in Greensville county, Va.; was married July 5, 1866, at Warrenton, N. C., by Dr. William Hodges, to Eugenia Littlejohn Feild, who was born November 14, 1841, in Mecklenburg county, Va., a daughter of Dr. George and Frances Blount (Littlejohn) Feild. By occupation he was a merchant, in politics a Democrat, and in religion an Episcopalian. They resided in Warrenton, N. C., 1897. Children: i. Fannie

Littlejohn, born May 27, 1867; ii. Ernest Morelle, born July 12, 1869, married M. Willie Hunter; iii. Eugenia Littlejohn, born June 15, 1871, died September 28, 1872; iv. Junius Alexander, born January 31, 1873, died August 11, 1873; v. Mary Campbell, born May 7, 1875; vi. Junius Alexander, born February 23, 1878; vii. Edwin Ashton, born January 22, 1880; viii. George Feild, born June 26, 1882; ix. Bettie Mutter, born November 29, 1884.

Albert Thweat Goodwyn (Peterson, Joseph, Thomas) was born in Dinwiddie county, Va.; was married, first, May 26, 1825, to Martha King; he was married, second, to Amelia Meade. By occupation he was a planter, in politics a Whig, and in religion an Episcopalian. He resided in Greensville county, Va. Children by first wife: i. Dr. John Peterson, married Martha Greenway; ii. George Whitney, married Elizabeth Morrison; iii. Eliza, died young. Children by second wife: iv. Maria, married Charles Pannill; v. Mary Elizabeth, married —— Wilson; vi. David Everard, married Fanny Montgomery.

Dr. John Peterson Goodwyn (Albert Thweat, Peterson, Joseph, Thomas) was married to Martha Greenway. By occupation he was a physician. They resided in Belfield, Va. Children: Nine sons and one daughter, names not furnished.

David Everard Goodwyn (Albert Thweat, Peterson, Joseph, Thomas) was married to Fanny Montgomery. They resided in Belfield, Va. Children: Three boys and three girls.

Robert Goodwyn was born in Virginia, was married, and resided in Dinwiddie county, Va. Robert Goodwyn had land grant for 320 acres in Albemarle county, July 20, 1748, and at the same time a John Goodwin received land grant for 400 acres in same county. He is said to have had a brother Thomas, and to have been a relative of Joseph Goodwyn, perhaps his brother. Children: i. Capt. Stephen; ii. Robert (?); iii. Capt. Armistead, married, first, Nancy Wicke; second, Sallie (Willson) Dance.

Capt. Stephen Goodwyn (Robert) was born in Dinwiddie county and resided in Dinwiddie county. On November 20, 1783, 2,666⅔ acres of land were granted to Capt. Stephen Goodwyn, "heir-at-law" of Lieut. Dinwiddie Goodwyn, of Dinwiddie county, Va.* Capt. Stephen Goodwyn also had land surveyed, March 31, 1787,

*Query: How could this Capt. Stephen Goodwyn be "heir-at-law" of Lieut. Dinwiddie Goodwyn? Armistead, brother to this Stephen, was only first cousin to Dinwiddie, and was alive in 1777, when Dinwiddie died unmarried.

by Henry Morris, amounting to $38\frac{7}{10}$ acres. The plat of survey is in possession of Mrs Lillie (Goodwyn) Grigg, of Petersburg, Va. Children: i. Dr. William, married Eliza Blunt; ii. Dr. George.

Dr. William Goodwyn (Stephen, Robert) was married to Eliza Blunt. By occupation he was a physician. Children: i. William Stephen, married ——— Dewey; ii. Benjamin Archer; iii. Elizabeth; iv. Sarah; v. Julia; vi. Martha.

William Stephen Goodwyn (William, Stephen, Robert) was married to Miss Dewey, of Southampton, Va. Children: i. William Samuel, resides in Emporia, Va.; ii. Watkins; iii. Douglas; iv. Joseph; v. Elizabeth; vi. Sarah Meade.

Dr. George Goodwyn (Stephen, Robert) was married and resided in Dinwiddie county, Va. Children: i. Stephen Archer; ii. Robert A.

Capt. Armistead Goodwyn (Robert), born in Dinwiddie county, Va., was married, first, to Nancy Wicke. He was married, second, to Mrs. Sarah (Willson) Dance. By occupation he was a farmer, in politics a Democrat, and in religion a Baptist. He resided in Greensville county, Va. He was a captain in the Revolutionary War. Children by first wife: i. Francis, born 1774; married ——— Stith; ii. Fanny A., born 1775; died unmarried; iii. Mary Ann, born 1776; married Robert Stith; iv. John, born 1777; v. James, born 1778; married Mary Ann Tolly; vi. Dr. Charles, born 1779; married Mrs. ———; vii. Elizabeth, born 1781; married John Edwards. Children by second wife: viii. Armistead, born 1800; died unmarried; ix. Nathaniel, born 1802; died unmarried.

James Goodwyn (Armistead, Robert), born in 1778, in Greensville county, Va., was married, in 1818, in Brunswick county, Va., by Rev. Mr. Bacon, to Mary Ann Tolly, born in 1793, in Brunswick county, a daughter of Greex and Nancy (Cousins) Tolly. By occupation he was a farmer, in politics a Democrat, and in religion a Baptist. They resided in Brunswick county, Va. James Goodwyn was a lieutenant in the war of 1812. Greex Tolley was a captain in the Revolutionary War. James Goodwyn died in 1839. Mary Ann (Tolley) Goodwyn, called also Mary (Henry) Goodwyn, died in 1867, in Wilson, N. C. Children: i. Robert A., born April 30, 1820; married Elizabeth J. Kirkland; ii. Ann Frances, born 1822; married William W. Burnett; iii. Mary A., born 1824; married William Cousins; iv. Susanna A., born 1825; married Andrew J. Boisseau; v. Cornelia W., born 1830; married William Willson; vi. Polona A., born 1832; married Edward Organ.

Capt. Robert A. Goodwyn (James, Armistead, Robert) was born April 30, 1820, in Brunswick county, Va.; was married May 26, 1852, in Brunswick county, Va., by Rev. Gregory Claiborne, to Elizabeth J. Kirkland, who was born in 1836, in Brunswick county, Va., a daughter of David R. and Aminta S. (———) Kirkland. By occupation he was a farmer, and in religion a Baptist. They resided in Smoky-Ordinary, Brunswick county, Va. Robert A. Goodwyn served as a private in the Mexican War, and as captain of a volunteer militia company in the late war. He has held the office of justice of the peace. Children: i. James H., born 1853; married Mary Johnson; ii. Mary E., born 1855; married John H. Johnson; iii. Nathaniel B., born 1858; married, first, Mary Powell; second, ——— Stobles; iv. Robert A., born 1860; died; v. Nannie W., born 1865; married James Boisseau.

Ann Frances Goodwyn (James, Armistead, Robert) was born 1822, in Brunswick county, Va.; was married, 1843, in Brunswick county, to William Warner Burnett, who was born 1818. By occupation he was a speculator, in politics a Whig and Republican, and in religion an Episcopalian. They resided in Dinwiddie county, Va., and Wilson, N. C. Ann Frances (Goodwyn) Burnett died in 1870 in Wilson, N. C. William Warner Burnett died in 1890, in Wilson, N. C. *Burnett* Children: i. Rosa Goodwyn, born 1847; married Richard E. Boisseau; ii. Possie Donias, born 1849; died 1888 in Gaston, N. C.; unmarried; iii. Augustus Wich, born 1851; married Mrs. ——— Bridges; iv. James Marion, born 1853; married ——— Tompson; v. Josephine Ellen, born 1855; married Peter Christman; vi. Willie Ann, born 1863; married Loyal Stott.

Rosa Goodwyn Burnett (Ann Frances, James, Armistead, Robert) was born 1847, in Brunswick county, Va.; was married 1866, at Petersburg, Va., by Rev. J. Churchill Gibson, to Richard Edwards Boisseau, who was born 1842 in Dinwiddie county, Va., a son of Major Robert Goodwyn and Martha Epps (Harderway) Boisseau. By occupation he was a merchant, in politics a Republican, and in religion an Episcopalian. They resided in Dinwiddie Courthouse, Dinwiddie county, Va., and she has contributed nearly all the data concerning the descendants of Robert Goodwyn. *Boisseau* children: i. Randolph Burnett, born 1868; ii. Selden Richard, born 1870.

APPENDIX L.

THE GOODWINS OF AUGUSTA COUNTY, VIRGINIA.

The family tradition is that Joseph and his wife were part of an English colony to settle in Augusta county. It may appear, however, that Joseph was a descendant of Major James.

Joseph Goodwin was married to Margaret Thomas. By occupation he was a farmer, and in religion a Methodist. They resided in Augusta county, Va., but in their old age removed to near Columbus, Ohio, where some of their children had settled, and died there. Margaret's name is also given as Catherine. She died November 8, 1820. Joseph died October 10, 1824. The children are not given in order of their birth. At the time Joseph removed from Augusta county, his children, Enos, Joseph, Jr., and Jesse removed to Roanoke county, Va. Children: i. Levi, went West; untraced; ii. Joseph, married Mary (Polly) Jenkins; iii. Septamus, removed to Missouri in 1823; untraced; iv. Jane, born 1780; married Lewis Runkle; v. John, married Susan Daugherty; vi. Melton*; vii. Jesse, married Mary (Polly) Deaton; viii. Enos, born February 3, 1789; married, first, Elizabeth Early; second, Martha Mitchell; ix. Kate, married John Lefler; x. David, born October 17, 1793; married Elizabeth Teaford.

Joseph Goodwin (Joseph) was born in Augusta county, Va.; was married to Polly Jenkins, who was born in 1800 in Roanoke county, a daughter of ——— and ——— (Peas) Jenkins. By occupation he was a farmer, and in religion a Methodist. They resided in Roanoke county. Joseph was a pensioner of the war of 1812. Children: i. Martha, born 1823, married John D. Coleman; ii. Priscilla, born 1825, married David Trout; iii. Jesse, born 1825, married Jane Hawkins; iv. John T., born 1827, married Elizabeth Gaines; v. Mary, married William Yingling; vi. William, born 1830, married Jane Martin; vii. Eliza, born 1833, married, first, Charles Batt; second, J. W. Chinquepeel; viii. Elizabeth, born 1835, married G. A. Beemer.

Martha Goodwin (Joseph, Joseph) was born in 1823 in Roanoke county, Va.; was married in 1842 in Roanoke county, by Rev. Mr. Wheeler, to John D. Coleman, who was born in 1810 in Lynchburg, Va., a son of Capt. Robert and —— (Dewes) Coleman. By

* A *Malen* Goodwin is mentioned by a granddaughter as having lived in Missouri. Query—Were this Malen and Melton the same man?

occupation he was a lawyer, in politics a Republican, and in religion a Quaker. They resided in Roanoke, Va., where John D. Coleman died in 1891. Their son, Robert E., has furnished much of the data of this family. *Coleman* children: i. Mary A , born 1844, married Thomas E. Kizar; ii. Thomas B., born 1847, married Anna Chapman; iii. Ella C., born 1849, married Joseph Strickler; iv. Lewis E., born 1852; v. Eliza A., born 1855, married James Truemain; vi. Robert E., born 1858, married Sarah Huffman; vii. Charles D., born 1860, killed in Colorado, 1883; viii. Martha R., born 1868.

Jesse Goodwin (Joseph, Joseph) was born in 1825 in Roanoke county, Va.; was married in 1848 in Bedford county, Va., to Jane Hawkins. By occupation he was a farmer, in politics a Democrat, and in religion a Baptist. They resided in Bedford City, Va. Children: i. James T., born 1849, died 1880; ii. Lewis B., born 1851, died 1878; iii. William B., born 1854, married Cora Brazeal; iv. George O., born 1856, married M. J. Smith; v. Elliott W., born 1859, married Molly Lewis; vi. Albert J., born 1861, married J. B. Otey; vii. Ella B., born 1866, married O. W. Howard.

John T. Goodwin (Joseph, Joseph) was born in 1827 in Roanoke county, Va.; was married in 1850 in Roanoke county, by William Hatcher to Elizabeth Gaines, who was born in 1833 in Roanoke county, a daughter of K. and Mary (Beaser) Gaines. By occupation he was a farmer, in politics a Democrat, and in religion a Baptist. They resided in Salem, Va., where John T. Goodwin died June 9, 1895. Children: i. Thomas P., born 1851, married Mattie Coffman; ii. Charles, born 1856, married Margaret Phlegor; iii. Annie B., born 1859, married G. T. K——; iv. Jannie, born 1862, married E. M. Grace; v. Ballard, born 1865, married Mamie Hollinbrook; vi. Zella, born 1867; vii. K——, born 1872, married Sallie A. Price.

William Goodwin (Joseph, Joseph) was born in 1830 in Roanoke county, Va.; was married by Rev. Mr. Linthacum to Sarah J. Martin. By occupation he was a miller, in politics a Democrat, and in religion a Methodist. They resided in Eggleston, Giles county, Va. Children: i. J. R., born 1854, married M. E. Kirk; ii. Mary F., born 1856, married J. B. Camden; iii. J. A., born 1861; iv. William E., born 1865, married E. Dillon; v. Ida M., born 1870, married L. B. Williams; vi. Lillie M., born 1874, married E. Williams.

Jane Goodwin (Joseph) was born in 1780 in Augusta county;

was married to Lewis Runkle. They resided in Augusta county, Va. Jane (Goodwin) Runkle, after the death of her husband, removed to Ohio, making her home with her nephew, David Wall Goodwin, in Columbus. No children.

John Goodwin (Joseph) was born in Augusta county, Va.; was married to Susan Daugherty. They resided in Fairfield county, Ohio, and Newark, Ohio. Children: i. Margaret, born 1809, married Washington Benjamin; ii. Preston; iii. Sarah, married —— Blaze, and died *sine prole;* iv. John, married Phœbe Wesley.

Margaret Goodwin (John, Joseph) was born 1809; was married December 2, 1832, to Washington Benjamin. By occupation he was a farmer, in politics a Republican, and in religion a Baptist. *Benjamin* children: i. Martin, born October 20, 1833; ii. John B., born August 15, 1835; iii. Sarah A., born March 11, 1838; iv. Susan A., born October 15, 1841, married Orrin Teaford Goodwin.

Preston Goodwin (John, Jeseph) was married and resided at Newark, Ohio. Children: i. Mary Ellen; ii. Rachel; iii. Anna; iv. John.

John Goodwin (John, Joseph) was married in Fairfield county, Ohio, to Phœbe Wesley. They resided at Yelrah, Fairfield county, Ohio. Children: i. Mary; ii. Jane; iii. Sarah: iv. Preston; v. John; vi. Amos; vii. Judson; viii. Noah.

Jesse Goodwin (Joseph) was born in Augusta county, Va.; was married 1837, in Roanoke county, by Rev. Mr. Esqueridge, to Polly Deaton, who was born October 25, 1807, in Roanoke county, a daughter of John and Elizabeth (Forrest) Deaton. John Deaton was married six times, and was fifty-three years old at date of this marriage. By occupation he was a farmer, and in politics a Democrat. They resided in Roanoke county. Jesse Goodwin died in 1863. Polly (Deaton) Goodwin was living in 1896 near Salem. Children: i. John L., born 1839, married Laurine Haley; ii Annie, born 1840, married John Mitchell; iii. William, born 1843, married Sarah Batt; iv. Hester, born 1845, married Joel Clarke; v. Eliza, born 1848, unmarried; vi. Charles, born 1851, married Mary Allen; vii. Louisa, born 1854, married Charles Olson.

John L. Goodwin (Jesse, Joseph) was born 1839, in Roanoke county, Va.; was married in Roanoke county, to Laurine Haley, who was born 1842, in Roanoke county, a daughter of —— and Sarah (Hatt) Haley. They resided (1896) in Salem, Va. Children: i. Fullis; ii. Annie; iii. Mattie; iv. Laurina; v. Mason.

Enos Goodwin (Joseph) was born February 3, 1789, in Augusta county, Va.; was married, first, by Rev. Bartlett Martin, to Elizabeth Early, who was a daughter of James and Sarah (Wall) Early, and cousin to the late Bishop John Early. She died April 20, 1828. Enos Goodwin married, second, Martha Mitchell, who died in 1860. By occupation he was a farmer, in politics a Whig, and in religion a Methodist. He resided near Salem, Va. He volunteered in the War of 1812, and was rejected on account of disability. He died September, 1861, near Salem. Children by first wife: i. Abner Jubal, born 1813, married Sarah Deaton; ii. Joseph, born 1815, married, first, Leanna Windle; second, Worthy Duncan; iii. David Wall, born 1817, married Catherine Mitchell; iv. Sarah, born 1819, married Joseph Storer; v. Jeremiah Early, born August 19, 1821, married Sarah Jane Carr; vi. Martha (Patsy), born 1823, married Gustavus Beemer; vii. Matilda, born 1825, married Samuel Beemer. Children by second wife: viii. John Mitchell; ix. Enos Vaughn, minister, resides at Salem, Va. (No response.)

Joseph Goodwin (Enos, Joseph) was born 1815; was married, first, 1845, in Roanoke county, Va., by Rev. William Hatcher, to Leanna Windle, who was born 1813, at New Market, Shenandoah county, Va., a daughter of William and Sarah (——) Windle. Joseph Goodwin was married, second, in 1878, at Roanoke, Va., by Rev. Dinwiddie, to Worthy Duncan who was born in 1850, in Goochland county, Va., a daughter of Littleberry and Elizabeth (Cosby) Duncan. In politics he was a Republican, and in religion a Methodist. He resided in Salem, Va. Children by first wife: i. Roland, born 1847, married Melissa Maddox; ii. Nannie, born 1849, married James Jones; iii. Frank, born 1851, married Mollie Mitchell. No children by second wife.

David Wall Goodwin (Enos, Joseph) was born in 1817; was married in 1850, by Rev. Mr. Liggate, to Catherine Mitchell, who was born in 1823 in Roanoke county, Va., a daughter of James and Rebecca (Storer) Mitchell. They resided in Columbus, Ohio. Children: i. Henry, born 1854, married —— Eppley; ii. Lucy, born 1859, married Rev. Robert Scott.

Rev. Jeremiah Early Goodwin (Enos, Joseph) was born August 19, 1821, in Roanoke county, Va.; was married September 9, 1852, in Giles county, Va., by Rev. George Stewart, to Sarah Jane Carr, who was born May 2, 1830, in Giles county, a daughter of William C. and Elizabeth (Bane) Carr. By occupation he was a minister, in politics a Democrat, and in religion a Methodist. They resided in Walker's Creek, Giles county, Va., removing to Science

Hill, Ky., where they now (1897) reside. Children: i. William Jesse, born June 19, 1853, married Marietta Ingram; ii. Mary Matilda, born July 25, 1855, married V. T. Millis; iii. Elizabeth Ann, born June 18, 1864, married B. P. Heard.

William Jesse Goodwin (Jeremiah Early, Enos, Joseph) was born June 19, 1853, in Tazewell county, Va.; was married September 24, 1884, at Monticello, Ky., by Rev. J. G. Bruce, to Marietta Ingram, who was born October 1, 1858, in Monticello, a daughter of George W. and Lucinda (Cullom) Ingram. By occupation he was a merchant, in politics a Republican, and in religion a Methodist. They reside (1897) in Somerset, Ky. Mr. Goodwin is vice-president of the First National Bank, and is a very successful business man. His name was voted on in the caucus for United States Senator in the present Legislature. Mrs. Goodwin is a cousin of Senator Shelby Cullom, of Illinois. Children: i. William, born July 29, 1885; ii. George E., born August 27, 1888; iii. Joseph A., born August 27, 1890; iv. Marietta, born November 25, 1894.

Kate Goodwin (Joseph) was born in Augusta county, Va.; was married to John Lefler. After their marriage they removed to Missouri. On the journey they visited the family of John Deaton, then living in Illinois. One of this family was Polly Deaton, born in 1807, and then about ten years old. She afterwards married Jesse Goodwin, brother to Kate. Polly is still living, and resides in Roanoke county, Va.

David Goodwin (Joseph) was born October 17, 1793, in Augusta county, Va.; was married in Fairfield county, Ohio, to Elizabeth Teaford, who was born March 25, 1798, in Augusta county, a daughter of Lewis (?) Teaford. By occupation he was a farmer, in politics a Democrat, and in religion a Universalist. They resided in Franklin county, Ohio, near Columbus. David Goodwin died December 3, 1856; Elizabeth (Teaford) Goodwin died July 23, 1873. Children: i. Levi, born January 19, 1826, died September 7, 1830; ii. Lovinia, born October 3, 1828, married Samuel Maize; iii. Laney, born December 5, 1829, married Andrew J. Agler; iv. Elizabeth, born November 14, 1832, married Luther Agler; v. Mary Jane, born July 11, 1835, married Clinton W. Agler*; vi. Orrin Teaford, born August 9, 1839, married Susan A. Benjamin.

* Their only child, Eva A., is married to Bishop McMillan, M. D., Columbus, Ohio.

Orrin Teaford Goodwin (David, Joseph) was born August 9, 1839, in Mifflin Township, Franklin county, Ohio; was married January 14, 1864, at Columbus, Ohio, by Rev. Joseph Trimble, D. D., to Susan A. Benjamin, who was born October 15, 1841, in Fairfield county, Ohio, a daughter of Washington and Margaret (Goodwin) Benjamin, she a daughter of John,[2] Joseph.[1] By occupation he was a farmer, in politics a Populist, and in religion a Universalist. They resided in Mifflin Township. Mr. Goodwin is a justice of the peace, and has been a member of the school board for twenty-one years. Children: i. Courtland Llewellyn, born November 23, 1864, died March 4, 1884; ii. Emma May, born April 22, 1871, married Leo J. Lunn.

APPENDIX M.

THE GOODWINS OF CAROLINE AND AMHERST COUNTIES, VIRGINIA.

Warner Goodwin, born in 1773, was married to Miss Camden, a daughter of Jabez Camden. He resided in Caroline county, Va., until about 1800, when he removed to Amherst county, where he married, and where he died November 30, 1841, in his sixty-ninth year. Children: i. Marbell Camden, born 1804; married Sarah ———; ii. Nancy, married Samuel Bowyer; iii. Elizabeth, married ——— Thurman; iv. William, born 1811; died October 24, 1865, unmarried; v. John, born 1813; died October 22, 1856, unmarried; vi. Thomas, died in Texas, unmarried; vii. James Leroy, born 1817; married ——— Daniel; viii. Catherine, died unmarried.

Marbell Camden Goodwin (Warner), born in 1804, in Amherst county, Va., was married to Sarah ———. They resided in Amherst county. Captain Marbell Camden Goodwin served as sheriff of Amherst county. He died May, 1868. Child: i. Selena, married John P. Beard, sheriff of Amherst county.

APPENDIX N.

THE GOODWINS OF CARROLL COUNTY, MARYLAND.

Willam Goodwin was married, and resided in Carroll county, Maryland, in 1784. Children: i. William, born 1784; married Providence Buckingham; ii. a daughter, married John Gorsuch.

William Goodwin (William), born in 1784, near Westminster,

Carroll county, Md., was married to Providence Buckingham. By occupation he was a farmer. They resided on Deer Creek road, two miles east of Westminster. William Goodwin was a soldier in the war of 1812. He was taken ill while in the service, was sent home, and died in the fall of 1814. He was buried on the John Gorsuch farm, near Frizzellburg, Gorsuch being his brother-in-law. After William's death, his widow and children removed to West Virginia, near the Ohio River. She died in Hamilton county, Ohio. Children: i. Margaret, married Thomas Fisher;* ii. Nicodemus, born February 3, 1808; married, first, Harriet Linton; second, Martha McRoberts; iii. Perry Greene Harrison, born 1814; married Rosanna Harris; iv. Mary, married John McBride.*

Nicodemus Goodwin (William, William), born February 3, 1808, near Westminster, Md., was married, first, 1829, at Wilmington, Ohio, to Harriet Linton, who was born about 1810, in Wilmington, a daughter of William and Hannah (Buckman) Linton. She died in 1844, in Cincinnati. He married, second, Martha McRoberts, who died in Olney, Illinois, in 1889. By occupation he was a mechanic and farmer, in politics a Republican, and in religion a Universalist. He resides (1897) in Olney, Ills. Children by first wife: i. William Linton, born April 18, 1830; married Mahala South; ii. Thomas Linton, born 1832; married Kate ———; iii. Mary Ann, born 1834; married James Gunion; iv. Harriet L., born 1835; married John Parker; v. Amanda M., born 1836; married George Philhower; vi. Louisa M., born 1837; married Thomas Young; vii. Merrill P. (Charles Murray), born 1840; died; viii. Albert L., born 1844. Children by second wife: ix. Belle; x. Clara; xi. Ada; xii. Byron; xiii. General.

William Linton Goodwin (Nicodemus, William, William) was born April 13, 1830, in Zanesville, Ohio; was married January 25, 1857, at Cassville, Ga., by Dr. Roberts to Mahala South, who was born May 11, 1840, in Lawrence District, S. C., a daughter of Zachariah and Mary (Moore) South. He has retired from business. In politics a Republican, and in religion a Methodist. He resided in Ohio until 1852, when he went to Alabama, then to Georgia, where he has since made his home in Cartersville. He has held twenty-four different commissions as government official. Children: i. Mary L., born March 13, 1858, married H. Mason Randall; ii. Hattie L., born August 19, 1859, married Charles A. Moore; iii. Eugene P., born March 10, 1861, married Milla Ran-

* Resided near Zanesville, Ohio.

dall; iv. Thomas L., born July 13, 1863, died October 4, 1864; v. William L., born August 13, 1865, married Mrs. Alice (Harris) Laboure; vi. Thomas A., born August 19, 1867, married Mary Keefe; vii. Earl P., born April 26, 1869, married Belle C. Young; viii. Fannie Belle, born November 29, 1874; ix. Pearl Estelle, born September 18, 1876; x. Ruby Gulnare, born April 9, 1880.

Perry Greene Harrison Goodwin (William, William) was born in 1814 in Baltimore county, Md.; was married at Montgomery, Hamilton county, Ohio, to Rosanna Harris, who was born in 1820, in Ohio, a daughter of Jonathan and Sarah (Cowhorn) Harris. By occupation he was a farmer, in politics a Democrat, and in religion a Methodist. They resided in Montgomery, Ohio, and (1897) Russellville, Ky. Children: i. Thomas H. L., born 1840; ii. Lloyd S. B., born 1842; iii. Deborah Ann, born 1845; iv. Margaret P., born 1848; v. Mary R., born 1850, died 1858; vi. Kay, born 1856; vii. W. D., born 1859.

APPENDIX O.

THE GOODWINS OF BALTIMORE COUNTY, MD.

Joshua Goodwin was born in Baltimore county, Md.; was married to Matilda Price, who was born in 1785 in Baltimore county. By occupation he was a farmer. They resided in Baltimore county, where he died in 1821. Matilda (Price) Goodwin died December 3, 1851, aged 66. Children: i. Thomas Price, born January 13, 1807, married, first, Elizabeth Gorsuch, second Ellen Gorsuch; ii. Ruth, born 1809, married Benjamin Matthews; iii. David P., born September 30, 1814; iv. Mary, born July 26, 1817, married Charles Brooks.

Thomas Price Goodwin (Joshua) was born January 13, 1807, in Baltimore county, Md.; was married, first, April 17, 1845, at Franklin District, Carroll county, to Elizabeth Gorsuch, who was born June 22, 1816, in Franklin District, a daughter of Benjamin and Sarah (Gorsuch) Gorsuch. She died September 24, 1853, and he married, second, Ellen, sister to his first wife, born December 5, 1820, died February 5, 1897. By occupation he was a farmer and tanner, in politics a Republican, and in religion a Methodist. They resided in Westminster, Carroll county, Md.. He died March 29, 1891. Children by second wife: i. Charles E., born September 11, 1859, resides in Westminster, unmarried; ii. H. Price, born January 11, 1851, married Charles A. Read.

APPENDIX P.

AN EASTERN MARYLAND FRAGMENT.

Thomas Goodwin was married, first, to Frances Madelain Young; and second, to ——. He resided on the Eastern Shore of Maryland. Children by first wife: i. James W., born February 5, 1813; married Mrs. Eunice (Hoyt) Ralph; ii. John, died in New Orleans about December, 1863. Child by second wife: iii. Susan, married Charles Lutts, of Baltimore.

James W. Goodwin (Thomas) was born February 5, 1813, on the Eastern Shore of Maryland; was married August 23, 1835, to Mrs. Eunice (Hoyt) Ralph, who was born September 17, 1800, in Portsmouth, N. H., a daughter of Daniel H. and Abigail P. (Walden) Hoyt, and widow of Hiram M. Ralph. By occupation he was a pilot. They resided in Portsmouth, N. H. James W. Goodwin died May 15, 1863, in New Orleans. Children: i. James W., born August 26, 1836; ii. Thomas J., born February 22, 1842.

APPENDIX Q.

THE GOODWINS OF VIRGINIA AND NORTH CAROLINA.

Benjamin Goodwin was born in Virginia; was married to Miss —— Allen. By occupation he was a planter. They resided in Virginia, removing to North Carolina before 1750. Children: i. Lemuel, born 1752; married Frances Amis; ii. Samuel, married Keziah Tatum.

Lemuel Goodwin (Benjamin) was born in 1752, in Halifax county, N. C.; was married to Frances Amis, a daughter of John and Mary (Dillard) Amis. By occupation he was a planter. They resided in Granville county, N. C. Lemuel Goodwin enlisted April, 1776, as sergeant in Capt. Allen's, afterwards Capt. Thompson's, company, First North Carolina regiment of the Continental Line. The data concerning this family is furnished by Mrs. Margaret (Campbell) Pilcher, of Nashville, Tenn., her mother being Frances Isabella (Owen) Campbell, daughter of Dr. John and Mary Amis (Goodwin) Owen. Children: i. Mary Amis, married Dr. John Owen; ii. Frances Amis, married Rev. Maurice Smith.

Samuel Goodwin (Benjamin) was married to Keziah Tatum, a daughter of John Tatum. By occupation he was a planter. They resided in Granville county, N. C., where Samuel Goodwin's will was probated in February, 1775. Child: i. Samuel; untraced.

APPENDIX R.

THE GOODWINS OF VIRGINIA AND GEORGIA.

——— *Goodwin* was married to —— Cain. Children: i. Shadrack, married —— Horn; ii. James; iii. William.

Shadrack Goodwin was married to —— Horn. They resided at the close of the Revolutionary War in Wake county, N. C., and removed to Jones county, Ga., near the site of the present city of Milledgeville. Children: i. Mary (Polly); ii. Jesse; iii. James; iv. Gideon, born 1807; v. Ruffin.

Gideon Goodwin (Shadrack) was born in 1807, near Milledgeville, Ga. He resided in Talbot county, Ga., for more than fifty years, honored as a gentleman and beloved as a Christian. His life was an open book of love to God and of good deeds to men. He and his ancestors were large slave owners. Child: Rev. S. A.

Rev. S. A. Goodwin (Gideon, Shadrack) was a minister. He resided in 1892 at 104 Jones street, Savannah, Ga.

APPENDIX S.

THE GOODWINS OF GREENBRIER COUNTY, WEST VIRGINIA.

Charles Goodwin was born in London, England. Child: i. Henry, married Martha Alexander. Perhaps other children.

Henry Goodwin (Charles) was born in London, England; was married in Augusta county, W. Va., to Martha Alexander. They resided in Greenbrier and Augusta counties, W. Va., where Henry died. Martha (Alexander) Goodwin died in Madison county, Indiana. Children: i. William, born 1795, married Elizabeth Hoover; ii. Henry; iii. Margaret, married John Davis; iv. Sarah, married Theophilus Leopard; v. Harvey; vi. Matilda, died unmarried; vii. Alexander Monroe, born July 1, 1816, married Catherine Ann McFarland; viii. Robert, died unmarried.

William Goodwin (Henry, Charles) was born 1795 in Augusta county, W. Va.; was married to Elizabeth Hoover, who was a daughter of ——— and Mary (———) Hoover. By occupation he was a miller, in politics a Republican, and in religion a Baptist. They resided in Logansport, Indiana. William Goodwin died 1868 in Logansport, Indiana. Children: i. Samuel McFarland, born August 5, 1826, married Cordelia John; ii. Mary Aditha,*

* Resides in South Chicago, Ill.

born May 11, 1828, married, first, Wm. Harvey Miller; second, John B. Higel; iii. Henry A., died in infancy; iv. Vitellus, died in infancy; v. Martha Ann, married John Soward; vi. John Henry, married Emma Utter; vii. Giles Nettleton, died in army, unmarried; viii. Cyrus Alexander, resides in Peru, Ind., unmarried; ix. Nancy Jane, married Robert A. New; x. George Washington.*

Samuel McFarland Goodwin (William, Charles, Henry), born August 5, 1826, in Greenbrier county, W. Va.; was married December 11, 1851, at Logansport, Ind., by Rev. Post, to Cordelia John, who was born November 11, 1828, in Ohio, a daughter of James and Amy (Stout) John. By occupation he was a farmer, in politics a Republican. They resided in Logansport, Ind., where he died October 20, 1871. His wife died in Rochester, Ind., November 11, 1893. Child: Emma, born January 30, 1853, married Allan Alonzo Cooke, and resides in Gas City, Ind.

Alexander Monroe Goodwin (Henry, Charles) was born January 1, 1816, in Greenbrier county, W. Va.; was married, 1837, in Miami county, Ohio, by Burris Westlake, to Catherine Ann McFarland, who was born January 12, 1816, near Baltimore, Md., a daughter of William and Elizabeth (Kellar) McFarland. By occupation he was a carpenter, in politics a Republican, and in religion a Methodist. They resided in Perrysburg, Miami county, and Logansport, Ind. He died February 18, 1874, in Logansport. His wife died June 8, 1893, in Berwyn, Ill. Children: i. Amanda, born July 3, 1840, resides in Logansport, unmarried; ii. Martha, born December 29, 1843, unmarried; iii. Narina, born November 24, 1846, married Stephen Boyer; iv. Oscar, born 1849, married, first, Emma Patterson; second, Lillian Patterson; third, Irma Nemitt; v. Irene, born April 3, 1852, unmarried.

APPENDIX T.

THE GOODWINS OF ALBEMARLE COUNTY, VIRGINIA.

William Goodwin was born about 1772, in England, and came to America with a brother, who died shortly after arrival. He settled in Albemarle county, Va., where he died in 1822. He was a farmer. Child: i. John Austin, born 1809; married Lucinda J. Mayo.

John Austin Goodwin (William) was born 1809, in Albemarle

---

* Resides in Pueblo, Col.

county, Va.; was married, 1828, to Lucinda J. Mayo, a daughter of Gould Mayo. By occupation he was a farmer. They resided in Albemarle county, where John Austin Goodwin died in 1873. Child: Richard A., born 1848.

APPENDIX U.

THE GOODINS OF LOUDOUN COUNTY, VIRGINIA.

Amos Goodin, said to have come from Bucks county, Pa., purchased a farm in 1760, near Purcellville, Loudoun county, Va. He left three children: i. David; ii. John; iii. Samuel.

David Goodin (Amos) resided on the homestead farm, dying in 1828. He left, so far as known, one child: J. C., born 1826; resides on the home farm.

John Goodin (Amos) removed to Ohio; untraced.

Samuel Goodin (Amos) removed to Coshocton, Rochester county, Ohio; untraced.

APPENDIX V.

UNTRACED GOODWINS OF VIRGINIA.

Peter Goodwin married ——— Woodfolk; no children.

Samuel Goodwin was pewholder No. 34 in St. Paul's Parish church, Kent, Maryland, last century.

Dr. T. J. Goodwin resided in St. Mathew's Parish, S. C., in 1850.

Sheldon Goodwin married Constance ———. His will was dated 1751, leaving all to widow. Probably no children. York county.

John Porter Goodwin lived in York county about 1729.

Capt. John Goodwin's estate has accounts filed by John Moss in York county October 18, 1784.

Harwood Goodwin, 1759.

John and Rebecca Goodwin had daughter, Elizabeth, born July 29, 1772. (Parish Register of Charles or New Pocosin.)

Thomas, 1753.

Mathew, 1701.

Devorox, Joseph and Thomas, Jr., 1705.

John and Benjamin, 1711.

Robert Goodwin, York county, 1742, 1748.

Robert Goodwin, inventory, August 22, 1800. York county.

Martin Goodwin, inventory, January 18, 1805. York county.

Peter Goodwin, Commissioner of Deeds, 1812. York county.

Peter Goodwin, inventory, March 30, 1824. York county.

Peter and Elizabeth Goodwin, January 17, 1825. York county.

G. B. Goodwin married Louisa DuPuy. They resided in King William Parish, on James River. (See *Va. Hist. Doc.*, Vol. V., p. 174.) Children: i. John E.; ii. George; iii. Annie; iv. Louisa; v. Albert F.; vi. William; vii. Arthur; viii. Mary; ix. Martha; x. Lemira.

APPENDIX W.

Miscellaneous Notes.

Amos Goodwin, private in the Virginia Continental Line, received a warrant for 200 acres of bounty land as a soldier.

Benjamin Goodwin, born 1748; a sergeant of the Virginia Continental Line; was pensioned in 1820, then 72 years old and residing in Mississippi.

John Goodwin, whose birthplace is given as "Jersey," was born about 1735. He was a member of Major Andrew Lewis' Company, about 1755, and was then described as twenty years of age, five feet seven and one-half inches in height, a resident of Frederick county, Va., and a saddler by occupation. No further record.

John Goodwin, of the Fourth Virginia Troops, Continental Line, deserted October 30, 1781.

John Goodwin, born 1759, of the North Carolina service, was pensioned as a private in 1833, then aged 74 and residing in Mississippi.

Theophilus Goodwin, born 1744, a private of the North Carolina Continental Line, was pensioned in 1818, then aged 74 and residing in Alabama.

APPENDIX X.

The Goodwins of Preble County, Ohio.

Although Scotland is claimed as the birthplace of Richard Goodwin, the ancestor of this family, it must be noted that the only Richard Goodwin, so far as now known, who lived in Virginia and served in the Revolutionary War, was Richard, brother to Micajah, John, Nelson and George Goodwin. (See Appendix H.) The descendants of both Micajah and of a George Goodwin, supposed to be this George, had relatives in the Carolinas. This Richard lived for some years in North Carolina. Later data may confirm the connection between Micajah, Richard and George, and may show that Nelson, the only one wholly untraced, settled in South Carolina or Alabama, there being a large family of Goodwins in the latter State who have not responded to any inquiry.

The given names in this family are utterly dissimilar to those used by the Virginia Goodwins, but are in common use among the Goodwins of York county, Maine—*i. e.*, Miles, Stephen, Nathan, Jonathan, Didema and Richard.

Richard Goodwin was born in Scotland, according to one account, but removed to Virginia, where he served in the Revolutionary War. He married, removed to North Carolina, and then to Eaton, Preble county, Ohio, where he died. Children: i. Nathan, married Nancy Arlington: ii. William, untraced; iii. Joseph, untraced; iv. Miles, untraced.

Nathan Goodwin (Richard) was born in Virginia or North Carolina; was married in Virginia to Nancy Arlington, who was born in Virginia, a daughter of Judge Arlington. By occupation he was a farmer, in politics a Whig, and in religion a Quaker. They resided in Virginia, North Carolina, and Eaton, Preble county, Ohio. Children: i. Stephen, born June 14, 1790; married Mary Ann Pearson; ii. Nathan, died unmarried; iii. Richard, died unmarried; iv. Mary Ann, married William Jarvice; v. Nancy, married William McDaniel; vi. Axie; vii. Daughter.

Stephen Goodwin (Nathan, Richard) was born June 14, 1790, in North Carolina; was married November 15, 1810, at Eaton, Ohio, to Mary Ann Pearson, who was born October 1, 1790, in North Carolina, a daughter of Jonathan and Sarah (Eliott) Pearson. By occupation he was a farmer, in politics a Whig, and in religion a Quaker. They resided in Georgetown, Ill., where Stephen died. His wife died February 5, 1876, in Bloomingdale, Ind. Children; i. Jonathan, born March 15, 1812; married Malinda Cook; ii. Delilah, born June 18, 1813; married John Higgins; iii. Didema, born September 4, 1815; married David Newlin; iv. William, born February 6, 1817, married Cynthia Ann Strador; v. Mary Ann, born February 4, 1819; married Elias Newlin; vi. Nathan, born May 24, 1822; married, first, Rebecca Davis; second, Sarah Dillon; vii. Rebecca, born March 25, 1826; married Milton Cook.

Jonathan Goodwin (Stephen, Nathan, Richard) born March 15, 1812, in Preble county, Ohio; was married August 8, 1836, near Georgetown, Ill., by Friends' ceremony to Malinda Cook, who was born November 11, 1817, in Indiana, a daughter of Isaac and Eleanor (Thornton) Cook. By occupation he was a farmer, in politics a Republican, and in religion a Friend. They resided near Georgetown, Ill., where he died July 21, 1855. Children: i. Eleanor,* born August 6, 1839, married Joseph Reagan; ii. Sarah A., born October 13, 1839, married ———; iii. Mary A., born ——, died —— ; iv. Delilah, born ——, died —— ; v. Stephen, born ——, died ——.

William Goodwin (Stephen, Nathan, Richard) was born February 6, 1817, in Eaton, Ohio; was married August 6, 1838, at Georgetown, Ill., by Patrick Cowan, to Cynthia Ann Strador, who was born April 15, 1819, in Ohio, a daughter of Henry and Nancy (Moss) Strador. By occupation he was a farmer, in politics a Whig, and in religion a Quaker. They resided in Georgetown, Ill., and Vinton, Iowa, where William died September 4, 1893. His widow resides (1897) in Vinton. Children: i. Sarah Jane, born September 9, 1840; died August 29, 1851; ii. Henderson, born March 31, 1843; married Angerene Davenport; iii. Rebecca, born May 9, 1847; married George W. Edmonds.

Henderson Goodwin (William, Stephen, Nathan, Richard) was born March 31, 1843, in Georgetown, Ill.; was married December 28, 1865, at Georgetown, by Jacob Yapp, justice of the peace, to Angerene Davenport, who was born March 30, 1848, in Lewisville, Ind., a daughter of Henry and Mahala (Conradt) Davenport. By occupation he was a farmer, in politics a Republican, and in religion a Friend. They resided in Georgetown until 1881, removing to Indianola, Ill., where they now (1897) reside with their seven younger children. Henderson Goodwin enlisted in the Seventy-third Illinois; was wounded September 20, 1863, in the battle of Chickamauga, from the result of which his left arm was amputated in 1885; was again wounded in the battle of Lookout Mountain, losing part of his right hand. He has been road commissioner, mail-carrier, justice of the peace, postmaster, and is now police magistrate. Children: i. Edward Henderson, born September 22, 1866; married Isabelle Jackson; ii. Ulysses Stephen, born August 26, 1868; married Agnes Jones; iii. Estella Norman, born September 15, 1870; married Harvey Newell; iv. Myrtle Sherwood, born January 5, 1873; married Albertus Dickson; v. William Henry, born March 31, 1875; vi. Rebecca Elizabeth, born November 4, 1877; vii. Angerena Davenport, born April 7, 1880; viii.

* Resides in Newton, Kansas.

9

Barton Odbert, born January 6, 1883; ix. Wynona Gertrude, born July 19, 1885; x. Caroline Jewell, born October 12, 1887; xi. Garnet Logan, born March 6, 1893.

It is probable that the following family descends from either William, Joseph or Miles, sons of Richard Goodwin:

James Goodwin, born about 1800, married —— Ward, and resided in Preble county, Ohio. Child (perhaps others): Timothy, born 1823, married Sarah Parish.

Timothy Goodwin (James), born in 1823 in Preble county, Ohio, was married in Preble county to Sarah Parish, born in 1834 in Preble county, a daughter of William and Anna (——) Parish. He was a farmer and Republican. In religion a member of the United Brethren. They resided in Preble county. Child (others not given): C. E., born 1859, married Miranda Skinner, and resides (1897) in Cowan, Delaware county, Indiana.

APPENDIX Y.

PROBABLE DESCENDANTS OF ROBERT GOODWIN.

Robert Goodwin, eldest son of Major James, left several children. One was Martin, who died *sine prole*. It is thought that perhaps many of the fragmentary Goodwin families in Virginia and Maryland descend from children of this Robert, unknown at present. A Robert Goodwin was patron of a York county school in 1711, and another Robert Goodwin was born in York county in 1703. It seems probable that the following may be a partial list of children in this family:

Robert Goodwin (James) married Anne ——. (See page 7.) Children: i. Martin, d. s. p.; ii. Robert; iii. John.

Robert Goodwin (Robert, James) was probably the patron of the school in 1711, and father of Robert, born in 1703.

The will of Samuel Hill, of York county, proved February 10, 1770, mentions Rebecca, daughter of Mr. *Robert* Goodwin, and gives to Anne Goodwin "my late wife's part of the estate of her deceased father, Mr. *Robert* Goodwin." These fragments, taken with the data of a John Goodwin given herewith, presumably a son of Robert first, show that a considerable family of Goodwins was living around York county, and, with reasonable certainty, it may be claimed that Major James was its ancestor. Reference may also be had in this connection to Appendix H.

John Goodwin (probably *Robert*, James) was married, April 22, 1705, in Christ Church parish, Middlesex county, Va., to Mary Elliot. Mary (Elliot) Goodwin died November 24, 1734. Children: i. George, married, first, Jane Haselwood; second, Elizabeth Warwick; ii. John, married Jane ———.

George Goodwin (John, *Robert*, James) was married, first, August 14, 1729, at Christ Church, Middlesex county, Va., to Jane Haselwood, who died January 28, 173⅞. George Goodwin married, second, June 15, 1738, at Christ Church, Elizabeth Warwick. Children by first wife: i. Robert, born July 23, 1730; died September 26, 1730; ii. George, born October 12, 1734; untraced.

John Goodwin (John, *Robert*, James) was married to Jane ———. Children: i. Robert, born December 30, 1732; ii. Jane, born February 27, 1735; both untraced.

APPENDIX Z.

THE GOODWINS OF HALIFAX COUNTY, VIRGINIA.

Walker Goodwin was born about 1775. He married and resided in Halifax county, Va. By occupation he was a farmer. Child (only one known): i. Walker, married Elizabeth Emanuell, or Manuell.

Walker Goodwin (Walker) was born in 1801, in Halifax county, Va.; was marrried in 1834, in Davidson county, Tenn., by Peter Fergus, to Elizabeth Manuell, who was born in 1817, in Davidson county, a daughter of Thomas and Fanny (Bragg) Manuell. By occupation he was a mechanic, in politics a Democrat. He resided in Halifax county, Va., and Davidson county, Tenn. She died in 1852. Walker Goodwin, Jr., died in December, 1881. Children: i. William, born 1836; married, first, in 1854; second, in 1871; ii. Susan, born 1839; died in 1860, unmarried; iii. Francis, born 1841; died in 1872, unmarried; iv. Mary, born 1843; died in 1870, unmarried; v. John Abraham, born 1847; married Rachel Frances Wagoner; vi. Elizabeth, born 1849; died in 1869, unmarried.

John Abraham Goodwin (Walker, Walker) was born 1847, in Davidson county, Tenn.; was married June, 1871, in Davidson county, by Tobias Tergus, to Rachel Frances Wagoner, who was born in Davidson county, a daughter of Abraham and Surilla (Spain) Wagoner. By occupation he was a farmer, in politics a Democrat, and in religion a Christian. They reside (1897) in Una, Davidson county. Children: i. John T., born May, 1872; died; ii. Paul, born October, 1873; iii. Laura E., born November, 1875; iv. Anne, born July, 1878; v. Pearl, born ———, 1881; vi. Charles, born February, 1883; vii. Mary, born October, 1884; viii. Eugene, born December, 1886; ix. Ruth, born November, 1893.

APPENDIX W.

ADDITIONAL MISCELLANEOUS NOTES.

On page 127, at the end of Appendix W., appears the name of Theophilus Goodwin, born in North Carolina and residing in 1818 in Alabama. It has long been known to the compiler of these records that a large Goodwin family was living in Alabama, but the most persistent requests for information remained unanswered until Mrs. Turner Myrick Goodwin, of Maplesville, Ala., was written to, and from her, from Mrs. Nettie Goodwin Crossland, of East Lake, from Mrs. Gertrude G. Stewart and Col. John W. Portis, all of the following data has been obtained.

One account is that this family was living in North Carolina about 1725–'50; that the name of the first ancestor is not now known; that he was twice married, and had by his first wife one son, name unknown, and another son named Young, and a son David by his second wife. The unknown son was the father of Theophilus, born in 1744, and Theophilus, with his uncles, Young and David, they being about his own age, or perhaps David was even younger, went South through South Carolina and Georgia to Alabama. Theophilus married Rebecca Bledsoe, and a daughter Sarah, born in 1803, and who is still living, but from whom no reply has been received, stated years ago that Young Goodwin was her father's own uncle and her mother's own cousin.

Another account, and apparently the more nearly correct, although it does not explain or conform to the statement of Sarah, daughter of Theophilus, is as follows:

——— *Goodwin* resided in Virginia, and had at least two sons: i. ——— married ———, and was the father of Theophilus; ii. Samuel married ———.

——— *Goodwin* resided in North Carolina, married and had child (perhaps others): Theophilus, born in 1744, married Rebecca Bledsoe.

Theophilus Goodwin was born 1744 in North Carolina; was married to Rebecca Bledsoe. By occupation he was a farmer, in politics a Whig, and in religion a Baptist. He resided in North Carolina, South Carolina, and in Bibb county, Ala. He was a private of the North Carolina Continental Line, and was pensioned in 1818. He died in Bibb county about 1840. Chilton county is now the name of that part of Bibb county where Theophilus resided. Children: i. William; ii. Harris, married Mary Turner; iii.

Gillie, married B. Forrest; iv. Julius, born 1784, married Margaret Kinnard; v. Wiley; vi. Henry; vii. Jefferson; viii. Charity, married Dempsey Hatcher; ix. Frances, born 1798, married, first, Thomas Wright; second, John Salter; x. Young G., born June 4, 1801, married Elizabeth Wright; xi. Sarah, born January 8, 1803, resides near Maplesville, Ala.; xii. Elizabeth, married William Andrews.

Harris Goodwin (Theophilus) was married to Mary Turner. They resided in Tennessee and Alabama. Died in the latter State. Children: i. Warren, married Nancy Bogle (untraced); ii. Thomas, died unmarried.

Gillie Goodwin (Theophilus) was born in Edgefield, South Carolina; was married at Edgefield to B. Forrest. By occupation Mr. Forrest was a farmer and in religion a Baptist. They resided in South Carolina where they died. *Forrest* children: i. Jefferson; ii. Elza, married, first, ———; second, Mrs. Jane Satcher; iii. Ellen, married Jack Chapman; iv. Rebecca, married William Jester.

General Julius Goodwin (Theophilus) was born in 1784 in Edgefield, South Carolina; was married at Edgefield, to Margaret Kinnard, who was born in South Carolina. By occupation he was a farmer, in politics a Whig, and in religion a Baptist. General Julius Goodwin was twice chosen as a representative from Bibb county. He died September 5, 1848. This family is all dead except John Kinnard and Mary Ann. No data concerning any except Aquilla Miles and John Kinnard. Children: i. Aquilla Miles, born January 20, 1813, married Rebecca S. H. Goodwin; ii. John Kinnard, married Ann Eliza Lloyd; iii. Jefferson, died unmarried; iv. Myrick, died unmarried; v. James, died unmarried; vi. Julius Pickens, married Eustatia Reid; vii. Lafayette, died unmarried; viii. Mary Ann, married John W. Suttle, and resides in Centreville, Ga.; ix. Theophilus, died unmarried.

Aquilla Miles Goodwin (Julius, Theophilus) was born January 13, 1813, in South Carolina; was married in Bibb county, Ala., to Rebecca South Hall Goodwin, born near Macon, Ga., a daughter of Young and Martha (Andrews) Goodwin. In religion they were Methodists. They resided in Selma, Ala., where Mrs. Goodwin now resides. Children: i. M. Gertrude, married James J. Stewart; ii. Walter Young; iii. Fitz Julius, married Marie Stillé; iv. Margaret Mae, married John D. Wilkins.

John Kinnard Goodwin (Julius, Theophilus) was born in South Carolina; was married at Selma, Ala., to Ann Eliza Lloyd, who was born in Bibb county, Ala., a daughter of David and Martha (Goodwin) Lloyd, she a daughter of Young Goodwin. By occupation he was a merchant, in politics a Democrat, and in religion a Methodists. They reside (1897) in Selma, Ala. Children: i. M. Carlene; ii. Mary; iii. Kate Ellen, died; iv. Lillie, died; v. John, died; vi. Ernest, died; vii. Julius Aquilla; viii. William Lee David, married, first, Lottie Cooper; second, Lillian ———; ix. Alice, died.

Charity Goodwin (Theophilus) was born in Edgefield, South Carolina; was married in Bibb county, Ala., to Dempsey Hatcher. By occupation he was a farmer, in politics a Democrat, and in religion a Baptist. They resided in Bibb county, Ala. *Hatcher* children: i. Jackson, married Mrs. ——— Lenoir; ii. Elizabeth, married ——— Lawley; iii. Rebecca, married ——— Cashat; iv. Dempsey.

Frances Goodwin (Theophilus) was born in 1798 in Edgefield, South Carolina; was married, first, to Thomas Wright, who was born in Newberry, South Carolina, a son of James and Elizabeth (Buzherdt) Wright. Frances Goodwin married, secondly, John Salter in Edgefield. *Wright* children: i. Henry T., married Frances Kenney; ii. Theophilus S., married Nancy Elder; iii. Julius Pickens, married, first, Jane Mathena; second, Elizabeth Bolton; iv. Ann, married George Crouch. *Salter* children: v. ——; vi. Charity, married —— Crouch; vii. Margaret, died unmarried; viii. Simpson Goodwin, married Eliza Denny; ix. Larkin, died unmarried; x. Savannah, died unmarried.

Major Young G. Goodwin (Theophilus) was born June 4, 1801, in Edgefield, South Carolina; was married December 25, 1822, at Edgefield to Elizabeth Wright, who was born May 12, 1804, in Newberry, South Carolina, a daughter of James and Elizabeth (Buzherdt) Wright. By occupation he was a farmer, in politics a Democrat, and in religion a Baptist. They resided in Edgefield, S. C., removing to Georgia and then to Maplesville, Chilton county, Ala., where Elizabeth died in 1865 and Major Goodwin in 1867. The initial G. in Major Goodwin's name was used by him to distinguish his name from that of the numerous other Young Goodwins. Children: i. Jasper Tompkins, born October 24, 1824, died in Magnolia, Ark., unmarried; ii. Ausmus Allen, born July 17, 1826, married Mary Dickson; iii. Margaret Amanda, born October 24, 1829, married George Ferguson, and died *sine prole;* iv. Enoch Hays, born 1831, died young; v. Thomas Sumter, born December 5, 1833, married, first, Lurana Griffin; second, Ann Griffin; third, Sarah Shaver; vi. Mardis Gale, born September 13, 1835, killed in the Confederate army in 1863; vii. Marion Lee, twin with Mardis Gale; viii. Elizabeth Ellen Savannah, born 1837, died in 1847; ix. Rebecca Jane, born July 17, 1840, married John Joseph Wimbish; x. Henry Clay, born August 29, 1842, killed in battle in Virginia in 1862; xi. Mary Antoinette, October 23, 1844, married Edward Davidson Crossland; xii. Eustatia Paralee, born July 18, 1847.

Ausmus Allen Goodwin (Young G., Theophilus) was born July 17, 1826, in Edgefield, S. C.; was married in Calhoun county, Ark., to Mary Dickson. By occupation he was a carpenter, in politics a Democrat. They reside (1897) in Magnolia, Columbia county, Ark. Children: i. Alice, married Peter Baker; ii. Elfleda, married —— Moody; iii. Minnie Eustatia, married Dr. —— Brown; iv. Daisy.

Thomas Sumter Goodwin (Young G., Theophilus) was born December 5, 1833, in Bibb county, Ala.; was married, first, in 1859, in Bibb county, to Lurana Griffin, who was born in Bibb county, a daughter of Robert and Nancy Griffin, who died in 1862. By occupation he was a farmer, in politics a Democrat, and in religion a Baptist. They resided in Bibb county. After the death of his wife he removed to Perry county, where he was married, secondly, in 1865, to Ann Griffin, sister to his first wife, and after the death of Ann he was married, thirdly, to Sarah Shaver. Children, both by first wife: i. Laura Elizabeth, born February 22, 1860, married Isaac Abercrombie; ii. Addie V. Clay, born 1862, married Jesse Sandford.

Rebecca Jane Goodwin (Young G., Theophilus) was born July 17, 1840, in Bibb county, Ala.; was married in 1871, in Chilton county, Ala., by Rev. Mr. Green, to John Joseph Wimbish, who was born in Clark county, Ala., a son of James and Mary Wimbish. By occupation he was a farmer and probate judge, in politics a Democrat, and in religion a Methodist. They resided in Alabama until about 1880, when they removed to Palmetto, Fla., where Judge Wimbish died in 1895. *Wimbish* children: i. Mary Fredonia, born November, 1872, married Thomas M. Strickland; ii. Elizabeth Eugenia, born October, 1874, died in 1888; iii. Willie Antoinette, born October 12, 1876; iv. Ada Hawthorne, born 1878; v. Maggie W., born September, 1893.

Mary Antoinette Goodwin (Young G., Theophilus) was born

October 23, 1844, in Bibb county, Ala.; was married October 18, 1883, at Selma, Ala., by Rev. J. L. West, to Edward Davidson Crossland, who was born May 18, 1855, in Autanga county, Ala., a son of Edward D. and Elizabeth Jane (Woolley) Crossland. In politics he was a Democrat and in religion a Baptist. They resided in Selma and in (1897) East Lake, Ala. Mrs. Crossland has furnished all the data relating to the descendants of Theophilus Goodwin. *Crossland* children: i. Goodwin, born March 25, 1885, died in infancy; ii. Clayton Edward Ferguson, born July 25, 1886; iii. Lizziebel Mae, born October 21, 1888.

Samuel Goodwin was probably born in Virginia; was married to ———. They resided in Virginia, removing to North Carolina about 1800. It is suggested that Samuel was twice married, and that Young was a son of the first wife. Children: i. Young, born ——; married Martha Andrews; ii. Mary Anne, born May 7, 1780; married Ira Portis; iii. David, born ——; married Temperance Andrews.

Young Goodwin (Samuel) was born in North Carolina; was married to Martha (Patty) Andrews, who was born in North Carolina. By occupation he was a planter, in politics a Whig, and in religion a Baptist. They resided in Bibb county, Ala., until their deaths. Children: i. William Wyche, born February 23, 1792, married, first, Jane Sanders; second, Susan Swift; ii. Elizabeth, married, first, William Hill; second, James Reid; iii. Mary, married Richard Bird; iv. Theophilus, married, first, Stacey Thompson; second, Mrs. Elizabeth (——) Sime, and died *sine prole;* v. Young, married Lucy Grubbs*; vi. Emily, married Rev. Daniel M. Norwood; vii. Martha, married Rev. David Lloyd; viii. Robert, married, first, Elizabeth Norvell; second, ———; third, ———; ix. Nauphlet, married Mary A. Portis; † x. Turner Myrick, married Nancy E. McCary; xi. John,‡ married Ann C. Neighbors; xii. Ann, married William Kinnard; xiii. Rebecca South Hall married Aquilla Miles Goodwin.

William Wyche Goodwin (Young, Samuel) was born February 23, 1792; was married, first, January 19, 1815, to Jane Sanders, who died in 1823. He was married, secondly, December 4, 1823, to Susan Swift, who was born August 25, 1802. By occupation he was

---

* Name also given as Stubbs.

† Mary A. Portis was daughter of Mary Anne (Goodwin) Portis, sister to Young Goodwin. She was first married to Samuel McColl. After her death Nauphlet married her younger sister, Maria Henrietta Portis.

‡ Wife's name also given as Ann Moore.

a very extensive planter, and in religion a Baptist. He resided in Macon, Miss., where Susan (Swift) Goodwin died April 13, 1851. William Wyche Goodwin died October 21, 1874, in Columbus, Miss. Children by first wife: i. Nathaniel Young, born January 13, 1816; ii. Thelston, born June 29, 1818; iii. William Wyche, born April 13, 1820; iv. Jane Sanders, born May 13, 1823. Children by second wife: v. Levina, born November 12, 1824; vi. John Swift, born August 7, 1826; vii. Frances Ann, born March 12, 1829; viii. Wiley Swift, born October 20, 1831; ix. Turner Swift, born September 21, 1834; x. Martha Elizabeth, born September 21, 1837; xi. Theophilus Swift, born November 7, 1839; xii. Ernestine Amanda, born February 2, 1842; xiii. Thomas Jefferson, born October 4, 1844; xiv. George Henry, born January 20, 1847, married Mollie Benjamin Harlan.

George Henry Goodwin (William Wyche, Young, Samuel) was born January 20, 1847, in Macon, Miss.; was married in 1868, at Harlan, Miss., by J. M. Stone, to Mollie Benjamin Harlan, who was born in 1853 in Harlan, a daughter of William Sims and Mary Ann (Hunter) Harlan. By occupation he was an extensive farmer, in politics a Democrat, and in religion a Methodist. They reside (1897) in Paulette, Noxubee county, Miss. Children: i. Mary Ernestine, born 1869, married Thomas Francis Scott; ii. Edward Eugene, born 1872, died May, 1877; iii. John Elmer, born 1875, resides in Sali, Miss.; iv. George Hunter, born 1877; v. Annie Belle, born 1880; vi. William Harlan, born 1883.

Elizabeth Goodwin (Young, Samuel) was married, first, to William Hill; she was married, secondly, to James Reid. *Hill* children: Martha, married Resin Woolley; ii. William. *Reid* children: iii. Mary Ann, married William White; iv. Jane, married Dr. Samuel Randall; v. Eustatia, married Julius Pickens Goodwin; vi. Richard.

Martha Goodwin (Young, Samuel) was married to Rev. David Lloyd. By occupation he was a minister and in religion a Baptist. They resided in Alabama, removing to Mississippi, where they now (1897) reside. *Lloyd* children: i. Levi; ii. William; iii. Ann Eliza, married John Kinnard Goodwin; iv. Judson.

Nauphlet Goodwin (Young, Samuel) was married first, to Mary A. Portis; secondly, to Maria Henrietta Portis, her sister, both daughters of Ira and Mary Anne (Goodwin) Portis. By occupation he was a minister and in religion a Baptist. They resided in Clark county, Ala. Children, names not given.

Turner Myrick Goodwin (Young, Samuel) was born March 2, 1808, in Hancock county, Ga.; was married January 7, 1847, in Bibb county, Ala., by Rev. David Lloyd, to Nancy E. McCary, who was born September 6, 1829, in Bibb county, a daughter of St. Clair and Elizabeth (Atchinson) McCary. By occupation he was a farmer, in politics a Democrat, and in religion a Baptist. They resided in Maplesville, Ala., where Turner died October 18, 1875. Mrs. Nancy E. Goodwin has furnished almost all the data of Young Goodwin's descendants. Children: i. Martha, born September 9, 1848, died; ii. Jane E., born February 14, 1851, died; iii. Anna M., born August 21, 1854, married Dr. F. D. DuBose; iv. Jackson L., born March 10, 1857, died; v. Charles E., April 25, 1859, died; vi. Mary G., born September 8, 1867, died.

Ann Goodwin (Young, Samuel) was married to William Kinnard. By occupation he was a farmer. They resided in Bibb county, Ala., removing to Arkansas. *Kinnard* children: i. Theophilus; ii. Luther, married Agnes Blakey; iii. Jefferson; iv. James; v. Helen; vi. Dullina; vii. Rebecca; viii. Ella.

Rebecca South Hall Goodwin (Young, Samuel), born February 11, 1816, near Macon, Ga., was married March 14, 1837, in Bibb county, Ala., by Rev. D. H. Norwood, to Aquilla Miles Goodwin, who was born January 20, 1813, in Edgefield District, South Carolina, a son of Julius and Margaret (Kinnard) Goodwin, he a son of Theophilus Goodwin. By occupation he was a farmer, in politics a Whig, and in religion a Baptist. They resided in Selma, Ala., where Mrs. Rebecca S. H. Goodwin now (1897) lives. Her daughter, M. Gertrude, has furnished considerable data on behalf of Mrs. Rebecca S. H. Goodwin. *Goodwin* children: i. M. Gertrude, born May 17, 1840, married James J. Stewart; ii. Walter Young, born April 16, 1845; iii. Fitz Julius, born July 4, 1847, married Marie Stillé; iv. Margaret Mae, born May 15, 1850, married John D. Wilkins.

Mary Anne Goodwin (Samuel) was born May 7, 1780, in Franklin county, Ransomsbridge, N. C.; was married October 5, 1800, in Franklin county, by Rev. Joel Rivers, to Ira Portis, who was born November 17, 1777, in Nash county, Ransomsbridge, N. C., a son of John and Sarah (Wilder) Portis, who had moved from Isle of Wight county, Va., to Nash county, N. C. By occupation he was a farmer, in politics a Democrat, and in religion a Methodist. Portis children: i. Mary Anne, born January 13, 1807, married first, Samuel McColl; second, Nauphlet Goodwin; ii. Joseph Pernelle, born November 4, 1807; married Epsy Jennings O'Neal, September 2, 1826; was a judge in Alabama; removed to Texas in 1847, and died in 1848; he was a Royal Arch Mason; iii. Solomon Wilder, born August 12, 1810; married Julia Curtis, January 10, 1828; iv. Samuel Goodwin, born October 6, 1812; married first, Rebecca Torry in 1829, and second, Martha Gordon, on March 2, 1830; v. David Young, born April 5, 1814; married Rebecca Cuming February 8, 1846; was a judge in Texas when he died, in 1880; vi. Maria Henrietta, born January 10, 1812; married Nauphlet Goodwin May 6, 1831; vii. Lavinia, born November 16, 1815; died October 10, 1817; viii. John Wesley, born September 9, 1818; married Rebecca G. Rivers January 7, 1840; colonel of the Forty-second Alabama; wounded at Corirth; was in the siege of Vicksburg; surrendered, and paroled by Gen. U. S. Grant; lawyer and farmer; resides (1897) in Suggsville, Ala.

David Goodwin (Samuel) was married to Temperance Andrews. Perhaps David was only a half-brother to Young Goodwin and to Mary Anne (Goodwin) Portis. Children: i. Elijah, married Nancy Page; ii. Luan, married William Wilson; iii. Mary; iv. David, married Miss —— Pounds; v. Lorrain, married —— Carruther; vi. Temperance, married —— Pounds; vii. Henrietta, married —— Whately; viii. Andrew Jackson, married Susan Berry.

Andrew Jackson Goodwin (David, Samuel) was married at Selma, Ala., to Susan Berry, who was born in Selma. By occupation he was a clerk, in politics a Democrat, and in religion a Baptist. They resided in Selma, Ala., where Andrew died in October, 1896. Children: i. David T., resides in Anniston, Ala.; ii. James Berry, married Sally Boggs; iii. Minnie, married Isaac Eskew; iv. Robert Lee; v. Andrew Jackson; vi. Curran; vii. Jasmine.

NOTE.—The Samuel mentioned at the foot of page 123, Appendix Q., there stated to be untraced, is thought by Col. Portis to be Samuel Goodwin, his grandfather.

NOTES

ON THE YORK COUNTY, VIRGINIA, GOODWINS.

BY THE EDITOR.

It appears to be the popular belief that Virginia was settled by the emigrants who came with John Smith. But, as a matter of fact, a large majority of all who arrived previous to the Indian massacre of 1622 died from exposure, disease, or massacre. The real settlement of Virginia occurred during the civil wars in England. The majority of these were merchants and shipping people from the cities, who had little sympathy with the quarrels of either Puritans or Cavaliers, but who were interested in making money and securing comfortable homes. From this class came James Goodwin, of York county, descended from a line of merchants. While the tombstone of his first wife states that she had seven children, and while seven children survived their father, I am inclined to think that Robert and Martin were by the last wife, Blanche, as she mentions them in her will, and omits the other sons. The Robert, son of the first wife, probably died without issue. (See page 7.)

The connections of the Goodwins were highly respectable. The Moores, Mosses, Chismans, Reades, Robinsons, Tipladys, Beales, Nuttings, Calthorpes, Sheldons, etc., were all justices of the county, and three or more of their representatives were councillors of State.

Moores. This family begins with Augustine Moore about 1651. Augustine Moore owned Temple Farm at the surrender in 1781. (See article "Temple Farm," QUARTERLY, Vol. II., pp. 3–21.)

Mosses. This family begins with Edward Moss, and intermarried with all the leading families of the section. To a deed of his, the clerk affixes on the record a rough drawing of a shield, evidencing heraldic charges. Like the Goodwins, they were probably from London. (See letter of Richard Banckes, p. 142.)

Reades. James Goodwin married Mildred Reade, who was daughter of Robert Reade and Mary Lilly (daughter of John Lilly). Robert Reade was eldest son of Col. George Reade, once colonial Secretary for State of Virginia, and brother of Robert Reade, private secretary to his uncle, Sir Francis Windebank, Secretary of State to Charles I. The Reades traced far into English chronicles. (See QUARTERLY, Vol. II., p. 9; Vol. III., pp. 29, 40, 50; *Virginia Magazine of History and Biography*, Vol. IV., p. 204.) George Washington, commander of the United States Army, and General Thomas Nelson, commander of the Virginia forces at the surrender at Yorktown, were alike descended from Col. George Reade. There were in York county contemporaries of Col. George Reade, Benjamin Reade, and Francis Reade, and in Warwick county, Thomas Reade. Benjamin and Thomas are called "kinsmen" of Col. George Reade, in the records. Thomas Reade married Elizabeth Tiplady, sister of Captain John Tiplady, and had issue, Francis, who had Thomas, who had, probably, Thomas, of Elizabeth City county, father of Hawkins Reade, "cabinet maker and wheelright," who is connected with the Sheild, McCandlish, and Pescud Families. (See QUARTERLY, Vol. IV., p. 59.)

Chisman. Lieutenant-Colonel John Chisman, who came to Virginia in 1621, was one of the first settlers to take up land in York county. Chisman's Creek is named for him. He was a member of the Virginia Council. He returned to England and resided in the parish of St. Mary Magdalene, Bermondsea, county Surry. His brother, Edmund Chisman, remained behind, and his son, Major Edmund Chisman, was prominent in Bacon's Rebellion. The Virginia family is, however, descended from the second son, Captain Thomas Chisman, who married Elizabeth Reade, a daughter of Col. George Reade. (See QUARTERLY, Vol. I., pp. 89-99, for Chisman pedigree.)

Robinson. Mr. Hayden in his *Virginia Genealogies* gives an interesting pedigree of this family. One of Virginia's greatest lawyers was Conway Robinson, lately deceased.

Beale. (See page 9.) The family begins with Col. Thomas Beale, member of the Virginia Council, who was in York county as early as 1645. The late Gen. Richard Lee Turberville Beale, United States member of Congress and General in Confederate State's Army, was a descendant. For Beale, see QUARTERLY III., pp. 40, 65, 69; II., p. 25.

Nutting. Captain Thomas Nutting left no male descendants. His wife was Elizabeth Booth, daughter of William Booth, J. P., who was a son, I think, of Robert Booth, clerk of York county. For Booth, see QUARTERLY, Vol. II., p. 11, iv., p. 53; v., pp. 180, 266.

Calthorpe. This family began with Col. Christopher Calthorpe, who came to Virginia in 1622 He was son of Christopher Calthorpe, Esq., of Blakeney, in Norfolk county, England, who was a scion of one of the proudest families in England, being connected with Queen Elizabeth. (See QUARTERLY, Vol. II., pp. 106, *et seq.*, for Calthorpe pedigree.)

Sheldon. Captain William Sheldon must have been a relation of Gilbert Sheldon, Esq., of London, who executed a power of attorney to him about lands in Virginia in 1715. This Gilbert was son and heir of Daniel Sheldon, Esq., who owned lands in Virginia, and married Judith, daughter of Sir John Chapman, and widow of Sir Maurice Digges. (See QUARTERLY, Vol. II., p. 8.)

It is believed that the following abstracts from the records will be of special interest, as they will enable the reader to verify in great part the work of Judge Goodwin. The assessor's books, for instance, seem to show that Peter Goodwin, who married Frances Chapman, or Toomer, was, indeed, son of Captain John Goodwin, son of Col. John Goodwin. (See page 9.) These books prove that the tract that Robert I. Williams now lives on, twelve hundred acres on south side of Back Creek, was assessed to Harold Goodwin, who was preceded (before 1833) by Peter Goodwin (whose wife was Frances), and that this Peter succeeded about 1785 Captain John Goodwin, deceased. There was another tract on the other side of Back Creek (being one hundred and seven acres) in Charles parish, which in 1782 was assessed to John Goodwin, from whom it came to Peter Goodwin (called Peter Goodwin, Sr.), who died about 1824, and was succeeded by his son, Peter R. Goodwin, who married Mahala, and had two children. A sister of this Peter R. Goodwin, Virginia E., married John Curtis.

EXTRACTS FROM THE RECORDS, YORK COUNTY.

Deed of William Smith, citizen and weaver of London, appoints in his place Mr. John Tiplady, of York River, in Virginia, planter, to receive all sums, etc., due him by virtue of one writing in covenant from Moses Davies, in the penalty of 20 hogsheads of tobacco. (September 8, 1668.) Witnesses: John Smith, Wm Swinnerton, Tho. Swinnerton.

Nov ye 10th, 1670. Upon ye peticon of Mr Thomas Read as intermarrying with Elizabeth Tiplady, Mrs Ruth Tiplady Administratrix of Mr John Tiplady deced. Is ordered to deliver the said Read his full Estate in Right of his wife, due from her father's estate & [Read] to give Receipt of the same to aquitt the Administratrix.

LONDON, 10th August, 1678.

Mrs Ruth Tiplady

I have yo^{rs} wth a bill of exchange to receive of Jn Presson wch money you ordered to discharge another bill of exchange drawne on me. I severall tymes Demanded the money of said Presson wch he absolutely denyed soe have sent you the enclosed p^{test}. That bill you drawne on me I could do noe other then to deny that, haveing no money from Presson, but if you had given me order to pay it in case that had been denyed I would a done it in favour to you. If you had sent home tobacco it would have come to a good markett I sold my coz Mosses tobo at 6d.$\frac{1}{4}$ ℘ ℔. and it is now worth as much and I believe will beare a good price next year I shall be glad to serve you or any of yor friends

My service to yo^{r}selfe and sonne I am

Yo^{r} serv^{t} RICHARD BANCKES

Record^{r} March 19th 16$\frac{79}{80}$ ℘ R. A. Cl Cur [Richard Awborne, Clerk.]

Power of attorney from Thomas Reade to his friend and brother, John Smyth, 1675.

Will of John Smyth, of York county. Gives his land in New Kent, purchased of Capt. William Smyth,[1] of Bristol, to be equally divided between his two sons, Henry and John Smith; to his daughter Sarah Smyth land on Back Creek, in York county; his housing and land at a place called Walton, fifteen miles from London, to be sold, and the proceeds to be invested in negroes to stock his plantation in New Kent county; his plate to be sold after his decease and the proceeds to be converted into nails and axes for the benefit of the said plantation in New Kent; legacies of horses to his three children and to his daughter-in-law Ann Dixon, the wife of Richard Dixon, who is to have all her mother's apparel [from a subsequent order it appears that Ann Dixon's father was James Moore]; makes brothers Ralph Walker and John Rogers executors. Dated December 22, 1687; proved Feb. 24, 1687–'8.

Inventory of John Smyth deceased, £209 12*s.* 6*d.* Among the items "4 hhds of tob. which lyeth in the hands of Mr Tiplady in England."

[1] For will of Captain William Smith, see *New England Hist. and Gen. Register*, Vol. XLVII., p. 547.

[John Hethersall died in York county in 1679, and left a widow, Rebecca. —*Va. Mag. of Hist. and Biog.*, Vol. II.] Deed of Rebecca Hethersall for 25 pds. to John Tiplady, who is about to marry her daughter, Rebecca Wythe. Witnesses: John Wythe, Hen^r^y Watkins. Dated May 7, 1687; proved June 24, 1690.

Bond of Rebecca Wythe, of the county and parish of York, to Elizabeth Tiplady and Rebecca Tiplady, of the county and parish aforesaid, for £300, to be paid in London by bills of exchange when said Eliz. and Rebecca come of age or married. The condition is, that John Tiplady, being about to marry Rebecca Wythe, confirms a part of his personal estate to his said two daughters; but the bond is to be void if said Rebecca Wythe gives them each a young negro. Witnesses: Jno [X] Phillips, John Watkins. May 3, 1687.

Will of John Tiplady, "of the parish and county of York Octob^r^ ye 23 Day Anoq. Decem 1688." To each of my two daughters Elizabeth & Rebecca Tiplady equal parts of my estate according to an agreement with my wife before our marriage, dated May 3, 1687. And I divide equally between my wife Rebecca Tiplady and my daus. Elizabeth, Rebecca & Susanna Tiplady 25£ part of the half part of my Mother Hethersall's Estate confirmed with her hand, May 7, 1687, the said half part being my wife, Rebecca's portion, due at my mother Hethersall's decease, and said 25£ to be paid within 3 years after date of agreement. And for remainder of mother Hethersall's Estate it shall be divided between my wife and daughter Susanna & the child my wife goes with. My two daus., Elizabeth & Rebecca, to stay with my wife until 18 years or married unless any of their relatives are willing to keep them. To York parish a thousand pounds of tobacco or 5£ sterl to buy a piece of plate with my name Engraved thereon, said tobacco or money to be paid by my overseers 3 years after my decease. To my natural[1] mother Ruth Tiplady one horse called by the name of Graye which I had by the marriage of my late wife. To sister Elizabeth Lucas and each of my overseers 20*s.* to buy them rings. To John Read, son of Thomas Read deced, of Warwick county one gunn which he hath already in possession. If all my children die without heirs, give my land to Robert Lucas and Charles Lucas, sons of John Lucas of Warwick Co. [Wife executrix. Friends m^r^ Edward Mosse and m^r^ Robert Reade overseers of his will.] JOHN TIPLADY.

Witnesses: Charles Minnis, Hen: Watkins, Thomas [X] Warde. Proved November 10, 1689.

December ye 18th 1689. An order that Elizabeth Tiplady be possessed of one negro given to said E. T. by her grandfather, Col. Thomas Beale.

Inventory of the estate of Major James Goodwyne, deceased, appraised by Edward Moss, ffrancis Reade, John Sheldon, Ralph Walker, according to an order, dated 24th November, 1687, produced in court January 5, 1687–'88. Total amount, £542.16.00.

November 7, 1689. Mr Thomas Ballard ordered to pay Mr Peter Goodwyn a legacy given him by Major Robert Baldry.[2]

---

[1] "Natural mother" meant at this time "one's own mother," as opposed to mother by law.

[2] Robert Baldry came to Virginia in 1635, aged 18. He became a justice and Major. Peter Goodwin was his godson. (Hotten's *Emigrants to Virginia*, and York county records.)

Susannah Goodwin, spinster, gives a calf to her god-daughter, Susanna Leightenhouse, daughter of Mr. Robert Leightenhouse, November 2, 1691.

January 25, 1691–'92. On petition of Mr John and Mr Peeter Goodwyn for their shares of their father's estate in the hands of their mother-in-law,[1] Mrs Blanche Goodwyn, ordered that Capt. Thomas Ballard, Capt. Thomas Mountfort, and Mr Edward Moss meet at her house and adjust Major Goodwin's accounts.

"Wee whose names are hereunder written, haveing in obedience to an ord^{r} of Yorke Co^{rt} bearing date ye 25th of January, 1691–'92, app^{ed} at ye house of Madam Blanche Goodwyn to Audite ye Accounts & Estate of Majo^{r} James Goodwyn, lately deceased, and doe finde y^{t} ye said Goodwyn dyed seized of ye psonall Estate of five hundred forty-two pounds & sixteen shillings as ye said Estate was appraised, & y^{t} ye above James Goodwyn stood indebted att y^{t} time unto John Jeffryes, Esqr, of London, Merchant, ye full sume of Three hundred seventy-two pounds, three shillings, five pence, And y^{t} after ye said debt is paid there remaines due to every childs pte ye full sume of Twenty-one pounds, six shillings, seven pence, there being seven children and ye widdow, and this wee make report of According to ye above ordo^{r} to ye Co^{rt}. Witnesse our hands this 4th day of ffeb^{ry}, 1691–'92.

"THO. BALLARD, THO. MOUNTFORT,

"EDWARD MOSS."

Will of John Aduston names wife Elizabeth, daughter Jane Rogers, wife of John Rogers; grandchildren Richard, Agnes and Elizabeth Dixon. Dated January 17, 1677.

An indenture between John Rogers, who married Agnes, daughter of Joane Adleston [Aduston], relict of John Adleston, deceased, and guardian to Adleston Rogers, his son, by Agnes, his wife, and Col. Thomas Beale. Recorded June 24, 1687.

Will of Richard Dixon names son James Dixon, wife Damazinah[2] Dixon, daughters Agnes, Rebecca and Anne, mother Agnes Rogers; to daughter Ann my brick house with yard, housing and orchard thereto belonging so far as a house commonly known and called the Hill house, 20 shillings apiece for rings to mother Agnes Rogers and Thomas Nutting. Proved January 24, 1706.

John Goodwin, churchwarden of Yorke parish, 1694.

ffeb^{ry} 24th, 1697–'98. M^{r} peter Goodwin's Deed of sail from Mr Robert Goodwin & Ann his wife was this day proved by acknol^{nt} in Co^{rt} to the said Peter, and is ordord to record.

November 24th, 1698. Peter Goodwin & Rebecka, his wife, daughter and Legatee of John Tiplady, deceased, Arresting William Watkins & Rebecka his wife, Adm^{r} of ye last will & Testament of John Tiplady, deceased, to this Co^{rt} in an account upon ye case for one-fourth part of ye Testat^{rs} estate amounting to ye sume of nineteen pounds, five shillings and three pence or thereabouts, & ye Def^{ts} failing to appe & answere y same ordo^{r} is granted ag^{t}. Capt

[1] Mother-in-law meant then step-mother.

[2] First wife was Ann Rogers.

Thomas Barbar, High sherr and ye next Cort to be Confirmed, if he causeth not ye said Deft then to appe & answere ye same.

Will of Ruth Tiplady [her marke and seal], proved November 24, 1698. Aged and infirm; daughter Elizabeth Lucas, grandsons John Read, Thomas Read, John Smyth; granddaughters Redley (?), Elizabeth Lucas, Margaret Lucas, Ruth Roscow, Sarah Vauson, Sarah Smyth and Susanna Tiplady; gives to William James "if he stayes to finish ye Crop, one cow calfe & hee to be cloathed from head to foot, and if tobaccoe bee made" 30 shillings shall be raised to buy rings for Henry Smyth, John Lucas & Elizabeth Powell.

Deed from Matthew Tiplady, of London, merchant, appointing his loveing unkle, Mr Jon Goodwin, of ye pish & county of Yorke, gent, his attorney, to make sale of all goodes as I shall at my departure out of the Collony of Virga leave with him, &c. 21 febry, 1695. Witnesses: John Rogers, Adduston Rogers, Thomas Rogers. Proved in court May 24th, 1699.

Mr John Goodwin, justice. 1699.

July ye 24th, 1701. Mrs Eliz. Goodwin granted admn of ye Estate of her deceased husband, Capt John Goodwin, who dyed without will, Mr Robt Goodwin, Mr John Wyth & Mr Jon Moore, securities.

Inventory and Appraismt of the estate of Capt. Jno Goodwin, deceased the 15th day of August, 1701, by Edward Moss, Jno Rogers, Thos Chisman, junr, William Watkins. Total value, £339, 5., 3. [Among the items: 1 Large Looking glass, 1 old silver Tankard, 2 old silver spoons, a large Tumbler, a large dram cup, and a money box; 1 large seale Ring, 1 cain wth an old silver head, 60lb of wool at 6d, 35 head of old and young cattle, valued at 61£, 5., 5., 8 calves at 10s, 30 old & young sheep, 2 negro men (Capt & Dick, 60 £); 3 negro women, Lucy, Rachell & ffranck, £84; 3 negro children (Humprey I., Sam, and ——, £45). Not included in the inventory were several bills due the estate, and a parcell of hoggs in ye wood.

Will of Blanche Goodwyn, "of Yorke Parish, in the County of Yorke, widow": one hhd of sweet-scented tobacco to daughter Elizabeth Blinkhorn; to grandchildren James & Elizabeth Duke, one cow apiece and "all the rest of my estate I give to my 2 sons Robert and Martyn Goodwyn to be equally divided," and make them my exors. Dated September 22, 1701.

Signed,

Her
BLANCHE B GOODWYN.
Mark.

Witness: James Sclater, Jn Morris, Sarah Brown.

Deed of Peter Goodwin, of ye parish and county of York, and Robert Goodwin and Anne his wife, of ye pish of Hampton in ye county of York, the latter for 10 pds sterling sell to former Waronimcock Island, on the north side of Pamunkey River, in ye upper part of King and Queen, formerly called Pamunkey Neck. 11 Nov., 1695. Rec. ffebry 24th, 1697. Witnesses: John Goodwyn, Matthew Goodwyn, and Martin Goodwin.

Alice Beale, "widow and exx of my husband Col. Thomas Beale, of the parish and county of York, deceased, out of the natural love and affection she bears her grandson Peter Goodwin," all her lands on Back Creek in the parish and county of York, to him the said Peter Goodwin and his wife's life, and after their decease to redound to my grandson Thomas Beale, of Rappahannock, and his heirs, male, but if he die without heirs, male, then the said land to be to the use of my grandson Peter Goodwin. And as to my personal estate in general unto my said grandson Peter Goodwin, excepting my bed and one negro girl that now waits upon me, hee paying me 600 pds of tobacco and caske to buy me necessaryes to support my old age, as also the said Peter Goodwin to find me with sufficient cloathing during my life, and pay all my debts, and to keep me from all the incumbrances of the world. This 23 September, 1702.

Her
ALICE X BEALE.
Mark.

Signed in the presence of John Rogers, John Aduston Rogers.
Rec. September 24, 1702.

Novemb^r^ ye 29th, 1702. Mary Banks, a mulatto and servant to Martin Goodwin, did this day in open court bind over her daughter Hannah Banks, a mullatto, unto M^r^. Peter Goodwin, wth him to dwell and serve untill shee attain unto the age of twenty-one years; and it is ordered that hee, the said Peter Goodwin, see the child baptized into ye Christian ffaith, and (as soon as she comes to maturity) to teach, or cause to be taught, her ye creed, ye Lords prayer, and the ten commandments in the vulgar tongue, if shee be capeable to attaine unto ye same, and 'tis further ordered that at the end or expiration of the said terme of twenty-one yeares to pay his said servant Hanah Banks three barrells of Indian corne and cloathing according to law.

Isaac Steele, commander of the ship *Reformacon* belonging to Whitehaven, makes over to Martin Goodwin one servant named Charles Roane, belonging to the city of Dublin, in Ireland, to serve 6½ years in consideration of 1500 pds of sweet-scented tobacco and caske in hand. Dated 24 April, 1703. Proved May 24, 1703.

Will of John Morce[1]: To wife the use of plantation during life if she be not with child, but if she be with child the use only till my child is of age and half of it afterwards. Should the child die my lands shall fall to Martin Goodwin and Dixon Nailor, the two sons of my two sisters; viz., after the decease of my wife. To Elizabeth Nailor, daughter of Dixon Nailor, £10 sterling. To dear wife all personal and movable estate after debts are paid. Wife sole exec. June 6, 1702. Proved July 24, 1702.
Test: Philip Moody, Robert X Roberts, William Hansford.

Will of Alice Beale, "of the parrish and county of York, widdow of Thomas Beale, Esquire,[2] late of the said Parrish and county in ye Collony of Virginia, being weak in body but in sound and perfect mind and memory, praised be God," desires to be buried in her garden upon ye plantacon I now dwell at and neare the grave of my late deceased husband as possible; to grandson Thomas

[1] The name Morce is not the same as Moss. John Morce was son of Mrs. Jane Morce and left a child David (posthumous), as appears from a subsequent deed. It would seem from this will that Blanche Goodwin was Blanche Morce before she married Maj. James Goodwin.

[2] In the early part of this century only the members of the council were called "esquire."

Beale one shilling sterling money of England; to granddaughter Elizabeth Powell and her two children each of them one shilling sterling; to great-grandson Thomas Reade, son of ffrancis Reade, the sum of 25 pds sterling to be paid at 18 years by Peter Goodwin, one of my executors; to my great-grandson Benjamin Reade, son of Francis Reade, 25 lbs. sterling at 18 years to be paid by Sarah Brown, one of my executors; either dying the survivor to enjoy both legacies, and if both die before 18, then the 2 legacies to be to the proper use of my executors; loving Cousin Robert Jones a heifer; various legacies of beds, negroes, etc., to grandson Peter Goodwin; to Cousin Sarah Brown, wife of William Brown, 2 negroe women, etc., and household furniture, and the plantation known as the "Bay Trees," containing 200 acres, which my deceased husband Col. Thomas Beale, Esquire, was possessed with, and to her heirs, and for want of such heirs the same to Peter Goodwin my grandson and his heirs; to Cousin Sarah Brown, wife of William Brown, the plantation on Back Creek about 300 acres, during her life and after her death to my said grandson Peter Goodwin. My grandson Peter Goodwin is to have at all times egress and regress for his or their stock, to feed and range upon y^{e} "Bay Trees" plantation. Grandson Peter Goodwin and loving Cousin Sarah Brown to be executors of this will.

Signm.
ALICE § § B BEALE. [Y^{e} Seal.]

Signed, sealed, and published in psents of Hugh Owen, John Walker,
Signm. Signm.
Samuel Cooper, Thomas E Edmuns, Elizabeth R Ridge. Proved ffeb. 24, 1702.

Jno Rogers, of York-Hampton pish, his gift to Elizabeth Goodwyn, ye eldest daughter of Martin Goodwyn[1] and Barbara his wife, one negro girl about 2 years old, named Lucy; should she die before age or marriage, then I, the aforesaid Jn . Rogers, in the parish, etc., give the said Lucy to all the rest of my grandchildren that now or shall be born of my daughter Goodwin's body according to priority of years. Martin Goodwin, Dixon Naylor. Acknowledged October 8, 1713.

September 19, 1715. Ann Goodwin permitted to keep an ordinary at Gabriel Maupin's house in Williamsburg. Securities: Philip Moody and William Hansford.

Will of Capt. Thomas Nutting, of Charles parish in ye county of York: Gives his daughter Jane Nutting the plantation where I now dwell and her heirs, failing such then to my granddaughter Elizabeth Sclater and her heirs; the plantation at the head of Charles river to his daughter Katherine Sheldon, and if she dies without issue, then to my son-in-law William Sheldon. To daughter Eliz^{a} Doswell a negro and a negro girl, one silver cann, and an equal share of my cattle I have in the Islands; to son-in-law Capt. William Sheldon my seal ring, cane and sword; 4 choice negroes to my daughter Jane Nutting, and after my wife's share is taken out, one good feather bed and all furniture to it, my riding horse called ffox and all my money in England, in whose hands soever, and four cows. In case my daughter Mary Sclater dies before division, her estate to go to her 3 children Elizabeth, Agnes, and Mary. Son-in-

[1] From this it appears that Martin Goodwin (p. 7) married Barbara Rogers, daughter of John Rogers.

law Capt. William Sheldon and Jane Nutting, executors. Dated July 11, 1717 Proved September 18, 1717.

Will of Martin Goodwin, dated May 12, 1718. To daughter Elizabeth 5 shillings & to every one of my children 5s A piece. His wife, Barbara Goodwin, to have the whole care, and to be executrix. Witnesses: William Moss, Jno. Cary, Peter Goodwin. Proved March 16, 1718–'19.

Will of Elizabeth Goodwin, widow, of the parish of Yorkhampton,[1] in the county of York, in the Colony of Virginia. To daughter Elizabeth Moss a negro girl, six silver spoons marked E. G., six steers, & 1 hhd of Leafe Tobacco 700 neat & all my wearing apparell; to son James Goodwin, 4 negroes, old silver porringer, one dram cup marked J. G., one old silver spoon marked J. G.; to daughter Rachel Wise, 4 negroes & one silver tumbler marked J. T. & one hhd of Leafe tobacco 700 neat & p^{r} of blue China Curtains & Vallins, the best bed bolster, blankett, pillows & rugg; to son John Goodwin, 4 negroes, the 3d best bed bolster, blankets, rugg & pillows & one silver tankard marked E. G. To Susanna Goodwin, 4 negroes, the second best bed, bolster, blankett, Rugg & pillows, six silver spoons marked with E. G. & one young sorrell horse with my riding saddle & bridle. All my tobacco in England and all that shall hereafter be left to be equally divided between my 3 children, Rachel Wise, John Goodwin, & Susanna Goodwin. All the rest of my estate to be equally divided between my 5 children Eliz^{a} Moss, James Goodwin, Rachel Wise, John Goodwin, & Susanna Goodwin. John Goodwin and Rachel Wise, executors. Witnesses: William [X] Hillsman, Rebecca [R] Goodwin, Peter Goodwin. Dated December 23, 1718; proved March 16, 1718–'19.

In the action of trespass upon the case between Mildred Goodwin (late Mildred Reade) vs Robert Philippson. March 21, 1719–'20.

Will of James Goodwin, in the year of our Lord 1719, September 21. "I, James Goodwin of the parish of York Hampton." Gives his property to his child, if his wife should prove with one; otherwise, to his brother and sisters, John Goodwin, Rachel Wise, and Susanna Goodwin. His brother John Goodwin is "to keep the estate, to have the use of the land, wasting no timber nor clearing no ground, keeping the old fields cleared; to school and bring up the child." Proved November 16, 1719. (See page 8.)

Will of Richard Slater, of Charles parish, names daughters Elizabeth, Agnes, and Mary Slater; his children to remain till of age with their grandmother, their uncle and aunt William Sheldon and Katherine, his wife; and their uncle and aunt, John and Jane Lowry. Appoints as executors William Sheldon, Elizabeth Nutting, and Katherine Sheldon. Proved November 17, 1718.

Lawrence Smith & Mildred his wife, late Mildred Goodwin, complts., vs. John Goodwin, ex^{or} of James Goodwin, deced., &c. 1720.

Will of John Doswell, jr., of Charles parish, in York county. Names sons Edward, John, and Thomas Doswell. To his son Edward, one silver tankard marked J. D., one gold ring posy "in Christ & thee my comfort be," one pair silver shoe-buckles; to son John, my silver-hilted sword marked J. D. on the hilt, one

---

[1] The two parishes of York and Hampton were united in 1706, and called York-Hampton.

gold ring marked P. S., and all my silver shirt-buttons, seven pair, one silver brooch, and one negro boy; to Thomas Doswell, a silver cane marked T N E,[1] one large-sight square-barrel gun; names father, John Doswell, wife Elizabeth, and friend Thomas Chisman. Dated April 25, 1718; proved December 15, 1718.

Will of Elizabeth Reade [widow of Col. George Reade], proved January 24, 1686–'7. Names sons Robert, Francis, Thomas, and Benjamin—the two last under age; daughter Elizabeth Chisman, and grandchildren, Mildred, Elizabeth, and Thomas Chisman; son Mr. Thomas Chisman, Mr. Edward Moss, and Mr. Thomas Barber made overseers to see her will performed.

Will of Mary Read [mutilated]. Legacies to children, of my large silver tankard, silver porringer, silver tumbler, and silver spoons; names sons Francis, John, and Samuel; granddaughter Mary Nelson, and grandson William Nelson. Makes son John sole executor, and desires Mr. Benjamin Reade and Thomas Reade to be trustees of her will. Proved November 20, 1722.

Will of Robert Reade, of York-Hampton parish, names children: John, of King and Queen county; Margaret, wife of Thomas Nelson; Thomas, George, Samuel and Mildred. Division to be made of 745 acres (bought of my son John Reade) being in St. Stephen's parish, King and Queen county, between my three sons, George, Samuel, and Francis Reade, when George comes of age, by Mr. John Baylor, Mr. Thomas Nelson,[2] Capt Law. Smith, brothers Benjamin and Thomas Reade, and my son John Reade. Wife, Mary Reade. Bro. Thomas Reade, Cosen Capt Lawrence Smith, & my son-in-law Mr. Thomas Nelson, appointed overseers of this will. Proved March 16, 1712.

Will of Thomas Chisman[3] names children, Ann, Mildred, George, Thomas, and Elizabeth, to each of whom he gives a negro girl; names Edmund, another son, to whom he gives one feather bed and furniture, six head of female cattle, and other stock; similar legacy to son John. "I give 57£ 16*s.* & 10 pence in hands of Micajah Perry, merchant of London—30£ thereof to son Edmund, the residue to son John." Residue of estate to wife for life, and after her decease, to children Ann, Mildred, George, Thomas, and Elizabeth, except my silver-hilted sword, my long gun, and my little paper trunk, which I give to my son Edmund Chisman; and my two Guns called Warner, and old little gun, which I give to my son George Chisman, and my short gun to my son Thomas. Wife, Ann Chisman, executrix, and son Edmund executor. Dated November —, 1722; codicil obliterated, dated November 6, 1722; will proved January 21, 1722–'23.

On the petition of Aduston Rogers and Mary Wagstaff, widow of Basil Wagstaff, deceased, setting forth that the said Rogers and her husband were securitys for Barbara Goodwin's faithful admin. of ye estate of Martin Goodwin, her deceased Husband, and said Barbara having since intermarried with one John Powers [ordered that, on petitioners giving sufficient bond, the es-

---

[1] Evidently Thomas and Elizabeth Nutting.

[2] Grandfather of General Thomas Nelson.

[3] This Thomas Chisman was son of Captain Thomas Chisman (who died in 1715), and grandson of Edmund Chisman, who settled with his brother, Lieutenant-Colonel John Chisman, in York county.

tate of said orphans to be surrendered to them]. May 18, 1724. John Powers appeared in court.

March 17, 1728, John Goodwin's peticon against a Road into his neck is continued till next court.

Will of Rev. Jas. Sclater.[2] Legacies of negroes and a hundred pounds apiece to each of his daughters, Martha Sclater and Mary Tabb, names sons John and James, to the last of whom he gives one silver tankard, one pair of hand-irons, and one-half of my books; the other half of my books I give to son John Sclater, excepted those I have given to my wife. A codicil mentions that Martha Sclater has married John Brody. Proved August 17, 1724.

Will of James Sclater,[3] of York county. Eldest son Richard Sclater, mother Mary Sclater his other son, William Sheldon. Captain William Sheldon appointed executor May 15, 1727.

Will of Elizabeth Doswell[4]; names sons Thomas Doswell and Edward Doswell, daughter Elizabeth, grandson John Moss; makes sister Katherine Sheldon, executrix. Proved January 15, 1727.

Will of Capt Wm. Sheldon[5]; his wife Katherine to have his whole estate for life, and then to go to William Sheldon [Sclater] and his next of kin, to remain in the name of Sheldon forever, legacies to Agnes Sclater and Mary Sclater, to cousin Elizabeth Conier, cousin Mary Lansdale, and daughter Anne Pamer; 2 bbls. Indian corn to Anne Sutherland, she alway so fetch it away yearly before Christmas. In case of William Sheldon [Sclater] dying without heirs, I lend my estate to Mary Sclater for life, daughter of Richard Sclater. Proved May 15, 1727.

November 17, 1727. Elizabeth Goodwin[6] prays an order for her estate in the hands of Albritton Wagstaffe.

August 18, 1730.

The action upon the case between Benjamin Catton and John Porter Goodwin,[7] is dismissed.

November 15, 1731.

On the petition of John Goodwin and Elizabeth, his wife, ag[t] Robert Armistead, the settlement of the estate of John Doswell is admitted to Record, &c.

Will of Peter Goodwin, of York-Hampton parish, in the county of York. Legacies to son John, grandson John Goodwin [under age], daughter Anne,

---

[1] The neck between Wormeley's Creek and Back Creek is still called Goodwin's Neck.

[2] Minister of New Pocoson, or Charles Parish.

[3] Son of Rev. James Sclater, next above.

[4] Daughter of Captain Thomas Nutting, and wife of John Doswell, Jr., of York county.

[5] Captain Wm. Sheldon married Katherine Nutting, daughter of Captain Thomas Nutting. She married, secondly, Robert Armistead, son of Anthony Armistead, of Elizabeth City county, brother of Col. John Armistead, of the council. (See Armistead pedigree, beginning with July QUARTERLY, 1897.)

[6] This Elizabeth Goodwin was not, as I take it, a daughter of Captain John Goodwin, but of Martin Goodwin. (See page 9.)

[7] This name confirms the suggestion on page 6, that Rachel Goodwin's mother was a Porter.

son Peter, his land in King William county, known by the name of Warranimcock Island, to son James for life, half the highland of the same within the swamp, paying to his brother half the quit rent; daughter Rachel Goodwin, grandson Peter Goodwin, wife Rebecca Goodwin, daughter Ann Goodwin, cozen John Goodwin. Dated 3 October, 1731. Pr. March 20, 1731-'2. Witnesses John Worledge.

Rebecca Goodwin's executor's bond, security John Goodwin and Edward Moss, dated March 20, 1731-'2, in the penalty of £1,000 sterling.

Report of Lawrence Smith, Tho[s] Nelson and Philip Lightfoot, appointed to settle the estate of John Doswell, deceased, that the share of Eliz[a] Doswell, who lately intermarried with John Goodwin, the younger, is 55 Pounds curr[t] money, and Robert Armistead, Gent. in behalf of that Estate agreed to pay that sum. 13 November 1731. (Page 10.)

February 19, 1732. In the action of debt between Matthew Goodwin, plf. and Wm. Hansford, Deft., the Deft. being dead the suit is abated.

John Goodwin sworn cornet to Capt. Rogers' troop; John Goodwin, jr., appointed constable, February 17, 1734-'5; John Goodwin, one of the justices, 1739, etc.

John Goodwin produces his commission as sheriff. Edmund Smith and Robert Sheild, his securities. July 21, 1740.

Robert Goodwin, aged 33, in 1736, his affidavit.

At a court for York county, &c., May 15, 1738. Peter Goodwin and Mary, his wife, one of the daughters, and Starkey Robinson, grandson of John Robinson, deceased, by Judith Robinson, widow, his next friend, plfs., *vs.* Mary Robinson, widow, and admix. of said John Robinson, and Anthony Robinson, infant grandson and heir of the said John, defts, &c. (Page 13.)

Will of Elizabeth Nutting,[1] of the parish of Charles, in the county of York, widow, being very aged and infirm, to grandson Robert Armistead, son of Robert Armistead and Catherine, his wife, the tract of land where she now lives, legacies to grandson Booth Armistead, to Elizabeth Rogers, daughter of Adduston Rogers & Catherine, his wife, grandson William Lowry, granddaughter Angelica Armistead. To Robert Armistead, my grandson as aforesaid, her silver tankard; granddaughter Elizabeth Goodwin, my seal-skin trunk; to each of her grandchildren and great grandchildren under 14 years, 20 shillings to be paid in current money, except my grandson Richard Sclater, to whom I give my half-pint silver can; grandsons Thomas Doswell, Edward Doswell, granddaughter Elizabeth Moore, to youngest son lately born of William Lowry & Jane his wife, my silver pint can, on condition that he be christened Thomas Nutting, otherwise I give the can to grandson, Booth Armistead. All residue of estate to daughter Catherine Armistead for the benefit of her 3 children, Booth, Robert and Angelica. To Frances Armistead, daughter of Ellyson Armistead, 20 s. to buy her a ring. To Elizabeth Lowry, my negro boy called James. Catherine Armistead sole ex .

---

1 She was the wife of Captain Thomas Nutting.

Witnesses: Thomas Kerby, James Kerby, James Manson. Dated September 13, 1733. Proved September 15, 1735.

March 15, 1741: In the suit in chancery between Peter Goodwin and Mary[1] his wife; Frances Calthorpe and Mary Calthorpe, spinsters, infants under the age of 21 years, by the said Peter and Mary their guardians, Plaintiffs, vs. James Calthorpe, Defendant, Ordered that the line determined by Francis Heyward and Danl Moore, Gent, in company with the surveyor of this county be the established line of division. (Page 13.)

February 18, 1744. James Goodwin exhibited an account of the estate of Thomas Chisman, an orphan. Appointed surveyor of the roads.

John Goodwin, a justice of the Peace, 1744.

Will of Peter Goodwin, of Charles Parish, "in the county of York, being very sick," etc. To son John all my landes in King William county, and my other parcel of land in York county bought of Wm. Sheldon Sclater; to him also my silver Tankard and my silver-hilted sword and my new arms. Legacies of negroes, etc., to daughters Rebecca, Mary, Ann Goodwin, and to son John all the residue of my estate. My exors to have the rents of my lands and property to bring up and school my children, & my son John to have the benefit of his part of the estate when he comes of age, and my daughters to have their parts when they come of age or marry. Appoints brother John Goodwin executor. Witnesses: Seymour Powell, Thos Charles, John Goodwin. September 8, 1747. Proved 21 September, 1747. (Page 13.)

Will of Rebecca Goodwin, of York-Hampton Parish. Legacies of plate and negroes to son John Goodwin, and his brother James Goodwin, granddaughters Rebecca Goodwin and Alice Goodwin, daughters of Capt. John Goodwin, daughter Rachel Charles, son Peter Goodwin's three daughters, Rebecca, Mary & Anne Goodwin, grandson Peter Goodwin. Rest of estate to be divided into 5 parts: 3 parts to my children John Goodwin, Rachel Charles & James Goodwin; & the other two parts, one for my daughter Anne Goodwin's two daughters, Rebecca Goodwin & Alice Goodwin, to be divided at age; but if either should die, her part to go to grandson John Goodwin, son of Capt. John Goodwin, & the other part to be divided between my son Peter Goodwin's 3 daughters as aforesaid. My 2 sons John & James Goodwin executors. Dated September 12, 1748. Proved 21 November, 1748. Witnesses: William Aduston Rogers, Elizabeth X Burcher, Barbary Aduston X Rogers.
Her mark. Her mark.

Settlement of the Estate of Rebecca Goodwin, by which it appears that Capt. John Goodwin for Rebecca & Alice Goodwin received one-fifth part of the estate = £56, 19, 9; Jno Goodwin, jr., received one-fifth, James Goodwin the same, Thos Charles for his wife one-fifth part, and Rebecca Goodwin, Mary Goodwin & Ann Goodwin received one-fifth part. February 20, 1748.

Will of Sheldon Goodwin, of the county of York. To Constance Goodwin, his wife, all his estate. Witnesses: H. Wythe, Edw. Wright, Mary Wythe. Dated September 5, 1751. Proved December 16, 1751.

---

[1] She was Mary Robinson and married, first, Elimelech Calthorpe (son of James, son of James, son of Christopher Calthorpe, who came to Virginia about 1622).

Will of James Goodwin, of York-Hampton parish. Legacy of slaves, money and his silver-hilted sword to his son John Goodwin; to son Peter my land in King William county, six negroes, silver tankard and £35; son Robert Goodwin the half of my land in Louisa, half the water mill & 5 negroes, a bed, etc., and half my stock that is on the plantation at my death; to son James the other half of my land in Louisa and the other half of my water mill & 5 negroes, as well as the other half of my stock on the land in Louisa at my death, with one bed & furniture. To daughter Rebecca 2 negroes and £200 current money at age or marriage, & one feather bed & furniture and my young mare; to daughter Elizabeth Goodwin a similar legacy; to daughter Diana a similar legacy; to daughter Rachel a similar legacy; gives to Ann Chisman 2 young negroes for life. Residue of estate to wife, Elizabeth Goodwin, for life, to be disposed of at her death, but if she should marry, then to be divided between my wife and six daughters, Rebecca, Elizabeth, Diana, Rachel Goodwin, Mary Moss & Ann Chisman. Elizabeth Goodwin sole ex[x]. Proved December 14, 1757. Witnesses: John Goodwin, James Goodwin.

Appraisement of James Goodwin's Estate in York,	£1986	9	0
" " " " King William,	323	16	8
" " " " Louisa,	597	0	0

Will of John Goodwin "in the year 1759, March 2[d], of the parish and county of York, weak in body." Lends to his son John his plantation in Hanover county if he allows my wife the liberty of living there as long as she lives; my widow to bring up my children, and at the marriage of my wife I give the land in Hanover to my son James Goodwin. To son John nine negroes for life, & at his death to be divided between my two granddaughters, Frances & Mary Goodwin, daughters of John Goodwin; legacies of negroes to children: James, Thomas, Peter, Rebecca, Susanna, Mary, Anne, Reuben, Alice; to wife the cattle & sheep on the plantation whereon I now live, except my silver-hilted sword & one silver spoon, which I give to my son John Goodwin. My stock in King William county of cattle & hogs is to be sold, & if there is any overplus after settling my brother Peter's estate, the said overplus to go to my wife. If any of my children who are under age should die before age, their part or parts to be divided equally among the survivors, excluding my eldest son, John Goodwin, etc. Wife & son John Goodwin executors. Proved May 21, 1759. Witnesses: James Goodwin, Elizabeth X Moss, Rebecca Goodwin. (Page 10.)

The settlement of the estate June 16, 1760, reported:

By the am't of the Personal Est. as p[r] acc[t] in King William county,	£ 534	0	0
By Do in Hanover county,	217	0	0
By Do in York county,	1672	18	10
By a silver-hilted sword, omitted in the appraisement,	1	0	0

John Goodwin, orphan of Peter Goodwin, in account with John Goodwin, his guardian. Mentions "*suit* vs. *my brother, James Goodwin.*" 1748.

Robert Goodwin, orphan of James Goodwin, deceased. "By your net proceeds of the plantation in Louisa ℘ Mrs. Eliz[a] Goodwin." 1759.

Ann Goodwin, orphan of Peter Goodwin.

James Goodwin, orphan of James. Eliz^a Goodwin, guardian. 1762.

Peter Goodwin's will. (Record mutilated.) To my honored Father two negroes, also my large silver shoe and knee-buckles, and my saddle and housing; to brother John Goodwin, also two negroes and all my wearing clothes; to nephew John Goodwin, son of my sister Rebecca, 2 negroes; to sister Rebecca Goodwin, my desk and two tables, all my tea ware and my plain gold ring, and a piece of fine Irish linen, if my goods arrive safe from London; nephew Jno. Chisman, son of my cousin Diana Chisman, £15 current money; all the remainder of my estate to my cousins Anne Moss, Elizabeth Moss, and Lucy Moss, daughters of my deceased sister, Elizabeth Moss. Proved December, 1763. (Son of Col. John Goodwin, page 8.)

Will of John Goodwin, of York-Hampton parish, in the county of York. To son J—— the plantation where I now live and to his heirs, and for want of such heirs, then to my grandson John Goodwin and his heirs, and for want of such heirs, to my grandson Martin Goodwin and his male heirs, and if he should die without such issue, then it to return to my lawful heirs forever; to grandson Jno. Moss a small tract I lately purchased of Wm. Moss and Robert Smith, upon condition that he pay to my executor on arriving at age £40 to the use of my estate, but if he should die, then my grandson, Sheldon Moss, to have the estate on the same terms; 20 shillings to grandson John Moss for a ring; names son John Goodwin and 3 granddaughters. . . . ner and Lucy Moss; names Rebecca Goodwin, son-in-law James Goodwin, of Hanover county; my 3 granddaughters, Diana Chisman, Elizabeth Toomer, and Lucy Moss. The parts of my two grandsons, John Goodwin and Martin Goodwin, to be kept in the hands of my son John Goodwin until they arrive of age, and appoints my son John Goodwin ex'or. September 10, 1766. Proved February 16, 1767.

Teste: Francis Brown, Edward Wright, John Aduston Rogers.

Division of John Goodwin's estate agreeable to an order of York court, bearing date 16 February 1767: (Mutilated.)

To the heirs of Rebecca Goodwin, deceased, daughter of the deceased, 12 negroes,				£367	10	0
To the heirs of Elizabeth Moss, deceased, decedent's, daughter, 12 negroes,				360	10	0
John Goodwin's negroes, value,	£362	0	0			
To receive from the heirs of Rebecca Goodwin, deceased,	1	6	8			
	363	6	8			
The heirs of Rebecca Goodwin, deceased, their negroes' value,	367	10	0			
To pay to the other two parties,	4	3	4			
	363	6	8			
The heirs of Edward Moss, deceased, the negroes' value,	360	10	0			
To receive from the heirs of Rebecca Goodwin, dec'd,	2	16	8			
	363	6	8			

The negroes belonging . . . Elizabeth Moss, deceased's daughter, &c., -------------------- £360 10 0

. . . . .

To Dianna Chisman, daughter of Elizabeth Moss, deceased, &c., --------------------

To Elizabeth Toomer, daughter of Edward Moss, deceased, --------------------

To Lucy Moss, daughter of Eliz[a] Moss, deceased, ----

Will of Eliza Moss names sons John, Sheldon, daughter Diana Chisman, Elizabeth Moss, and Diana and Lucy Moss, son-in-law Thomas Chisman. Dated 1760.

Will of Mary Sclater,[1] cousin Martha Cary, granddaughter Mary Sclater, grandson William Sclater, who is to have his father's picture now in my possession; all cattle and sheep to John Tabb,[2] except what are marked for my granddaughter Martha Brodie; granddaughters Mary Tabb and Mary Brodie (under age) all my silver plate; husband James Sclater, deceased, Mary Tabb's sister Elizabeth; names Rachael Tabb, Mary Brodie's sister, Martha, names Sarah Brodie, grandson Richard Slater, and his brother William Sheldon Sclater, Jr., granddaughter Rachel Tabb; equal parts to the children of James Sclater, John Tabb, and John Brodie. May 27, 1737; July 21, 1744.

[Mrs. Elizabeth Goodwin, of York county, advertises for a mare. Deliver her to Mr. Thomas Doswell, of Hanover county, or to Mr. David Jameson, of York county.—*Virginia Gazette*, 1771.]

John Goodwin, jr., exor. of John Goodwin, Gent., and likewise his eldest son and heir—deed to John Moss. Acknowl[d] Sept. 21, 1772.

The estate of Col. John Goodwin, deceased, settled June 11, 1774, by Aaron Phillips, Edmund Curtis, William A. Rogers.

Among the items:

To John Goodwin, Jun[r], account, --------------------	£ 5	16	11
To balance due Peter Goodwin's estate, --------------------	3	1	10½
To John Goodwin for the trouble and expence he has been at in collecting, --------------------	6	10	0
Contra.			
By cash of Martin Goodwin, --------------------	2	10	0
By cash received of John Moss for the land bought of Moss & Smith, --------------------	40	0	0
By balance to Cap[t] John Goodwin by discharging the aforesaid debts, --------------------	49	17	7

The estate of Peter Goodwin, deceased, with the estate of Col[o] John Goodwin, deceased, 1774. (Son of Col. John Goodwin.)

Will of Elizabeth Goodwin (dated August 2, 1780, proved 17 June, 1782) of the county of York, in the parish of York-Hampton. To granddaughter Elizabeth Pescud, 50 pds. due me from Mr. Pescud for the mill rent. To grandson Edward Moss, 50 lbs. current money; to granddaughter Mary Hob-

[1] Widow of Rev. James Sclater.

[2] Col. John Tabb, of Elizabeth City county, burgess, etc.

day, negro Lucy and her increase, she paying to her two sisters, Mildred Hobday and Nancy Buckner Hobday, ⅓ part of the valuation of said slave, to be valued by two men on oath, when the youngest of said legatees shall arrive at 18 years; to each of the surviving children of deceased son, Thomas Chisman, £12 current money, except grandson Thomas Chisman, and to him I give £25; to grandsons George Brown and John Brown, £50, and to granddaughter Elizabeth Philips, £40; to son John Chisman, a negro, or £106, and one bed and furniture; to son Peter, a negro; to son Robert, negro woman; granddaughter Elizabeth Garland Goodwin, negro girl; lends to daughter Rebecca Mask, negro girl called Black Sal and £40 current money, and after her death give the same to my granddaughter Elizabeth Mask, and in case of her death, to be divided among surviving children of said Rebecca Mask; a negro girl, Billy, to daughter Elizabeth Blackwell; to daughter Diana Wallace, negro Rose and youngest child; to daughter Rachel Mallory, negro Nancy, and £50, and a negro boy; to granddaughter Anna Chisman, daughter of son John Chisman, a negro child now up the country; to son-in-law John Goodwin, his bond; to friend Barbara Rogers, £10; to my negro men Hazard and Dick, 40s. apiece. Residue of my estate to be equally divided between my children John Chisman, Elizabeth Blackwell, Diana Wallace, Rachel Mallory: grandsons James Goodwin, Littleton Goodwin, and Wilson Bailey; sons John Chisman and Robert Goodwin, and friend Thomas Pescud, my ex'ors. Witnesses: Bernard Elliott, Ann X Elliott. (Widow of James Goodwin.)

Inventory and appraisement of Peter Goodwin's, Sen., estate, 30th March, 1784.

John Moss, appointed guardian of Peter Goodwin, an infant orphan of John Goodwin, deceased, March 21, 1785.

Appraisement of Capt. John Goodwin's estate, £1,427.12.8.

Martin Goodwin *vs.* John Moss, administrator of John Goodwin, deceased. A committee appointed to settle all accounts of John Goodwin, deceased, who was executor of John Goodwin, deceased. November 22, 1787.

Susanna Goodwin, orphan of Capt. John Goodwin, deceased, in account with Martin Goodwin, her guardian. 1794.

Appraisement of estate of Robert Goodwin, deceased, taken August 22, 1800.

Estate of Robert Goodwin in account with Martin Goodwin. Dr. £45 12s. 10d.; Cr. £53 0s. 9d.

Martin Goodwin constable. 1803.

Martin Goodwin, deceased, estate 15th September, 1805, £126.18.0.

Deed of Martin Goodwin, conveying certain slaves to Peter Goodwin, Jr., and Allen Chapman, his security. July 3, 1792.

Peter Goodwin, of York-Hampton Parish, and Frances, his wife, to Bernard Elliot, 120½ acres on Back Creek. November 1, 1794.

Peter Goodwin, Jr., and Frances, his wife, to Kempe P. Elliott. November 20, 1818.

Peter Goodwin, Jr., bond as commissioner of wrecks. Securities, Bernard Elliott, John Stedman, John A. Rogers.

Peter Goodwin's, Sen., land being on north of Back Creek, adjoining James Ironmonger, divided between the widow, Peter Goodwin, and John Curtis in right of his wife Virginia. Mrs. Goodwin is the guardian of Peter, and the land is of small extent. 1824.

Elizabeth Goodwin's will, dated October 9, 1831, proved December 19, 1831. To son Peter R. Goodwin the silver tankard and family Bible; to Mrs. Elizabeth Tomkins my bell metal skillet; names my two children, Virginia E. Curtis and Peter R. Goodwin.

Peter Goodwin, Jr., deceased. Inventory and appraisement taken 29th November, 1832. In account with F. B. Power, administrator.

Will of Peter Goodwin—wife Mahala, two children, friend and brother-in-law, John Curtis, executor. Witnesses: Robert F. Elliott, Harold Goodwin, F. W. Power.

ELIZABETH CITY COUNTY.

Will of John Moore, of Elizabeth City county, names nephews John, Edward, Merritt, and Daniel Moore. Gives to Merritt Moore the plantation whereon John Merritt now lives; but if he dies, to my nephew Daniel Moore. Nieces Martha Moore, Anne Moore, Rachel Wise, Susannah Goodwin, sister Elizabeth Goodwin, Nephew William Moore, Uncle William Lowry, and Aunt Rachel Lowry, Cozen John Lowry. Dated December 11, 1715; proved January 18, 1715–'16. (See page 8.)

Will of Richard Hawkins names daughters Mary, Phebe, and Elizabeth Reade, son Anthony Tucker and Thomas Reade, executors. Dated June 12, 1737, proved September 21, 1737.

Deed of Thomas Reade to Robert Armistead, of York county, for an island near the new mill-dam on Back River, being part of a greater tract, formerly belonging to Thomas Reade, deceased, father of the said Thomas, and devised to said Thomas by will of said Thomas, recorded in Elizabeth City county September 19, 1738.

Hawkins Reade, son of Thomas Reade and Elizabeth Hawkins, married, first, Rachel Curtis (sister of Robert Curtis, of York county), and second, Elizabeth Moss, widow of Thomas Pescud. His daughter Mary married Robert Sheild. (See QUARTERLY, IV., p. 59.)

ASSESSOR'S BOOKS.

York County, 1784.—107½ acres on the north side of Back Creek assessed to John Goodwin, deceased, and 1,200 acres on York River, Chesapeake Bay, and Back Creek assessed to John Goodwin.

1785.—The first tract to John Goodwin's estate, and the second to John Goodwin, deceased.

1798.—The first to Peter Goodwin, Sr., and the second to Peter Goodwin, Jr.

1824.—The first tract to Peter Goodwin's, Sen., estate, the second to Peter Goodwin, Jr.

1829.—The first tract to Peter Goodwin, Jr., and the second to Peter Goodwin, Sen.

1832.—The first tract to Peter Goodwin, Jr., and the latter to Peter Goodwin's, Sen., estate.

1833.—Harold Goodwin succeeds to the second tract.

NOTE.—The assessor's books explain the relationship between Peter Goodwin, Sr., who married Elizabeth ——, who died in 1831, and Peter Goodwin, Jr., who married Frances Chapman, or Toomer. On page 13 it is said that Peter Goodwin, of Charles parish, son of John Goodwin, "perhaps did not survive." This seems to be an error, as he was doubtless the Peter, Sr., who, dying in 1824, left one son, who became Peter, Jr., while Peter, Jr. (son of Capt. John Goodwin, of Yorkhampton parish, on the other side of Back Creek, the dividing line of the parishes), became Peter, Sr. Upon the death of this last Peter, about 1833, his son Harold inherited the twelve hundred acre tract. The following data should, therefore, have followed the paragraph devoted to John Goodwin on page 13.

Peter Goodwin, Sr. (John, Peter, Peter, James), married Elizabeth, and had issue: i. Peter R. Goodwin, who married Mahala ——; and ii. Virginia E., who married John Curtis.

Peter R. Goodwin (Peter, John, Peter, Peter, James), born in York county, Va., married Mahala, living in 1832. His will mentions wife Mahala and two children.

ACKNOWLEDGMENT.

It is but right and proper that acknowledgment should be made of the liberality of Mr. James J. Goodwin, of Hartford, Conn., without whose pecuniary assistance this publication would probably not have been made. A similar generous spirit on the part of Mr. Goodwin rendered possible the researches of Henry F. Waters in the English archives. Mr. Waters' "Gleanings" are published in the New England *Historical and Genealogic Register*, and are invaluable to those interested in old Virginia families. Judge John S. Goodwin puts it too strongly (on page 1) when he says of the English origin of the Goodwins of Connecticut that it has "so far eluded the most diligent search." In fact, much has been accomplished, though the information is not yet as precise as might be desired.

LAND GRANTS TO THE GOODWINS OF VIRGINIA.

NAMES.	BOOK.	PAGE.	COUNTY.	DATE.	NO. ACRES.	DESCRIPTION.
Major James Goodwin, . . .	4	279	Westmoreland, ...	March 15, 1657, . .	1,000	On S. side Potomac River.
Major James Goodwin, . . .	4	341	"	December 24, 1658, .	400	On small creek Po. River.
Matthew Goodwin, ...	9	316	Warwick, ...	April 25, 1701, . . .	134	
John Goodwin, ...	25	359	Prince George, ...	January 12, 1746, .	1,503	
John Goodwin, ...	26	512	Albemarle, ...	July 20, 1748, . . .	400	
Robert Goodwin, ...	26	523	"	July 20, 1748, . . .	325	
John Goodwin, ...	27	81	Surry, ...	December 1, 1748, .	1,190	
Thomas Goodwin, ...	33	496	Dinwiddie, ...	April 28, 1748, . . .	71	
Thomas Goodwin, ...	33	496	"	April 28, 1748, . . .	80	
John Goodwin, ...	33	880	"	August 20, 1760, . .	381	Near cor. Jno. Winfield's.
John Goodwin, ...	33	881	"	August 20, 1760, . .	114	
Harwood Go(o)dwin, ...	34	397	"	August 10, 1759, . .	300	
Harwood Goodwin, ...	34	435	"	August 10, 1759, . .	400	
Thomas Goodwynn, ...	36	619	Sussex, ...	August 15, 1764, . .	100	

CORRECTIONS AND ADDITIONS.

PAGE 6.—In fifth line, for "swear to his father's will," read "qualify on his father's will."

PAGE 7.—*Major James Goodwin* seems to have had two children by his second wife, Robert and Martin, which would indicate the early death of Robert, the son by the first wife. Martin Goodwin married Barbara *Rogers*. See Dr. Tyler's notes.

PAGE 8.—*Elizabeth Goodwin,* here given, may not have been the Elizabeth Goodwin who was the ward of Albritton Wagstaffe. It may have been Elizabeth Goodwin (Martin, James) on page 58, who was the ward. In that event, the date of birth given on page 8 would not be the date of birth of that Elizabeth.

PAGE 9.—*Peter Goodwin.* Strike out the last two lines (in parenthesis), as Dr. Tyler's notes show the correctness of this line of descent.

PAGE 9.—*Mary Goodwin* (Peter, John, John, James), should read *Mary Goodwin* (Peter, John, John, John, James).

PAGE 10.—*Rachel Goodwin,* ninth line, married *Thomas* Charles.

PAGE 18.—*Barker* is incorrect; the name is *Barbee.*

PAGE 34.—*William F. T. Garnett* is correct.

PAGE 58.—*Elizabeth Goodwin,* see correction to page 8.

PAGE 126.—Appendix V., add *John Goodwin* and Alice Spencer were married March ye 21, 1738. Perhaps this is a second marriage of the John Goodwin mentioned on page 130, who married Mary Elliott, she dying November 24, 1734.

PAGE 130.—Appendix Y., *Robert Goodwin* appears from Dr. Tyler's notes not to have been the eldest son of Major James Goodwin, that Robert presumably having died, and this Robert being a son of the second marriage.

INDEX TO NOTES

ON THE YORK COUNTY, VIRGINIA, GOODWINS.

INDEX.

THE APPENDICES ARE EACH INDEXED SEPARATELY.

THE GOODWINS OF YORK COUNTY, VA.

APPENDIX A.

THE GOODWINS OF BROOKVILLE, INDIANA.

APPENDIX B.

THE GOODWINS OF WASHINGTON COUNTY, IND.

APPENDIX C.

THE GOODWINS OF FAYETTE COUNTY, PENNSYLVANIA.

APPENDICES D and E.

THE GOODWINS OF WHEELING, W. VA., THE GOODWINES OF WARREN CO., IND., and THE GOODWINS OF YORK CO., PA.

APPENDIX F.

THE GOODWINS OF HARRISON COUNTY, WEST VIRGINIA.

APPENDIX G.

THE GOODWINS OF SAINT MARY'S COUNTY, MD.

APPENDICES H, I, J, X, and Y.

THE GOODWINS OF BOTETOURT AND TAZEWELL COUNTIES, VIRGINIA; THE GOODWINS OF DAVIDSON CO., TENN.; THE GOODWINS OF PREBLE COUNTY OHIO; ALL PROBABLE DESCENDANTS OF ROBERT GOODWIN.

APPENDIX K.

THE GOODWYNS OF DINWIDDIE COUNTY, VIRGINIA.

APPENDIX L.

THE GOODWINS OF AUGUSTA COUNTY, VA.

APPENDICES M, Q, R, T, V, W, and Z.

THE GOODWINS OF CAROLINE, AMHERST, ALBEMARLE and HALIFAX COUNTIES, VA., and THE GOODWINS OF VIRGINIA and NORTH CAROLINA and of VIRGINIA and GEORGIA, with UNTRACED GOODWINS and MISCELLANEOUS NOTES.

APPENDICES N, O, and P. THE GOODWINS OF CARROLL CO., BALTIMORE CO., and EASTERN MARYLAND.

APPENDIX S.

THE GOODWINS OF GREENBRIER CO., W. VA.

APPENDIX U.

THE GOODINS OF LOUDOUN COUNTY, VIRGINIA.

www.ingramcontent.com/pod-product-compliance
Lightning Source LLC
Chambersburg PA
CBHW071121280326
41935CB00010B/1075

9780788402050